David Webster

The angler and the Loop-Rod

David Webster

The angler and the Loop-Rod

ISBN/EAN: 9783337759476

Printed in Europe, USA, Canada, Australia, Japan

Cover: Foto ©Lupo / pixelio.de

More available books at **www.hansebooks.com**

THE ANGLER

AND

THE LOOP-ROD

BY

DAVID WEBSTER

"Forty Years a practitioner in this Art."
—Robert Howlett (1706).

WILLIAM BLACKWOOD AND SONS
EDINBURGH AND LONDON
MDCCCLXXXV

All Rights reserved

PREFACE.

IN the following pages I propose to record some of the results of my experience in the art of angling, and especially in that most delightful branch of the art known as fly-fishing.

The work is a small one, though the field which it covers is wide. It does not pretend, therefore, to be exhaustive; its only aim is that it may be found exact. It begins at the beginning. It takes the angler to the river-side, puts the rod into his hands, and shows him both how to fish and where to fish. It treats in more or less detail of angling for trout, salmon, grayling, and pike, and of the various lures that are employed in different conditions of water and at different seasons of the year.

Fly-fishing for trout, however, receives the first

and fullest treatment; and although one would suppose that surely nothing remained to be said on this well-worn theme, it is believed that several facts of importance, especially in regard to the influence of the wind on the success of the sport, appear here for the first time.

Into the list of flies I have admitted only those which, from close observation and actual trial, I have proved to be most worthy of the angler's regard. All of them, with the exception of the sand-fly (which attains its maturity in the sand and gravel at the side of the water), are hatched in the bed of the stream, and constitute the ready and natural food of the fish. The remarks under this head are more particularly applicable to the Clyde and the Tweed; still I believe they will hold good for all rivers and streams in this country, for the common natural flies are found more or less on all alike, and differ merely in the times of their development. No apology is offered for introducing into the text a few facts concerning their natural history and habits; for while there is no need that the angler be an entomologist, it goes without saying that he who takes an intelligent interest in all that relates to his craft, will both do greater things in it, and derive greater pleasure from doing them.

The instructions offered regarding the dressing of the artificial flies are based on the practical experience of years, and are directed towards securing in each case as perfect an imitation of the natural prototype as materials and skill can produce. In this connection I have endeavoured to meet the arguments of those who hold that a close imitation of the natural insect is not only unattainable in any appreciable degree, but, even if it could be attained, would be both unnecessary for all the purposes of the angler, and inimical to his success. Whether I have entirely succeeded in theoretically demonstrating the unsoundness of these views, I will not presume to say; for failure in this, as in other pleas, may be due quite as much to a poor advocate as to a bad cause, and it has been my fate all life long to deal more in experimental tests than in logical proofs. But the *facts* are against them; and if my friendly opponents will permit me to choose as our weapon the rod in place of the pen, I shall be quite prepared to pit my practice against their theory, and stake my reputation as an angler on the result.

Some space is devoted to night-fishing as followed during June and July; for though I respect, I do not share, the opinions of those " honest anglers " who regard it as little better than poaching. With legitimate lures, and under proper regulation, it may yield good, and withal true sport, at a time when day-fishing is utterly barren.

But the distinctive features of the book are the prominence which it gives to the art of fishing with what may be styled the loop-rod and line, and the pre-eminence which it claims for such over the ordinary appliances of jointed-rod and reel. Not that these latter should be entirely discarded—indeed, in certain circumstances they alone are admissible—but my experience of both has gone to show that, for the most part, in ordinary trout-fishing, the loop-rod and line are immeasurably superior in everything that makes for skilful and successful angling.

For more than forty years, from early spring until the close of autumn, I have followed this method of fishing, chiefly on the Clyde and the Tweed, not only with the keen relish of the sportsman for his sport, but with the zeal born of necessity. For, as in the fishing season my livelihood was entirely dependent on the success of my rod, I have been wont to regard the net result of the day's exertion with a pardonable amount of interest, if not of anxiety; and it may therefore be safely assumed that I would adopt that method which promised the greatest results. In more recent years other "brothers of the angle" in the south of Scotland have admitted the claims of the looprod, and attested its superiority; but I am inclined to believe that to the large majority of fishers in these days it will prove at least novel. And if neither its novelty nor its success should be alone sufficient to recommend it to the true Waltonian who would see the artist in the sportsman, I can confidently add that the angler who gives the looprod a fair trial, and attains to even a moderate degree of skill in its use, will be in little danger of regarding fly-fishing as being merely or primarily an ingenious method of filling a creel, but will be led to admit that it may rise to the dignity of an art whose pursuit is its own chief charm.

One word more. This little work was undertaken at the solicitation of an old friend, himself a skilful and enthusiastic angler; and to him my grateful acknowledgments are due for his kind assistance in giving expression to my views and form to my facts. Whatever may be its value as a contribution to the already extensive literature of angling, or whatever practical hints the young angler may derive from this record of the observation and experience of an old "hand," I trust that my humble efforts may at least be recognised as a tribute of my devotion to an art which, in spite of their many foibles and crotchets, has ever linked its disciples, both old and young, in the freemasonry of a genial brotherhood.

D. W.

LANARK, *April* 1885.

CONTENTS.

CHAP.		PAGE
I.	THE ANGLER'S TACKLE AND EQUIPMENT,	1
II.	TROUTING-FLIES,	16
III.	FLY-DRESSING,	64
IV.	ARTIFICIAL-FLY FISHING,	69
V.	NATURAL-FLY FISHING—	
	THE MAY-FLY,	131
	THE GREEN DRAKE,	142
	THE BLACK ANT,	148
VI.	INSECT-BAIT FISHING—	
	THE CREEPER,	152
	THE CADDIS,	158
	THE GRUB,	162
VII.	WORM-FISHING,	165
VIII.	MINNOW-FISHING,	190
IX.	NIGHT-FISHING,	217

X. GRAYLING-FISHING,	. . . . .	233
XI. SALMON-FISHING,	. . . . .	252
XII. PIKE-FISHING,	. . . . . .	301

APPENDICES—

I. CLOSE-TIME FOR TROUT,	. . .	332
II. SUMMARY OF LURES,	. . . .	337
III. PRINCIPAL OPEN REACHES OF THE CLYDE AND THE TWEED, WITH THE WINDS THAT BLOW UP-STREAM ON EACH,	. . . . . .	339

LIST OF ILLUSTRATIONS.

COLOURED PLATES.

PLATE		PAGE
I. TROUT-FLIES,	. . . . .	42
II. MINNOW-TACKLES,	. . . . .	196
III. SALMON-FLIES,	. . . . .	261
IV. DO.	. . . . .	263

ANGLES AT WHICH TO CAST,	. . . .	99
MINNOW-BAIT,	. . . . . .	197
DO.	. . . . . .	212

THE ANGLER

AND

THE LOOP-ROD.

CHAPTER I.

THE ANGLER'S TACKLE AND EQUIPMENT.

" You see the ways a fisherman doth take
To catch the fish, what engines doth he make.
Behold how he engageth all his wits,
Also his snares, lines, angles, hooks, and nets."
—BUNYAN.

"I TELL you, scholar, fishing is an art; or, at least, it is an art to *catch* fish." So said old Izaak Walton; and his cautious limitation has been abundantly justified in the experience of many who have found that, while it may be given to all to fish, it is certainly not given to all to catch fish.

The forest of rods seen at our railway stations on a Queen's birthday or a bank holiday, might lead one to suppose that, if fishing be an art, there must indeed be many artists. Every day, too, seems to add to their number, while the cry is "still they come." In this increasing crowd of votaries the true angler will find no cause for alarm; for whatever leads to greater wariness on the part of the fish, will call for only a higher degree of skill on the part of the fisher. Although the multiplication of rods can hardly be said to be the only reason why trout are scarcer now than they were forty years ago, it is at all events sufficient to assure us, and delight us with the assurance, that the innocent and healthful joys of angling are no longer confined to the few who caught the big baskets of former days, but are now being more universally recognised and more ardently pursued.

Nor is this throng of disciples likely to suffer from lack of instruction, or at least from lack of instructors. For, from the days of Dame Juliana Berners until now, there have issued from the press about six hundred works on angling, and these chiefly in English,—a collection ample enough, it might be supposed, to contain every principle of the fisher's art, and every rule for its practice. Much, however, I am convinced, remains to be discovered or explained before the angling fraternity can be said even to be in full possession of every fact which bears upon their art, much less to have attained to the highest perfection therein.

Observation and experiment alone must lead to further progress here; and in the hope that my long experience as an angler, differing as it does from that of most authorities in several important particulars in regard both to tools and methods, may reveal a few facts to stimulate or direct the intelligent practice of others, I have ventured to take advantage of the proverbial long-suffering of the brethren of the rod, and to inflict upon them another book on angling.

I promise, however, not to trespass so far upon their good-nature as to attempt to give a history either of the fish to be caught, or of all the various means of catching them that have obtained in the world, from that distant time when the divers of Antony adopted the mean method of fastening the fish on to his hooks to ensure him success in his contest with Egypt's dusky queen, until these days of truly scientific angling and highly educated fish. Neither shall I be at pains to set forth for the hundredth time the joys of angling, and the enthusiasm of the angler, as he sallies forth to the dales and to the uplands, his spirits in full accord with nature in her spring-time, and his heart beating high in anticipation of his triumphs. I shall dare to dispense even with an apostrophe to the tutelary deities of the stream, and this, too, when an apology would be more fitting from one who makes bold to venture within the precincts of their temple, and sacrilegiously rob them of their scaly treasures. And although no work on angling would be considered complete without an allusion to the ill-tempered sally of Dr Johnson, regarding "the fly at one end of the line, and the fool at the other," I can afford, in the presence of anglers, to dismiss the Doctor with "the retort courteous," that I suspect he must have tried the gentle art himself, and in his chagrin at the poverty of his "take," uncharitably based his definition of angling in general on what it had proved to be in his own case in particular.

But I have no desire to be hard upon the Doctor, for I could not accept his description as correct even of unsuccessful angling. Indeed, in the case of not a few, it is the pleasurable pursuit of health, rather than of fish, that brings forth rod and basket. In view of the fact that many of those who, when occasion offers, leave town for a day's "fishing," and hie to the breezy river-side, are confined to the stuffy office or the shop for months together, I am constrained to exclaim, Would that all "fools" were as wise!

> "Trust me, there is much 'vantage in it, sir;
> You do forget the noisy pother of mankind,
> And win communion with sweet Nature's self,
> In plying our dear craft."

Without the fatigue which accompanies the more violent exercises of hunting and shooting, angling, as a sport, possesses more than their attractions; for the less engrossing character of the pursuit permits of a greater enjoyment of the fair scenes amid which it is followed, and fosters a closer acquaintance with life in water and in air, which is not only in itself a source of pleasure, but an aid in the further prosecution of the sport; while as an art angling demands higher powers of intelligence and caution, decision and patience, with quite a host of resources and cardinal virtues. Yet the angler need be no slavish follower of his craft. It may be to him no more than a sport which furnishes an outlet for the exercise of his wits, a rational way of enjoying his holiday, and a restorative of his exhausted power. But surely the recreation will be all the more rational, and the enjoyment none the less keen, if the sport is pursued with some degree of skill and with some chance of success. Of the success, indeed, even the accomplished angler cannot be always sure, but every "honest angler" will admit that the skilful pursuit alone deserves it. In this art, as in others, it is practice of course that makes for perfection. But the practice, to be effective, must be with good tools and after good methods; and in so far as a competent knowledge of tools and methods is conducive to success, this little work, I trust, will not be entirely without value. And first, then, as to the angler's tools.

The Rod.—The trouting-rod which I am in the habit of using is a two-handed spliced rod, measuring from 13 feet 6 inches to 13 feet 8 inches. It consists of three pieces. The butt is made of ash, the middle piece of hickory, and the top of lancewood. When greater lightness is desired, limetree may be used for the butt: what the rod gains in this respect, however, is lost in durability. Attached to the extremity of the top piece is a strong loop of twisted horse-hair, through which is passed the loop of the hair-line used in casting. If the rod be well balanced, nicely tapered, and neatly and firmly tied together, its sweep and action in casting will be smooth and even throughout its entire length. But it is as well to have the middle piece somewhat stiff when one is using the loopline. For undue suppleness in a rod—and in the middle piece lies the test—is just as fatal to good casting as too great rigidity. A spliced rod of this kind is much lighter than the ordinary brass-jointed rod, and casts a much better line.

The butt, middle piece, and top may be made of equal length, but I frequently use a short middle piece and a long top; and this arrangement, I think, improves the spring. The following measurements will give a good spring: butt, 4 feet 8 inches; middle piece, 3 feet 7 inches ; top, 5 feet 5 inches. This form of rod, however, is not so convenient for carrying about, as the top projects somewhat beyond the other pieces, and is therefore more liable to be broken, unless care is used, especially in railway-travelling.

Any one who has never handled a well-balanced spliced rod of this description can have no conception of its immense superiority to the ordinary jointed rod as regards lightness and elasticity. The angler who gives it a fair trial will never, I believe, exchange it for any other; and should he still prefer to use a reel, notwithstanding the manifold advantages of the loop-line system of fishing, which I am about to describe, he may have the rod fitted up in all respects in the same way as the jointed rod, minus the joints. In artificial fly-fishing, where the true and prompt action of the rod is a matter of the utmost importance, the spliced rod, as affording the best means of obtaining a combined and easy play of all the parts from the butt to the tip, is without any rival. From its inestimable advantage of responding at once to the action of the wrist, it enables the angler to cast with the utmost delicacy and precision, and to strike with all requisite promptness and certainty. Thus any dexterity and skill in casting which the angler may possess, are turned to the fullest advantage when he employs the spliced rod; and, with it in his hands, he will be ready to admit that the good results of his hard day's fishing, especially if the trout have been "taking" well, were in no small degree attributable to the superiority of his tools.

The Casting-Line.—This line is made of horsehairs, not too firmly twisted—the lengths of hairs being knotted at their junction, and the ends neatly tied with well-rosined silk thread. It tapers gradually from the loop to the gut. The number of hairs composing the thickest part of the line at the loop ranges from thirty-six to forty-five, according to fineness, diminishing gradually to five or six at the point where the gut-line is attached. The length of the casting-line should be from 18 to 20 feet. The loop at the top is about three inches long, and is passed through the corresponding loop of smaller size attached to the rod.

The Gut-Line.—The gut-line, as distinguished from the casting-line proper, measures from 16 to 17 feet, and so the total length of line from the loop to the trail-fly is from 34 to 37 feet. The gut should be tapered as well as the hair-line—the strongest lengths being selected for the portion next the casting-line, and the finer for the remainder, so as to preserve the tapering of the line throughout its entire length from loop to fly.

I am thoroughly opposed to the use of dyed gut, so much vaunted by almost every writer on angling. Natural gut, if sufficiently transparent, round, and even in substance, is undoubtedly the best for all angling purposes. This, however, is not always to be obtained in the shops, and drawn gut is frequently substituted for it. The great variety in the stains recommended—some anglers advocating a red water-stain, others a slate tint, others again a blue or a walnut tint, and so on—proves, at all events, that there is no agreement as to the precise stain least likely to be seen by the fish. I maintain that natural, transparent gut—not the white glistening material that is so frequently sold—is less visible to the eye of the wary trout in clear water than any coloured gut can possibly be. This any one may prove for himself, by placing two hairs of gut, the one dyed and the other in its natural condition, in a crystal vessel of pure water, and looking at them carefully from all positions. He will find that even when the hairs are suspended a short distance from the surface of the water, and viewed from below, the pure transparent gut is scarcely visible, while the dyed material is detected at once. The greater part of the gut sold in shops is really unserviceable for fine fishing in clear water, on account of its coarseness and irregularity. Fine colourless gut is indispensable for angling in clear water, and the rounder and more regular it is the better. On the other hand, when it is reduced and drawn out, as it often is, till it resembles nothing so much as gossamer, it will make neither a strong line nor a good "cast."

The threads of gut which have been carefully selected to form a perfectly tapered line, are first well soaked in cold water to render them more pliable and to prevent their breaking, and then united by means of the double slip-knot, which is the safest, and for all practical purposes the best. Remembering that the strength of a chain is the strength of its weakest link, the angler will take care that no faulty hair find its way into the line.

I always use nine flies on my cast, and as they are all tied on very fine looped gut, the droppers are easily attached by bringing the loops over the knots of the line. I place one over every alternate knot, thus allowing a space, according to the general length of the hairs, of 20 or 22 inches from fly to fly. The length of the droppers need not exceed 2 inches, and ought to be the same for each. Some authorities on angling recommend that they should hang from $2\frac{1}{2}$ to 3 inches, increasing in length in proportion to their distance from the trail fly. But experience will prove to any angler that this is a mistake, as the fly on the long dropper then comes in contact, and even gets entangled, with the line, and deprives the trout, which has risen to feed, of the proper facility for working its own destruction. Prejudice also exists against the system of fixing the droppers by means of loops, on the ground that it is a clumsy and inartistic method. But if fine gut is used, and the loop drawn tight, the connection can be formed as securely and as neatly as in any other way; and when occasion requires that one fly be replaced by another, the dropper can be immediately detached by inserting the point of a pin between the loop and the line.

The Fishing-Book. — I recommend a full-sized fishing-book, well provided with pockets and divisions. In addition to the ordinary tackle of casting and gut lines, the book should contain a small pair of scissors, pins, white wax, two or three varieties of silk thread, and some spare gut. The angler will also provide a spare fly-cast or two and some spare flies, similar to those on the gut-cast, so that damage to tackle may be repaired without loss of time; for every moment is valuable, and should be utilised to the utmost when the "take" is on. Of course, several bait-lines and hooks, with some sinkers and swivels, should also find a place in the book. Some authorities, or would-be authorities, evidently of the opinion that if trout refuse the flies that are on the water, they may be induced to accept imitations of others with which they have never formed any previous acquaintance, advise the angler to have beside him several casts, with a different selection of flies on each, not only of such as might possibly be in season or out of season, but of others whose prototypes have at no time been seen on this earth, at least since the Flood. Now this is hardly a scientific method of going to work; and the error, though common, is not likely to be committed by any practical angler. Casts of flies are not made up by selecting flies of various sizes and colours at random, on the bare chance of their proving acceptable to the fish. Every observant angler knows what kind of natural flies are "on the water" during any particular portion of the fishing season, and makes up his cast accordingly, feeling assured that if trout will not "take" the imitation of the fly that is in season, it is useless, in general, to offer it, as a more tempting bait, any imitation of other flies which have at that time no existence. The failure to secure a basket in that case will not, I suspect, be found to lie with the flies.

Fishing-Creel. — Notwithstanding its somewhat pretentious appearance, I recommend a large pannier capable of holding from 20 to 25 lb. of fish. It is not much heavier than a smaller basket—

unless when it is full—and it is quite as handy. While it affords room for a good "take" of fish, when one is fortunate enough to get it, such a creel gives facility for stowing away all that an angler can possibly require in the way of tackle-book, minnow-tackle-box, bait-bag, lunch, and last, but not least, the flask. As an improvement on the ordinary basket, I would suggest that a division be inserted to separate the fish from the fishing gear; or, what is better, that the basket carry inside, and attached thereto, a waterproof bag, in which both gear and lunch might be kept. The best baskets are those made of round willows. The belt should be broad, so as not to press unduly on the shoulder, and a strap might be fitted to the outside of the basket to hold a waterproof. Bags for holding fish are worse than useless. Through pressure on the back the closely packed fish get soon heated and destroyed, assuming the appearance of having been caught some days before, while the bearer is subjected to great discomfort, especially in hot weather.

The Angler's Equipment.—As to dress, a grey tweed suit of good strong material, with several side-pockets, will be found the most serviceable. Trout do not like loud colours, and the angler will do well to avoid anything likely to render him a conspicuous object in the water.

The wading-stockings should be made the full

length of the legs, and be carefully adapted to the feet; for they are equally uncomfortable when too long as when too short. If the material is thoroughly waterproof, the lighter it is the better, as the weight will necessarily be considerably increased in the course of a long day's wading. Before putting on the stockings, pass an elastic band round the ankle and over the trousers, to prevent the latter from being disarranged; and over the wading-stockings put on a pair of strong worsted socks of large size, to keep the boot, and the gravel which insinuates itself into it, from abrading the fishing-stocking. The socks are held up by elastic garters. The boots are made specially for the purpose, a size or two larger than ordinary walking-boots. They should come well up the ankle, be strong but not too heavy, and have a few nails in the soles to prevent slipping.

After a day's fishing, turn the wading-stockings inside out, and dry them slowly before a fire during the night, if they are to be required next day. Where this is carefully attended to, they will last much longer than they would otherwise do. It is advisable, however, to have two pairs, and to use them alternately. The angler should, if practicable, put on his fishing-stockings before starting for the day, so that on reaching the river he may be ready to commence operations without loss of time. He will thus also save himself the trouble of carrying his walking-shoes in his basket all day, as well as the labour of transporting a dead weight of fishing stockings and boots to and from the riverside. If the start has to be made from town, however, it is sometimes inconvenient to go forth fully equipped. In these circumstances, straps may be attached to the outside of the basket, both on the front and on the bottom, in such a way as to carry the boots and wading-stockings without interfering with the proper use of the basket or the free movements of the angler.

CHAPTER II.

TROUTING-FLIES.

" So just the colours shine through every part,
That Nature seems to live again in Art."
—GAY.

" Wel cowde he dresse his takel yemanly."
—CHAUCER.

THERE are two considerations which guide me in the selection of my trouting-flies. First, that although trout may feed more or less on a great number of natural insects, they have a decided preference for certain flies at certain seasons; and secondly, that seeing they take an artificial fly for a natural, the more closely that artificial resembles its prototype, the more likely are they to take it. These statements, though wide and general, are not mere assumptions, the principles of some visionary theory of the angler's art, but the well-grounded beliefs of most practical fishers, and, in my own case, the product of a close observation of insect-life and long study of the habits and whims of fish.

Following their guidance, I select for each season those flies which have been proved to be in greatest favour with the trout at that season, and endeavour to have in each case as perfect a representation of the natural insect as art and materials will allow.

The fault which I have to find with most writers on angling is, that though they do not offer to contest the position that all flies are not equally in demand with the trout, the principle of the selection of the fittest seems to have no place in their works. Their lists are crowded with insects which are rarely seen on the water, and still more rarely accepted by the trout. Indeed the number and varieties given by some authors are almost endless, and can only prove as bewildering to the amateur as they certainly must be useless to him for obtaining sport. Should he be persevering enough, he may find that they will all kill now or again; but this, I fancy, is not the assurance that he seeks. What he needs to know is—Have all these flies been shown by actual trial to be equally acceptable to the fish? That is—Will they all kill equally well? And if not, which are the best? It is in answer to these most legitimate questions that the subjoined lists of flies have been drawn up; and it is with the confidence which their practical success has inspired that they are submitted to his notice.

Though authors most frequently err in recommending too many flies, it is quite possible to have too few. A recent writer on angling, Mr Cholmondeley-Pennell, who has entered very fully into this subject, and propounded a remarkable theory of his own, gives a collection of artificial flies which certainly cannot be said to be either too large or too varied; for the conclusion to which he comes, after much disquisition and not a little speculation, is, that six flies—"three for salmon and grilse, and three for trout, grayling, and dace"—are amply sufficient for all the angler's needs. Whether they may satisfy the prevailing tastes and habitual cravings of the fish, is quite another question, though to me it seems the chief one.

But not only do I maintain that the selection should include only such flies as the trout most commonly prefer, but that the artificial imitations of these flies should be as nearly as possible the exact counterparts of the natural insects. It is the latter position which has been most frequently and most vigorously assailed. It has been attacked, too, on all points, and each successive assailant having, to his own satisfaction, scored a signal success and fairly demolished the theory, considers himself bound to set up in its place a new one of his own. The result is, that the opinions of the theoretical anglers who write on this question bid fair to equal in number the writers themselves; and ere long the statement that *anglers* differ, though not perhaps fraught with such eventful issues, will become quite as proverbial as the trite one that *doctors* do. In the interests of a successful career as flyfishers, let me hope — as I in truth sometimes suspect — that however much they may differ in their theories, they may, even at the expense of their consistency, be more uniform in their practice.

Some philosophers — possibly those who, as "Ephemera" suggests, "read insect nature through the glass cases of museums"—assert that there is no resemblance whatever between the natural fly and what appears to be the best artificial imitation ever dressed. Others, such as a writer in 'The Angler's Souvenir,' take up a different standpoint, and assure us that, whether possible or not, it is at all events needless to make a good imitation of any fly, as "the greatest number of trout is caught with flies which are *the least like* any which frequent the water." Stoddart, Stewart, and others of a more sober frame of mind, hold that "a neatly made natural-looking fly will, where trout are shy, kill three trout for one which a clumsy fly will;" but that, to kill at all, "it is only necessary to make the artificial fly resemble the natural insect in shape," as "it is not likely that trout can see the colour of a fly very distinctly."[1] I shall take only another, and, so far as I know, the most recently advanced theory—that of Mr Pennell. The views of this author on the character of the artificial flies an angler should use are much more startling than his conclusions, already given, in regard to their number; and as some of his positions have been maintained by others who are considered authorities in angling, and all of them involve the errors of the theories stated above, I may be excused if I examine his propositions in some detail, and endeavour to bring them to the infallible touchstone of experience; for angling is necessarily a practical art, and the evidence of experience must in this, as in weightier matters, have precedence of plausible theories and *a priori* arguments.

After dividing trout fly-fishers into two classes, which he names respectively the "colourists," or those who consider "colour" everything and "form" nothing, and the "formalists," who hold "that the natural flies actually on the water at any given time should be exactly imitated by the artificial fly used, down to the most minute particulars of form and tinting," Mr Pennell proceeds to state what, in his view, are the arguments by which the opposing theories are maintained, and then to show that he occupies a position quite distinct

[1] Stewart's Practical Angler, pp. 74, 75, and 80.

from either and superior to both. To quote his own words :[1]—

"The position of the 'formalists' is as follows :—

"'Trout take artificial flies only because they in some sort resemble the natural flies which they are in the habit of seeing: if this be not so, and if *colour* is the only point of importance, why does not the "colourist" fish with a bunch of feathers tied on the hook "promiscuously"? why adhere to the form of the natural fly at all? Evidently because it is found, as a matter of fact, that such a bunch of feathers will not kill: in other words, *because the fish do take the artificial for the natural insect.* If this be so, it follows that the more minutely the artificial imitates the natural fly, the better it will kill; and also, by a legitimate deduction, that the imitation of the fly on the water at any given time is that which the fish will take best.'

"To the above argument the 'colourists' reply :—

"'Your theory supposes that trout can detect the nicest shades of distinction between species of flies which in a summer's afternoon may be numbered actually by hundreds, thus crediting them with an amount of entomological knowledge which even a professed naturalist, to say nothing of the angler himself, very rarely possesses; whilst at the same time you draw your flies up and across stream in a

[1] The Modern Practical Angler, p. 67 *et seq.*

way in which no natural insect is ever seen, not only adding to the impossibility of discriminating between different species, but often rendering it difficult for the fish even to identify the flies as flies. The only thing a fish can distinguish under these circumstances, besides the size of a fly, is its colour. We therefore regard form as a matter of comparative indifference, and colour as all-important.'"

Now the division of the great fly-fishing fraternity into "colourists" and "formalists" is neither a scientific nor a happy one, not only because, according to our author's own showing, the "formalist" argues for both colour and form, but also because, if it be adopted, no place in the brotherhood will be found for Mr Pennell. Passing this, however, I hold that the so-called formalist occupies a perfectly safe position in affirming that trout "do take the artificial for the natural insect," and that "the more minutely the artificial imitates the natural, the better it will kill." But, says Mr Pennell, the argument of the "colourist" that "from the way the artificial fly is presented to the fish it is impossible they can distinguish minutiæ of form and imitation, equally commends itself to common sense and common experience." Now I hold that trout not only *can*, but actually *do*, detect the nicest shades of distinction between species of flies presented to them; but not, indeed, if we "draw our flies up and across stream in a way in which no natural insect is ever seen;" for then, undoubtedly, it would not only be impossible for the fish to "discriminate between different species, but it would be difficult for it even to identify the flies as flies." Mr Pennell says that this is the point in which the entomological theory entirely breaks down. No doubt it is; but this so-called entomological theory is not the theory of any practical angler with whom I am acquainted, although it may be an antiquated method of alarming fish by report. No one now with the slightest pretensions to the name of angler would in any circumstances ever dream of "drawing his flies up and across stream," as Mr Pennell himself advocates, in the hope of concealing the defects of his imitation by an unnatural mode of presenting it.

I maintain that where the imitation is good, the trout will take it, and that, as a general rule, the more closely any artificial fly resembles, both in form and colour, its natural prototype, the better will it kill; in other words, that trout can, and do, distinguish "minutiæ of form and imitation." During night-fishing in June, I use six flies of different colours or shades of colour; and I have times innumerable found that nearly the whole of my trout, amounting from 10 to 20 lb. and frequently more, were got with a particular fly, while scarcely a fish was killed with any of the remaining five, and this, too, in the darkest nights. The same fly, it is true, did not kill on every occasion; but a certain and single shade of colour, representing a particular species of fly, seemed to take their fancy one night, and another and different fly another night, to the almost complete exclusion of those presented with it. If fish cannot, as our author says, discriminate between different species even during the day, how would he and his " colourist " account for their selecting a particular fly during the darkness of night, and this not on one occasion, but on hundreds of occasions?

As an analogous case I might cite the following: When double-rod fishing was in vogue many years ago, it was the practice to place from forty to fifty hooks on the line, which extended across the stream from bank to bank. Fish would on certain days select certain flies, all of the same form and tint—imitations of the same species—and reject almost every other during the whole of the day's fishing. Again, during the season of the sand or gravel fly, which comes out in the early part of May, and, if the weather be favourable, is seen on the water till the middle of June, it has been my experience that for every fish that can be killed with any other artificial fly, ten will be killed with the sand-fly if properly imitated in size, shape, and colour. So with the March brown; in April the success of the angler will be measured almost entirely by the extent to which he avails himself of a good imitation of the natural fly.

In combating the "legitimate deduction" of the "formalist," that the imitation of the fly on the water at any given time is that which the fish will take best, Mr Pennell says,—"The experience of every fly-fisher teaches him that when a particular natural fly is on the water in abundance, trout will commonly take better an artificial fly imitative of any other species." It is now nearly forty years since "Ephemera"[1] held this doctrine up to scorn, and apologetically assured his English readers that "some Scotch writers were the first promulgators of it, and that they had carried it to ridiculous extravagance." But however excusable it might be in a "Scotch writer" so long ago, coming from an English authority on angling of to-day, and of "twenty years' experience" to boot, is it not enough to take away one's breath, and tempt another "Scotch writer" to ask where Mr Pennell obtained his experience? At all events it has not been my experience, and I have fished seven months in the year during a period double that over which the researches of Mr Pennell have ex-

[1] Handbook on Angling, p. 84.

tended; and many other practical anglers fully bear me out in my conclusions. No doubt when the natural flies, such as the March brown and the sand-fly, come on the water in abundance, the angler will usually find that the fish do not take his imitations of these insects so freely as when the natural flies are passing off—which is indeed the time when his artificial fly becomes most deadly. What is asserted is that, even in those less favourable circumstances, the fish will prefer the imitation of the insect which happens to be on the water to *every other imitation.* And the explanation of the fact that the angler is not so successful in capturing fish at the time when the natural flies are on the water in swarms is simply this: his eight or nine flies bear a very small proportion to the myriads of natural flies among which they are cast and with which they compete, and so the chances of a trout being attracted by his flies are in the same degree proportionally small. But let the March browns or the sand-flies become scarcer, or better still, let them pass off for the time being altogether, then, in the absence of their rivals, the angler's flies, if closely resembling them, will have little difficulty in securing the prompt attention, and with it the portly person, of the trout. This desirable result will not be attained, however, as our author imagines, by dangling the flies in the water, and drawing them up and across, but by casting *up-stream* and allowing them to float gently down.

"Because trout," says Mr Pennell, "take the artificial for the natural fly, the 'formalists' argue that the one should be the exact counterpart of the other, ignoring the fact that the two insects are offered to the fish under entirely different conditions. The artificial fly is presented under water instead of on the surface; wet instead of dry; and in brisk motion up, down, or across stream, instead of passively floating. Thus at the very outset we find ourselves compelled to simulate life instead of death in our flies, and for this purpose impart to them a wholly unnatural motion whilst swimming; and as it is found that a naturally proportioned insect is deficient in movement, an unnatural quantity of legs (hackles) are added to it."

Now our position is, that just as in our imitation of the fly we endeavour to approach as nearly as possible to an exact counterpart of the prototype, so in our mode of offering it to the trout we maintain the "dear deceit," by presenting the artificial fly under conditions corresponding as closely as possible to those under which the natural fly would appear. With this intention we adopt the method which the English school of anglers condemns, and fish up-stream. The manifold advantages of this method will be described farther on; but one of them is, that thereby our artificial fly is presented to the fish in circumstances the most favourable for luring it to destruction. When fishing upstream, our artificial fly, if deftly cast, will at the moment of its fall appear to the trout as a living insect alighting on the surface of the water; and, if allowed to float gently down with the current, will not cease to prove an attraction to the fish, for it will then have the semblance of an insect fairly in the stream and unable to resist it. In both cases the appearance and conditions are perfectly natural; and in the latter they are none the less natural, though they may not be so alluring, if the fly do not maintain a position exactly on the surface, but slightly under it. It will of course be "wet," as an insect helplessly borne along by the stream would be; but with proper tackle and skill it will not sink much beneath the surface before the next cast is made; and though, to the fish, the fly is deprived of some attractive features when slightly under the surface, the angler reaps several advantages from so presenting it. These considerations, however, belong to another chapter. What we argue here is, that even if there be something less alluring to a fish in a fly under the surface, there is nothing which it would regard as unwonted or suspicious. For, are not the vast majority of river-flies hatched in the bed of the stream, and must they not therefore be often seen and seized by the fish under water, as well as on the surface? How, then, can our author say that flies presented under water are in an "abnormal condition"?

But even granting that the artificial fly is, as it appears to the trout, in an unnatural condition, I do not see how matters are to be mended by adding to its unnaturalness in dragging it up and across stream. Mr Pennell says, "We must simulate life instead of death in our flies, and therefore we must impart to them a wholly unnatural motion whilst swimming." How does Mr Pennell make out, that in order to "simulate life" we should be "unnatural"? Is this the theory of an artist? Or would any one, while attempting to deceive a cat by an artificial mouse, atone for the imperfection of the imitation by arranging that the mouse should move backwards or walk on its hind legs? Is a trout less likely to take a perfect imitation of a fly passively, though, mark you, naturally going with the current, half drowned to all appearance, or wholly drowned if you will, than an admittedly defective imitation of a nondescript, frantically endeavouring to keep up a false appearance of exuberant life by what are acknowledged to be "unnatural movements"? Is it not at least just as likely that the fish will detect an unnatural movement as an unusual appearance? At all events, does it not seem impossible that the one defect can cover the other? To "simulate life" in a fly is a very worthy aim indeed; only it is not to be attained by making it unnatural in its movements,—but first, by constructing a lifelike imitation of the natural insect down to minute particulars of form and colour—and secondly, by a skilful cast up-stream presenting this imitation in the most natural manner possible. If life is to be "simulated" at all, let it be for any sake the life of a fly, not of a monstrosity. Certain *natural* movements the angler may imitate; *unnatural* ones he had better not devise. The hovering and flitting of the insect over the surface of the water is a natural movement he cannot copy; to attempt it by a jerking motion of the wrist will only result in exciting the suspicions of the trout, if not in filling them with alarm. But what natural motions are within reach of the angler's imitative art—the alighting of the fly on the water, and its floating gently down as if carried by the stream—*these* let him attempt by fishing up-stream, and he will discover that his imitation insect will be "unmistakably identified as a fly."

Mr Pennell, in his criticism of Mr Stewart's argument for fishing up-stream and allowing the fly to come gently down, says that it is founded on "the analogical fallacy that because the natural *dry* fly usually floats passively *down*-stream, the artificial—*wet*—should do the same." Well, why shouldn't it? If we are not able to make our art compete successfully on all points with nature, let us not on that account outrage nature. The fallacy lies with Mr Pennell; for as we imitate a fly in the stream and helplessly carried along by it, the analogy is not between a *dry* fly and a *wet* one, but between a natural fly—*wet*—and an artificial fly—*wet*. Let both be placed on the water, and let us see which floats " briskly up."

Mr Pennell is as indifferent to the size of his flies as flies, as he is to their form and colour. For he says, " Size is a matter of no moment as regards the flies themselves, though of the utmost consequence in another point of view. For nothing is more certain than that some waters—usually large ones, whether rivers or lakes—require large flies; whilst small ones, almost equally universally, have to be fished with small flies. This necessity cannot be ignored by the 'formalists' any more than by the 'colourists'; and the result, as regards the former, is that they are obliged frequently to use a fly professing to be an exact imitation of the March brown, for example, and having no other advantages but such supposed resemblance, which is only about half, or a third even, of the natural size! This one fact, which is undeniable, is of itself almost a sufficient refutation of the 'exact imitation' theory."

I am astonished. Surely the author of 'The Angler Naturalist' does not imagine that all flies of one species are of one size, any more than all fish are—or even all "formalists," for that matter. It is true that, however long an insect may live, it never grows after it has attained its perfect form; yet the growth in the larval state is not always uniform, and in the same species it is quite common to find larvæ of very different sizes; and so, when full development has been reached, the diversity in bulk is wide enough. This is the case, more or less, in all flies; but in the green drakes, some instances appear in which one fly of the species is found more than double the size of another. The stone-flies, too, furnish conspicuous illustrations of such diversity; and moreover, in many species of this family, as the Rev. J. G. Wood informs us, though "there is great similitude in shape, there is great difference in size between the sexes, the males being scarcely one-third as large as the females."[1] In regard to the March browns, there are both large and small specimens on the water, and therefore it is difficult to understand what Mr Pennell means by their "natural size." I use an imitation of a March brown of a "natural size,"

[1] Insects at Home, p. 266.

and yet it is not so large as the largest, nor so small as the smallest, of those which frequent the stream.

In all these cases, and in others, we can scarcely be credited with practically furnishing "a sufficient refutation of the exact-imitation theory," when we dare to have some diversity in the size of our imitations of flies of the same species. It is quite open to the "formalist," so long as he does not "o'erstep the modesty of nature," to have, if he so please, his green drakes or his March browns of various sizes to suit various circumstances. Younger dressed his March brown on a No. 6 hook, and Stoddart used a No. 4, while Ronalds gives three different hooks; and yet they one and all fished with flies of the "natural size." It would be quite needless, however, even if it were possible, to have an imitation of all natural-sized flies, and therefore I select, as most generally suitable under all conditions, an average specimen, and dress it on a No. 3 hook. I am led to adopt this one because, in representing the largest sizes, there are produced a bulky dressing and a clumsy fly, which, in alighting on the water, is more apt to disturb than allure, especially if the river should be low and clear. On a "big" heavy water the larger imitations might possibly be the more deadly, but I prefer a fly of a medium size, as being, all round, the most advantageous.

In summing up the arguments, or rather such arguments as Mr Pennell adduces, on both sides, he gives what he calls his own "true rationale" of the matter in these words :—

"1. Trout certainly take the artificial for the natural fly.

"2. But as the artificial fly is necessarily presented in an abnormal condition — namely, wet instead of dry, sunk instead of floating, and as the resemblance which wet feathers and silk under water bear to dry insect-down, fluff, and wings on the water, is imperfect,—(3) it is necessary, for the purpose of hiding the counterfeit, and partly also to hide the hook, to give the fly an unnatural, lifelike movement in the water, adding to it also an unnatural quantity of legs (hackles) which open and shut, and move with the movements of the fly.

"4. These movements and alterations, however, make it quite impossible for trout to discriminate minutely between the various unnatural imitations of natural flies, whether in form or tint, (5) and render it doubly important that the imitation insect should be as characteristic and 'fly-like' as possible in shape, lest the fish should fail to perceive the resemblance altogether.

"6. General shape, general colour, and size, are all that can be distinguished by the fish. These are the points, therefore, to be kept in view in the construction of artificial trout-flies."

Mr Pennell then goes on to state his conclusion on the whole matter—that " it would be better to select two or three of the most favourite and distinctive families of flies, and imitate them only; not in their varieties or even in their species, but, as it were, in their types,—using those colours only which represent the prevailing tints in the families selected." Following out this idea he selects the Ephemeridæ and the Phryganidæ as the families from which these typical flies are to be drawn, employing in their construction only the colours green, yellow, and brown, as these are the tints which predominate in the families.

Reverting to this " true rationale," I should state it thus: " Trout certainly take the artificial for the natural fly;" but to induce them to do so the more readily—

1. Select as your prototype not any one natural fly, but an ideal fly—a creation of your own, a nondescript.

2. Of this ideal nondescript make an imperfect imitation both in form and colour.

3. Present this imperfect imitation in an unnatural condition—not as floating passively down, but as swimming vigorously up.

4. Conceal both the imperfect imitation and the

unnatural condition by furnishing the "fly" with an "unnatural quantity of legs," and by making it perform equally unnatural evolutions.

5. These legs and evolutions rendering it impossible for the trout to distinguish the "fly" either by form or tint, make the imitation "as characteristic and fly-like as possible, lest the fish should fail to perceive the resemblance altogether," for "trout certainly take the artificial for the natural fly."

There is very great danger indeed that the trout will "fail to perceive the resemblance altogether" of such a fly to the natural insect, but the danger will be considerably increased if the angler adopt a further recommendation which our author hastens to give ; for, to make "confusion worse confounded," after telling us that the fly should be "as characteristic and fly-like as possible in shape," and that " wings are an unmistakable characteristic of flies," he adds on the next page, "wings are therefore merely an encumbrance to the artificial trout-fly, and should be entirely rejected." Doubtless wings will be found an encumbrance and a snare to flies that are already provided with "an unnatural quantity of legs," and that are expected to perform such wonderful evolutions on the water to disguise their imperfections ; but it must surely be the dimness of vision in some aged trout, or the blind appetite of some young one, that would induce either to dine on flies without the "unmistakable characteristic."

Thus the whole theory carries with it its own refutation, and, like the fly which it advocates, requires "an unnatural quantity of legs" to support and render it acceptable. These, however, are still undeveloped; and therefore, while it may be only a graceful panegyric on our theory for Mr Pennell to say that it cost him "a pang of regret to write what may eventually prove its epitaph," we fear that he has thereby deprived us of the opportunity of reciprocating his good offices, for he has all the while been unwittingly, though we cannot say prematurely, performing that last loving labour for his own.

The position that, since trout take the artificial for the natural fly, they will be most readily deceived by an imitation as perfect as may be in all points of form, colour, size, and motion, has been assailed not only by those who say, with Mr Pennell, you *cannot* present such an imitation, but also by those who say, you *need not*. I have tried to show the possibility of doing so; and now a few words as to its advisability.

The idea that trout can detect the nicest distinctions of form and colour in flies, is held by some authors to be incompatible with the so-called defective structure of the eye in the fish, and by others to be inconsistent with its limited knowledge of entomology. But this is mere theorising. The eye of a fish is certainly peculiar in its structure, and, as the editor of 'Cuvier's Fishes' says, is "only an indifferent representative of the beautiful and animated eye of man." The crystalline lens is extremely dense and almost spherical; the iris can neither be dilated nor contracted, and therefore the pupil cannot be regulated to the degree of light. While all this is true, we must remember that we are not likely to ascertain what fishes can see with their eyes, by simply comparing them with our own; that they must be in this, as in other parts of their structure, perfectly adapted to the medium which surrounds them; and that what may be a defective eye for an animal on earth, may be the best possible for a fish in water. My belief in the economy of Nature's power leads me to suppose that they have no more than they need; my faith in her goodness assures me that they have no less.

Mr Erasmus Wilson, in "Ephemera's" 'Handbook,' sums up a minute consideration of this subject in the following words: "Whether, therefore, we regard the mechanical or the vital apparatus of the organ of vision, or whether we pursue the inquiry, by anatomical investigation, or by observation of the habits of the animals, we have the clearest evidence before us that the faculty of sight in fishes is one of their highest sentient endowments."[1]

Dr Günther, in his 'Study of Fishes,' while admitting that in the range of their vision and acuteness of sight fishes are very inferior to the higher classes of vertebrates, says: "At the same time it is evident that they perceive their prey or approaching danger from a considerable distance; and the discrimination with which they sometimes prefer one colour or kind of artificial fly to another, affords sufficient evidence that the vision, at least of certain species, is by no means devoid of clearness and precision."[2] The recent researches of Mr Dalrymple reveal the existence of particular muscles controlling the *position* of the lens of the eye of many fishes, and thus modifying the angle of vision for varying distances, precisely as the ciliary muscle of the human eye regulates the *form* of the lens, and adapts it to the required focus.

Much easy satire and some cheap raillery have been expended on the angler who, in insisting on an exact imitation of a fly, would seem to credit trout with an extensive practical entomological knowledge of its natural prey. But mere theorists are not very likely to discover what amount of entomological

[1] Handbook of Angling, p. 292.
[2] Pages 111, 112.

knowledge trout possess, any more than they are likely to settle the once vexed question as to how many angels can dance on the point of a needle. The knowledge possessed may be extensive or otherwise, but it is certainly sufficient and eminently practical. The tastes of fish may be variable, and even whimsical, but the angler will only ascertain what these are by studying them. Experience alone is the guide; and my experience, as already given, points to the conclusion that trout *do* discriminate between fly and fly even under the most unfavourable conditions; and I am quite content to accept this fact with all that it implies.

Mr Stewart, in his excellent manual on Angling, and Mr Stoddart before him, say that anglers who hold the view that successful fly-fishing requires the use of an imitation of one or other of the natural insects on the water, are therefore necessarily obliged to have an infinite variety of flies. I have already hinted that this is not my opinion. Very few varieties are really necessary, but those selected at any one time should be facsimiles of flies that are in greatest favour with the trout then. I have myself fished with flies of every form and colour, and have caught fish with all of them. But I would not recommend them all on that account as equally deadly: many of them, indeed, are practically of no value for good sport. The angler may catch trout with an imitation of a fly with which the fish have had previously no acquaintance; he may catch them with flies that have not the remotest resemblance to any natural fly seen on water or in air; he may even catch them with a frog for that matter. There is no accounting for the vagaries of fish, any more than of folk; for there are "queer fish" on land as well as in water. Yet eccentricity here and there is not taken as the prevailing taste, and what a foolish or frolicsome young trout may do occasionally is no criterion of the usual habits of the genus. All that is contended for is—and this, I suppose, is what an amateur would wish to be assured of—that an *exact* imitation of those flies which observation has proved to be most to the liking of the trout will kill better, vastly better, than an *imperfect* imitation of such flies, or even an imitation, however perfect, of any other flies.

Having premised thus much on the principles which regulate my choice of flies, I shall now present the angler with my list, classifying them according to the seasons in which their prototypes appear.

FLIES FOR FEBRUARY, MARCH, AND APRIL.

1. *The February Red.*—This fly, the first of any importance to the angler, makes its appearance in

February, should the weather be bright and genial, and continues in season until the end of March. It is a small insect with a dark-brown or reddish-black body, two sets of light mottled wings (of which the posterior are the larger), and legs of a reddish tinge. Though Father Walton says that "no man should, in honesty, catch a trout in the middle of March," his *collaborateur* Cotton begins his fly-fishing in January, and leads off with a "red brown," for which he substitutes the "lesser red brown" in February. I fancy that the angler's "honesty" is not so much a barrier to the enjoyment of the sport in February as the late seasons which are now the rule in this country, and which prevent the flies from making their appearance in any numbers during that month. On a fine day, however, good sport is occasionally got with the red; and I have seen a basket of twenty pounds taken with it in February.

It is dressed as follows: *Body*—A thread of black and one of pale-red silk twisted together, with black and red cock's hackle. *Wings*—The light side of a feather from the hen-pheasant wing, tied on a No. 2 hook.

It may be as well to state here, once for all, that my flies are dressed on Adlington's hooks, which I consider by far the best that are made.

2. *The Blae*, or *Blue Dun* of English anglers.— The blaes are a very numerous genus, and one

Pl. I. Trout Flies

variety or another, differing simply in shade, is to be found in the water during the whole of the season. The earliest representative comes out late in February or early in March, and continues to be a special favourite till June.

This species of the blae is dressed with the starling-wing and black hackle, tied with black silk on a No. 2 hook.

3. *The March Brown.*—With the exception of the sand or gravel-bed fly, there is perhaps no more deadly artificial lure than the March brown. In an open season it makes its appearance in March, but if the weather be cold, its advent may be delayed till April. It generally lasts till the beginning of May. When it is said that a fly is " in season," the reader is not to understand that he will find a representative of it on the water at all times during the fishing months. For the temperature of the water is always an important factor in the development of flies. Thus the blaes come out on what we should call a warm day in early spring; but when the season advances, and the temperature generally is raised, a comparatively cold day is more favourable for their appearance. The sand-flies, on the other hand, appear on the water only when the day is hot, with bright sunshine. If the morning be warm, the March browns may frequently be found on the water as early as nine

o'clock, but in colder days they may not appear till mid-day. In balmy weather they may be seen flitting o'er the surface of the stream in myriads, while the trout " in speckled pride " literally rise to the occasion, the water seethes from bank to bank, and the fun grows fast and furious. A " rise " of trout on Clyde or Tweed under the potent influence of this March charmer is a sight sufficient to disabuse the prejudiced mind even of a Johnson, and convert the most persistent detractor into an enthusiastic lover and " constant practiser of our art." It reaches its full development in the great red spinner, which is also a favourite fly with some anglers.

The brown is dressed thus: *Wings*—The dark side of the feather of the partridge-wing. *Body*—The reddish-brown of the hare's breast, mixed with a little of the hair from the ear, tied with yellow silk on a No. 3 hook.

4. *The Teal Drake.*—This is a small, slender-bodied fly, which makes its appearance in April or May, according to the season. The body and legs are of a dark colour, and the wings are mottled white and black. Though many anglers do not set much store by this fly, I find it an excellent lure till the end of May. As in other members of this order, the upper pair of wings forms a sheath or case for protecting the under pair when the

insect is at rest, and then the wings are incumbent; but to give the fly the appearance of alighting on the water, I adhere to the plan I adopt in all other imitations, and make the wings expanded.

It is dressed with a mottled feather from the teal drake (which, however, is rather lighter in colour than the wings of the natural insect, but is as close an imitation as possible), and black hackle tied with black silk on a No. 2 hook. At the end of May a red hackle is substituted for the black, and tied with yellow silk.

FLIES FOR MAY.

5. *The Sand-Fly*, or *Gravel-Bed Fly* of English authors.—This fly "comes on" in the beginning of May, usually about the 6th (later, if the season be cold), and lasts till the beginning of June. It belongs to the Tipulidæ family or crane-flies—so called from their having long legs. Unlike the other flies enumerated, the sand-fly is not hatched in the water, but in the sand and gravel-beds on the banks of the river. And this is the explanation of the fact mentioned without comment by both Ronalds and Francis, that "it is not found upon all waters," and that "none are to be seen on sedgy rivers which flow over a loamy or muddy bed." Whenever the sand and gravel-

beds become heated by the sun's rays, the insects, bursting from their larvæ, attain their full development as flies, and may then be seen skipping in thousands over the stream, to the intense delight and satisfaction of the hungry trout. This applies especially to the Clyde, as, for a great part of its course, it flows over a gravelly bed with sand-banks on each side. As the March brown is unquestionably the most effective fly from the middle of March till the beginning of May, so the sand-fly stands pre-eminent as a "killer" from that time until the beginning of June, when the May-fly makes its appearance. Should the weather in May be bright and hot—for then only are the conditions favourable—the sand-fly, closely imitated and properly used, will afford more sport than any other artificial fly that I know. At all events, in a "small" clear water during bright sunshine, and for days together, I have got heavier baskets with it than with any other artificial fly, or even with all the others combined, with the exception of the blae, which, occurring under many forms, is always represented on my cast in one variety or another throughout the entire season. A cold day, however, being unfavourable for the development of the natural flies, is unfavourable for the success of their imitations. The fly is a small one, with dark body and legs, and light brown and black mottled wings.

It is dressed with a tail-feather of the hen pheasant, with black hackle, tied with black and blue silk on a No. 2 hook.

6. *The Black Blae*, or *Iron Blue Dun* of some authors.—This is a small dark fly of the same order and family as the blae or blue dun. It is in season from the early part of May till the latter end of June. It generally comes on the water on cold days, and then, from the absence of the sand-fly, it is a good killing lure. To imitate every species of the numerous genus of duns would be a fruitless task. What the angler requires is a selection of the best representatives of this excellent fly; and among the many varieties of it which crowd the streams throughout the season, I consider there is none more deadly than the black blae. After some days' existence in the stage represented, the insect dons a brand-new dress-coat with a long tail, and attains his full development in the well-known "spinning Jenny." In this form also it is doubtless a great favourite with the fish, but the difficulty of imitating perfectly the wonderful delicacy and transparency of the wings is the principal reason why so many anglers discard it. For, as I have stated before, an imitation to be thoroughly effective must be perfect; and the angler had better use a close imitation of a less alluring fly than a poor imitation of a favourite.

The black blae is dressed with the wing of the hen blackbird and a little down from the back of the water-mouse, or a small black hackle mixed with a little yellow mohair, and tied with black and yellow silk on a No. 1 hook. For the wing, "Ephemera" prefers a tomtit's wing-feather; Ronalds, a cormorant's wing, or the breast of the water-hen; Jackson, a wing of the water-hen: and these may make good imitations, for the wings of the natural insect vary slightly in depth of colour.

7. *The Green-Tail* or *Grannom.*—This is one of the numerous species of the caddis-fly. It appears early in May if the weather be warm, and lasts a little longer than the sand-fly. The body has a slight yellowish tinge, the upper part being blackish, and the segments edged with whitish grey. The wings are shining; the upper pair are pale brown, and the lower are pearly in hue and slightly iridescent. Since the caddis family, both in their larval and winged states, furnish the angler with some of his deadliest lures, a few words on the development of this fly may not be considered out of place.

As in the case of the stone-flies, the female caddis collects her eggs and carries them about in a cluster at the extremity of the body. The green tint of this cluster gives the popular name to the fly. When about to deposit her eggs, she crawls down the stem of some aquatic plant a foot or so below the surface, and by means of a gelatinous secretion fastens them to the stem. There they remain till hatched. When they reach the larval stage the little creatures attach to themselves, by a glutinous cement, fragments of leaves, sticks, grass stems, shells, and grains of sand, until they have formed hard tubular cases; and in these remarkable habitations they pass the whole of their larval and pupal existence. In some species the caddis-cases are carried about by the larvæ; in others they are affixed to stones. When about to pass into the quiescent and helpless pupal state, the caddis fortifies its dwelling against the predatory hordes of the water by spinning a wonderful network across each end, which sufficiently protects it till the final stage is reached. In assuming the perfect form the larger species burst this network, and crawling up the stems of plants, find their way to the banks; while the smaller make use of their cases as rafts, on which they stand and spread out their bright new wings to the sun.

The green-tail is not a particular favourite with anglers, especially if the banks of the river are well wooded, as the insects find their nourishment in the leaves of the trees, from which they issue forth in swarms, to be in their turn nourishment for the expectant trout; and as said trout exercise a wise discrimination in preferring the genuine article when they can get it, the angler's imitation in such circumstances will bring him little success. If the banks are destitute of trees, and the day be wet, it sometimes affords good sport.

It is dressed with hare's ear for the body, with light side of a feather from the wing of the partridge or cock pheasant, tied with brown and yellow silk on a No. 2 hook. I prefer the pheasant dressing.

8. *The Yellow Dun.*—This is a small yellow fly which comes on the water towards the middle of May, when the days are warm and sunny. It lasts for several weeks; and during that time the trout show such a predilection for the natural fly that the imitation is not of much account. For my part I seldom use it.

Dress with straw-coloured silk, yellow hackle, and canary-wing on a No. 1 hook.

9. *The May-Fly,* or *Stone-Fly* of some authors, or *Green Drake* of others.—There are many pretenders to the title of the May-fly. Cotton enumerates four —the green drake, the stone-fly, the black fly, and the little yellow May-fly,—"all of which," says he, " have their champions and advocates to dispute and plead their priority, though I do not understand why the two last-named should—the first two having so manifestly the advantage, both in their beauty and the wonderful execution they do

in their season." If there is anything " in a name," the title of May-fly should certainly not be given to the green drake, seeing that it seldom appears on the water until the beginning of June. This Mr Francis admits, and yet he subscribes to the claims of the green drake. The stone-fly, our May-fly, comes out on Scottish rivers about the 20th of May, and remains in season for about three weeks. In its immature or larva state it is known as the creeper, crab, or gauger, and is, under certain conditions, nearly as deadly a lure as the fully developed insect. It is found in abundance under the stones and pebbles by the river-side, where it reaches its maturity. It will thus be readily understood that on those rivers which flow over a sandy or a fine gravelly bed—the home of the sand-fly —the May-fly is scarcely to be found; and even on the same river they may be plentiful in some reaches, and entirely absent in others. The insect attains a large size, and although clumsy in its flight, it is very active with its legs, which it uses with surprising effect in paddling its way through the water. The colour is generally described as "a fine brown, ribbed with yellow, and yellower on the belly than the back;" but my observation has shown me that in the early morning the body has a fine yellow hue, which deepens and passes into a brown as the day wears on; and further, that in the early days of their brief existence, the insects wear their brightest coats. I always capture them in the morning, as I find that in their yellow attire they possess the greatest fascination for the giddy trout, as is evidenced by the literally "devouring affection" which the finny tribe display towards them. The May-fly, indeed, is the most tempting and most deadly natural insect known to the angler. I seldom use the imitation when I can get the natural fly, seeing the trout have a like preference. But in places where the insect cannot be found at all during its season, or on waters from which it has just passed off, a good imitation may work some destruction.

I make one thus: *Body*—A piece of cork cut the same shape, and ribbed with yellow and brown silk. *Wings*—Whalebone scraped as thin as gauze. Hackle stained yellowish brown. A No. 5 hook is tied on at the tail, and another at the shoulder of the fly. The object in making the body of cork is to get a large fly of this kind to float. It is fished down-stream in the same way as we use the natural insect. The method will be explained in a subsequent chapter.

JUNE FLIES.

10. *The Black Mote* —This fly comes on the water in June, and lasts till August. It is a very small insect, with black body and dark dun wings. Born of the water, it is found all over the surface on bright sunny days, but disappears in rain or cold. In windy weather the angler may look for it in sheltered situations.

Dressing: *Body*—Herl of black ostrich-feather. *Wings*—Light side of a feather from the wing of the hen blackbird, tied with black silk on a No. 0 hook.

When the trout are rising well at this fly, it is useless to have any other imitation on the cast, especially during June and July. The angler should then make up a special cast of the finest gut.

11. *The Yellow Fly*, or *Green Drake* of English authors.—This large fly appears on the water about the beginning of June, and continues as long as the May-fly. As in the case of the March brown, its appearance during the season is accelerated by warm weather, and retarded by cold. In its larval condition it is an inhabitant of the muddy banks of rivers, where it burrows for itself a home of safety, in which to pass the two years of its im-

mature existence. When it comes out of the pupa, it takes to the reeds on the river-side, and is always found on that bank towards which the wind blows. Its habitat is thus chiefly on sluggish streams, bordered by rushes, where the May-fly is not to be met with. After a few days' existence as the green drake, it reaches a still further development; the male fly becomes the black drake, and the female the grey drake. In these later stages, however, it is not so valuable a fly as when it first appears—the bright colours, as in the case of the Mayfly, being most in demand. And, as Mr Wood in his 'British Insects' remarks on this fly, "the angler need care only for the female insects, because the fish prefer them, laden as they are with eggs, to the males, which have little in them but air."

When the natural fly cannot be had, I have recourse to the artificial, which is made up thus: The *wing* is dressed with a feather from the breast of the wild drake, dyed a pale yellow by means of fustic in a weak solution of alum; the *body*, with hog's-down dyed pale yellow, sparingly put on, and ribbed with brown silk. A light-yellow hackle is wound over it. Hook No. 7 or 8.

12. *The Black Ant.*—This is a somewhat large fly, with a black body and a light dun-coloured gauze-like wing. It appears in June or July, according to the season, and lasts till the end of

August. It loves the sunlight, and takes best on warm bright days.

Dressing : *Body*—Black ostrich herl. *Legs*—Black and red cock's hackle tied under the wings. *Wings*—Light side of a feather from the starling-wing, tied with black silk on a No. 4 or 5 hook.

The natural insect makes an excellent lure. The method of using it will be described subsequently.

JULY FLIES.

13. *The Partridge Tail* or *Frog-hopper.*—This is one of many species. It is found on bright sunny days hopping about the slender spires of grass. In taking its long leaps it sometimes alights on the water, when it falls an easy prey to the trout. The species I prefer is dressed with the mottled feather of the partridge-tail, and light ginger-coloured hackle tied with yellow silk on a No. 2 hook. Let it be the end fly of the cast.

14. *The Blue Dun* or *Blae*, already given as No. 2.

AUTUMN FLIES.

15. *Autumn Red.*—This is another species of the caddis-fly, and, along with those now to be mentioned, is found on the water during the months of August, September, and October. It is dressed

thus: A feather from the tail of the hen pheasant, and light ginger-coloured hackle, tied with yellow silk. Hook No. 2.

16. *Autumn Musk-Fly.*—This is a smaller species of what is known in England as the cinnamon-fly, and closely resembles the English sand-fly.

Dressing: A feather from the light side of the cock-pheasant wing, and a ginger-coloured hackle, tied with yellow silk. Hook No. 2.

17. *The Blue Dun* or *Blae*, as before described.

18. *The White Tip.*—This is one of the numerous small flies with variously coloured tips, to be found on the water on warm evenings before dark. Larger flies, also with light tips on the wings, make their appearance at night. Dressing: Feather from the back of the starling-wing, and starling hackle tied with black silk on a No. 1 hook.

19. *The Hare's-Ear Dun.*—Another representative of this well-known and favourite genus. Dressing: Starling-wing with down from the outside of the hare's ear, tied with yellow silk. Hook No. 2.

20. *The Autumn Brown.*—This fly may be best represented by dressing a March brown on a No. 2 hook.

21. *Pale Autumn Dun* (Willow Fly).—The "little pale blue dun" of Ronalds. This fly appears about the end of August, and lasts until the close of the fishing season. It is very abun-

dant, and is a good fly for both trout and grayling. Dressing: Starling-wing, and the light down from the inside of the hare's ear mixed with a little yellow wool for the body, or a small yellow hackle, tied with yellow silk on a No. 1 hook. A favourite fly in August and September on a black water is dressed thus: Orange-coloured feathers from the wing of the thrush—two feathers being necessary to form the wing; black hackle and a No. 2 hook. Tie with black silk.

GLOAMIN' OR EVENING FLIES.

During the months of June and July capital sport is sometimes obtained on warm evenings at dusk. Several species of the yellow and the blue duns come on the water at that time, and in their artificial forms often prove very deadly. The following are most effective:—

1. *The Evening Blue Dun.*—Dressed with starling-wing and black hackle tied with yellow silk on a No. 2 hook.

2. *The Gloamin' Red Hackle.*—This is the "pale evening dun" of Ronalds, but the representation of it in that authority is somewhat faulty. Dress thus: Light starling-wing with a light ginger-coloured cock's hackle, tied with yellow silk. Hook No. 2.

3. *Light-Red Dun.*—This is dressed like No. 2, substituting the light side of a feather from the partridge-wing for the starling-wing.

4. *Evening Teal* is one of the sheath-winged order of flies, somewhat resembling the teal drake already described. It is dressed with a mottled feather from the teal drake, with a light ginger-coloured hackle, tied with yellow silk on a No. 2 hook.

5. *Light-Yellow Dun.*—This fly appears during cold nights in June. Dress with canary or corn-bunting wing, and a light-yellow hackle, tied with pale straw-coloured silk on a No. 2 hook.

NIGHT-FLIES.

The following flies come into use after sunset during the months of June and July. They are imitations of those large moths that are seen towards nightfall flitting about the meadows in warm weather; and the angler whose enthusiasm for the sport is sufficient to take him to the waterside instead of to his bed, will often with their assistance score a big success ere the day dawn. The method of fishing will be explained further on, but meantime the flies are given.

1. *The Large White Tip.*—This fly is costumed thus: A white-tipped feather from the wing of

Night-Flies.

the wild drake or teal drake, with mixed red and black wool for the body. A black hackle tied with yellow silk on a No. 5 hook.

2. *Night Yellow Fly.*—This fly is similar to the green drake which appears during the day in June. The same dressing will do as is given for the drake; but as the night-fly is smaller, a No. 5 hook should be used instead of a No. 7.

3. *Pheasant-Tail Fly* (Black Hackle).—Dress the wing with a feather from the hen pheasant; the body with white tinsel, and a black hackle tied with yellow silk on a No. 4 hook.

4. *Pheasant-Tail Fly* (Red Hackle).—Dress with hen-pheasant tail and a light ginger-coloured hackle with yellow silk. Hook No. 4.

5. *Large Night Brown.*—This fly closely resembles the March brown, and is dressed somewhat similarly. *Wing*—The dark side of a feather from the partridge-wing. *Body*—The down from hare's breast, tied with yellow silk on a No. 5 hook.

6. *Large Blue Dun.*—It is dressed, like other blue duns or blaes, with starling-wing and black hackle, tied with black silk. Hook No. 4.

7. *The Night Teal.*—This is of the same family as the other teals already described. Dress with teal-drake feather and a light ginger-coloured hackle, with a little reddish hare-down underneath. It is tied with yellow silk on a No. 5. hook.

8. *The Down-looker,* or *Oak-Fly.*—This fly is generally found on trunks of trees or posts near the water-side, and is so named from the fact that whenever it alights it turns its head downwards. Dressing: Light side of a feather from the wing of the cock pheasant, with down from the hare's ear, and a grey hackle wound over it, tied with yellow silk on a No. 5 hook.

9. *Pheasant-Wing.*—Dress thus: Light side of a feather from the cock-pheasant wing, black and brown wool with black hackle over it, and tied with brown silk on a No. 5 hook.

10. *The Musk Brown.*—This is a caddis-fly, and receives its name from the odour which it emits when handled. Dressing: *Wing*—Very light-brown common hen or brown-pigeon feather. *Body*—The down of a hare's breast, wound over with light ginger-coloured hackle, tied with yellow silk. Hook No. 5.

Should the water be dark-coloured, all the above night-flies might be dressed on hooks of a larger size.

SPIDER-FLIES.

Spider-flies—or, as they are often called, hackle or buzz flies—are held in high repute by a large section of the angling community; and it is undeniable that on hot sultry days in June and July, when the winged fly is not on the water, they sometimes prove a very attractive lure, and even excel their winged competitors. For myself I have always preferred the winged insects, and have no doubt that, in the proper fishing season, they are by far the most effective. Besides, owing to the softness of the materials with which they are dressed, spiders do not last so long as the ordinary flies; and the angler will often find that after catching a dozen or so of trout, there is very little left of the "spider" to conceal the hook. This, of course, necessitates a change on the cast, with consequent loss of time, and, it may be, of temper. Now we would advise the angler to "taste life's glad moments" ere they pass, and avoid all unnecessary trials of temper and tackle at the very time when the lure is most taking and the sport most keen.

1. *The Black Spider.*—Dress with a small feather from the shoulder of the starling; or, if this cannot be had, a feather from the shoulder of the rook.

2. *The Red Spider.*—Use a small feather from the shoulder of the corn-crake or land-rail; failing this, a light ginger-coloured hackle.

3. *Golden Plover Spider.*—This is dressed with a black and yellow mottled feather from the golden plover, and as the season advances, with a small feather from the neck to suit a smaller hook. This spider is a great favourite with many anglers.

4. *Grouse Spider.* — Here is another favourite, dressed with a mottled feather from the grouse. I know of some anglers who use no other lure than this spider during the whole of the fishing season.

5. *Partridge Spider.*—Use a small mottled feather from the breast of the partridge, and tie with yellow silk.

As the season advances the hooks are reduced in size.

FAVOURITE FLIES OF SOME ANGLERS.

In the preceding lists will be found all the flies I use, and the dressing I consider best adapted for each. Of course there are many other flies given by good authorities; but to enumerate them all would be, as I have already said, an endless task. All I can do here is to give one or two different dressings of flies already described.

As a fly for May, the body made of down from the hare's ear may be dressed with a variety of wings. In the green-tail, I have used the partridge-wing; but a good fly may be dressed with the wing of the starling, corn-bunting, jay, woodcock, or teal.

The sand-fly or gravel-bed fly might be dressed with a small brown and black mottled feather from the root of the partridge-wing close to the back, or with a feather from the back of the grouse just above the tail; but the feather from the hen-pheasant tail I prefer to the others, as it more closely resembles the natural fly, although, at the same time, it is more difficult to dress.

CHAPTER III.

FLY-DRESSING.

"Thou, Nature, art my goddess: to thy law
My services are bound."
—King Lear.

ALMOST every writer on angling since the days of old Izaak, has prefaced his chapter on this subject with the observation that it is nearly if not quite impossible, by merely printed instructions, however explicit, to make any one an expert or even a tolerably fair fly-dresser. Certainly the art did not come to me through any such instructions; and a practical fly-maker myself, I am at one with others in the belief that a volume of details would fail to impart it to any. For fly-dressing is an art—a humble art, if you will, but still an art as much as painting is. In both we set ourselves to represent nature in form and tint, and equally in both we must follow nature as our guide. The principles of the art may be given, but the art itself, in the application of these principles, must be acquired. And should the tyro ask, How? I am inclined to answer him, as Opie answered his pupil who wished to know with what the great painter mixed his colours, "With brains, sir!"

But, postulating the "brains," I can instruct the beginner in the materials for fly-making, and tell him, as far as words can, what he is to do with them. I may tell him, too, that he must train his eye to discern the features of the natural fly, and his hand to reproduce these features in all their delicacy and grace. But I cannot give him the true eye and the delicate touch; they come not by instruction. They may come, however, through close observation and constant practice in intelligently following the natural model after a good method. "Practice makes perfection," says the proverb. Yes; but until we reach perfection, we shall never know how much practice leads thereto. There is no finality in this art, any more than in any other; and even our best imitation is, after all, only the "cunning'st pattern of excelling nature." And though the pattern must be submitted to the critical eye of the fish before I am able to boast its cunningness, I can, even in these days of secondary education of trout, always approach sufficiently near to the perfection of nature as to deceive the critics and fill the basket. And to encourage any angler who has the "ambition to become one of the greatest deceivers," I can only say to him, as Cotton said to his disciple, "A trout taken with a fly of your own making will please you better than twenty with one of mine."

I subjoin a few hints as practical in their nature as possible, in the hope that the beginner may be saved some needless trouble through following a wrong method.

There are several ways of dressing flies. Some dressers clip the feather to avoid breaking the fibre, and tie the wings on separately. I cannot commend this plan. A fly so dressed is very easily injured, and soon gets beyond identification by either fisher or fish; while from the very first the wings lie flat on the back when the fly is placed on the water, and thus rob the imitation of much of its attractiveness.

Another method consists in taking off the fibre in small sections, and placing them evenly and closely together until the dresser has sufficient to form both wings. These he ties upon the hook with four or five turns of the silk, and then, with a needle dividing the fibre, and so forming the wings, he whips the thread a few turns between them, reversing it each time as if describing the figure eight. The number of turns required depends upon the fineness of the silk.

But the plan I adopt is the following:—

1. Take the fibre from the feather in small portions until you have what will form the wings, moisten each portion with saliva, and place them evenly together.

2. Take now the gut, with the teeth render it flat at the end so as to give a secure hold in the tying, and having made two turns of the thread round the middle of the hook, place the gut along the under side of the wire, and wind the thread firmly until within four or five turns of the bend.

3. Lay on the fibre to the metal, whip to the end of the hook, and make two turns back to the root of the wings.

4. Split the fibre with the point of a needle, apportioning to each wing an exactly equal amount.

5. Roll the thread between the wings, taking care to keep them apart with the finger and thumb, and set well back at each turn of the silk.

6. If the fly is to be a hackle, work back with the thread a few turns and fasten the hackle; wind to the tail of the fly, and thence back to the wings; and lastly, roll on the hackle up to the wings, and finish off.

7. If you are making a fly bodied with dubbing, work back with the silk as far as the body is to extend, wind on the dubbing with waxed silk thread, and finish off at the root of the wing.

Many fly-dressers finish off at the tail, but the result is unsatisfactory. The fly won't be long in use till the trout have torn open the fastenings and exposed the cheat. When it is finished at the wings, the work stands much longer. I always use floss silk folded to the thickness required, slightly twisted, and well waxed. Some dressers use scissors to remove the surplus fibre; but by placing the nail of the left thumb under it, close to the end of the hook, and cutting it off with a sharp penknife, a much neater finish is made. Flies dressed in the way I have described, may be crushed or ruffled in the book or pocket almost to any extent without detriment to their killing qualities; for whenever they are placed in the water, they at once assume their original form, the wings set themselves widely apart, and stand out on the surface of the stream with all the appearance of life. The only possible objection to the method is its tediousness; but though this objection may have some weight with dressers who are not anglers, it can have no weight at all with the enthusiastic fly-fisher who dresses his own flies.

CHAPTER IV.

ARTIFICIAL-FLY FISHING.

" Mark well the various seasons of the year,
How the succeeding insect race appear ;
In this revolving moon one colour reigns,
Which in the next the fickle trout disdains."
—GAY.

" Give me mine angle : we'll to the river : there
.   .   .   .   .   .   I will betray
Tawny-finned fishes."
—*Antony and Cleopatra.*

" With the well-imitated fly to hook
The eager trout, and with the slender line
And yielding rod solicit to the shore
The struggling, panting prey."
—ARMSTRONG : *Art of Preserving Health.*

ALTHOUGH in sheltered districts and in a favourable spring fair sport may be obtained with the artificial fly early in March, in Scotland, at least, where for too many years past winter has " lingered in the lap of May," it would hardly be safe to set down in the angler's calendar that fly-fishing begins in earnest before the middle of April. At this time the natural flies generally begin to appear on the water in considerable numbers, to the evident satisfaction of the trout, that speedily and joyfully hail them with more than the familiarity of an "auld acquaintance," whom even a whole winter's enforced abstinence had not suffered them to forget.

In exposed and high-lying districts the flies are later in coming out, and it is not unusual for the angling season on one part of the river to be a fortnight later than on another. In April and early May the good baskets which may be got on Clyde below Lamington, or on Tweed below Peebles, will be looked for in vain on the upper reaches of those rivers, where circumstances are not so favourable for the early development of the flies.

From the commencement of the fishing season till the end of May, the angler may rely on obtaining better sport with the artificial fly than at any other time during the season. I admit the fact, and have elsewhere endeavoured to account for it, that even during this, "the height of the season," the angler's "take" is poor compared with the baskets of twenty or thirty years ago; but even in these altered and degenerate times, I should consider any day's fishing a failure were I to kill less than from ten to fifteen pounds of trout between ten in the morning and four in the afternoon.

I have stated that for artificial fly-fishing I prefer, and constantly use, the spliced rod and loop-line. A reel is of course dispensed with here, and the connection between rod and line is formed by simply passing the loop attached to the line through the corresponding hair-loop at the point of the rod. The length of the hair-line should be regulated by the size of the stream. For such a river as the Clyde I employ one of 18 or 19 feet, though some anglers use a considerably longer one. A combination of the two methods of loop-line and reel-line fishing is sometimes effected by using an ordinary jointed rod with reel, and attaching the loop-line to the end of the line wound off the reel. This answers very well in large rivers where big fish are abundant; but for ordinary trouting purposes, the simple loop-line and rod system is much to be preferred.

The advantages which such a line possesses over the ordinary line are manifest, and have been already alluded to. By its more gradual taper and greater weight, a longer line can be thrown, and this with much more ease and precision, than is at all possible with a reel-line, and consequently a larger number of flies may be used, and a wider stretch of water commanded. The direction and strength of the wind are always important elements in the success of a day's fishing, and the angler cannot afford to ignore them; but so far as mere facility in casting is concerned, the loop-line possesses a marked advantage over the ordinary line in rendering the angler much more independent of the assistance of the wind, and much less impeded by its opposition. The greater weight and consequent momentum of his line enable him to cast his flies to within a few points of the wind if necessary, where, with a lighter line, much good water might be lost, and much time spent in crossing and re-crossing to get a favouring breeze; while in the entire absence of wind he can take full advantage of the great length of his line, and cast with unerring precision. Unless in exceptional circumstances of wind and weather, the angler with the loop-line ought to be able to lay his flies on the water within a few inches of any given point —and this, too, from a distance of 40 or 50 feet. The value of such a cast in clear water can scarcely be overestimated, especially when it is remembered that the line carries three times as many flies as the advocates of the short-line system use when fishing up-stream. Every part of the river may thus be most favourably and easily reached without the necessity of deep wading, and the concomitant evil of unduly disturbing the water.

It should be noted that these advantages are

Advantages of the Loop-Line. 73

claimed for the loop-line only when applied to fly-fishing, and that when so applied the line has its truest action only in conjunction with a spliced rod of perfect taper and even sweep; for by no other arrangement can there be combined and homogeneous action of all the parts from butt to fly. Angling with such a rod and line is scientific angling. Every impulse of the arm imparted to the rod is transmitted directly to the cast of flies, and the response is true and prompt; the nicest calculations can be made for distance and direction with almost perfect accuracy; and it becomes as possible to cover a rising fish under overhanging trees, or straight up-stream within an inch or two of the bank, as to sweep the river in its broad expanse.

The novice will not, of course, expect to become an adept on first handling the rod; but with a little expertness, the results will astonish him: and not the least part of the astonishment will arise from the gradual discovery of the vastly superior capabilities of such a rod and line. If the excellence of the instrument has anything to do with the excellence of the performance, the angler may rest assured that in the loop-rod and line he is furnished with a guarantee that whatever skill he acquires in casting will be abundantly answered in the issue. In fact, with this rod and line, true angler cannot afford to ignore them; but so far as mere facility in casting is concerned, the loop-line possesses a marked advantage over the ordinary line in rendering the angler much more independent of the assistance of the wind, and much less impeded by its opposition. The greater weight and consequent momentum of his line enable him to cast his flies to within a few points of the wind if necessary, where, with a lighter line, much good water might be lost, and much time spent in crossing and re-crossing to get a favouring breeze; while in the entire absence of wind he can take full advantage of the great length of his line, and cast with unerring precision. Unless in exceptional circumstances of wind and weather, the angler with the loop-line ought to be able to lay his flies on the water within a few inches of any given point—and this, too, from a distance of 40 or 50 feet. The value of such a cast in clear water can scarcely be overestimated, especially when it is remembered that the line carries three times as many flies as the advocates of the short-line system use when fishing up-stream. Every part of the river may thus be most favourably and easily reached without the necessity of deep wading, and the concomitant evil of unduly disturbing the water.

It should be noted that these advantages are

claimed for the loop-line only when applied to fly-fishing, and that when so applied the line has its truest action only in conjunction with a spliced rod of perfect taper and even sweep; for by no other arrangement can there be combined and homogeneous action of all the parts from butt to fly. Angling with such a rod and line is scientific angling. Every impulse of the arm imparted to the rod is transmitted directly to the cast of flies, and the response is true and prompt; the nicest calculations can be made for distance and direction with almost perfect accuracy; and it becomes as possible to cover a rising fish under overhanging trees, or straight up-stream within an inch or two of the bank, as to sweep the river in its broad expanse.

The novice will not, of course, expect to become an adept on first handling the rod; but with a little expertness, the results will astonish him: and not the least part of the astonishment will arise from the gradual discovery of the vastly superior capabilities of such a rod and line. If the excellence of the instrument has anything to do with the excellence of the performance, the angler may rest assured that in the loop-rod and line he is furnished with a guarantee that whatever skill he acquires in casting will be abundantly answered in the issue. In fact, with this rod and line, true fishing down or across the water, let them match themselves for a day with fishers who fish up the water, and on comparing baskets, the follower of 'old saws' will gape with due wonder and dumb astonishment, when he finds how much he is outstripped by the follower of 'modern instances.'"[1]

Whence, then, this difference in the results? or wherein has the up-stream fisher the advantage? The first, and indeed the chief advantage is, that when the angler has raised and hooked a fish, he pulls it down-stream into water over which he has already fished; and thus the water above, where his next cast will be made, remains undisturbed. Whereas, should he be fortunate enough to hook a trout in fishing down-stream, he must, to ensure its capture, take it still farther down, thus disturbing the water which he has not fished, and throwing away any chance of fishing it to profit. Though this fact is undisputed and indisputable, a

[1] Though not a consistent advocate of fishing up-stream, Mr Richard Penn, in his 'Maxims and Hints,' published as early as 1833, enumerated two of the advantages claimed for this method. He says: "When you are fishing up-stream, you have a better chance of hooking those which rise at your fly, because the darting forward of a fish seizing it has a tendency to tighten your line, and produce the desired effect. If you are in the habit of catching a fish sometimes, there is another great advantage in fishing up-stream—viz., whilst you are playing and leading (necessarily down-stream) the fish which you have hooked, you do not alarm the others which are above you, waiting till their turn comes."

recent English writer, Captain St John Dick, attempts to minimise its importance; for he tells us that "in all ordinary rivers it is a matter of very little importance the small amount of water that may be disturbed when killing a fish in fishing down-stream."[1] Well, if in the case of one fish only, perhaps so. But if this be the angler's invariable style of angling, and if he multiply the number of fish he intends to kill by "the small amount of water" disturbed in killing each, he will, unless he has "thrown away ambition," require more than the Captain's "ordinary river," and much more than an ordinary day, either to fulfil his expectations or derive any satisfaction from the contemplation of his basket.

Our author says that "there might be some reason for fishing up a stream in which trout lay every two or three yards." Now it is precisely because trout are *not* nowadays to be caught in any stream "every two or three yards," that the angler must be all the more careful to fish up those places where he may expect to catch them; for if the capture of one scare the others, he will be guilty of extravagance in the now small mercies that remain to him in over-fished and depopulated streams. And when, as often, while "the take is on," in that "small amount of water" lie his main

[1] Flies and Fly-Fishing, p. 24.

chances of securing a good basket for that day, he will be advised to cast his flies up-stream, so as most effectually to utilise every inch of the water and every moment of his time. The fact is, that when the water is "small" and clear, trout are principally to be found in the necks of the streams —indeed, when the May-fly appears, they *crowd* the streams; and if the angler should hook a fish there while fishing down, it must needs bulk more largely in his imagination than in his eye, ere he can contentedly accept it as the only trophy from that water, which to the up-stream fisher might have yielded a goodly company to grace his basket and attest his skill.

The second advantage claimed for up-stream fishing was alluded to in a former chapter, where I urged the necessity of presenting the fly to the fish in the manner most likely to deceive it. This is certainly attained by casting up-stream, and allowing the fly to float gently towards the fish with all the appearance of a natural insect being carried down-stream.

But thirdly, not only is the trout then most likely to believe that he sees a real fly, but he is also then most likely to be hooked should he rise to it, as the slackness of the line at this critical moment gives the fish the most favourable opportunity for seizing the fly, and the angler the most favourable opportunity for striking against and securing the fish. In fishing down a clear stream these advantages are in great measure lost. For then the fly hangs against the current, if, indeed, it does not appear to the fish to be frantically endeavouring to stem the current; and even should the trout overcome his well-grounded doubt as to its nature and attempt to seize it in this position, the angler will, in two cases out of three, lose the fish through the necessity of striking up-stream. Captain St John Dick tries to escape the force of this argument by affirming that, "although fish always lie with their heads up-stream, they never by any chance take a fly in that position, but always make a decided turn in the act of rising, and take the fly with their heads pointing down stream." Now every observant angler can have no hesitation in characterising this statement as not only hypothetical but fabulous. The trout, seeing the fly coming down towards him, rises to meet it, and in doing so his head is up-stream towards the fly. He certainly makes a "decided turn" in the water; but, luckily for the angler, it is not "in the act of rising and taking the fly," but after having seized the fly, he turns to descend. Captain Dick himself thinks it necessary to qualify his statement, for he says, "It must be borne in mind that when trout are *gnatting* they do not follow this rule;"

and—shall I add?—it is only when *napping* that they do. Even with this reservation, however, I fear that the Captain is straining out his gnat only to swallow his camel.

Lastly, as the fish all lie with their heads upstream, the angler who fishes up approaches them from behind, and is consequently outside the range of their vision. To fish down in clear water brings him more under the observation of the trout, and thereby lessens his chance of catching them; for if a fish get but a glimpse of the fisher, it will require more than a deftly cast fly to reassure it that all's well. Of course the angler is more conspicuous on the bank than when wading; but even in the latter case, he should remember that the sharp eye of the fish serves it well, not only by direct vision to see the angler's feet in its own element, but also, through the influence of refraction, to discern strange appearances above it. In a black water the trout cannot, of course, see so well, and in that case the angler may fish down with less risk of being observed.

The reason why so many anglers prefer to fish down in all conditions of water is simply that they find it easier to do so. And no doubt fishing upstream is more difficult than fishing down. Even if we take no account of the greater physical exertion required to wade against the current, successful up-stream fishing implies more knowledge of the habits and habitats of the fish, more nicety and precision in casting, greater dexterity in managing the line when cast and in bringing it properly home, a quicker eye in detecting a rise, and a readier hand in responding thereto. But surely these attainments will follow intelligent practice; and the beginner will be less disposed to shirk the difficulties than to face them, when he remembers the *dictum* of Plato, that "what is good is difficult," and is assured on the word of many an "honest angler" that, be the difficulties what they may, they are not more real than the success which attends their overthrow.

There are circumstances, however, in which fishing down-stream may be practised; indeed there is one in which no other method will suit, and that is, of course, when the wind is too strong to permit of fishing either up or across. But should the element of wind not enter into our calculations, we have still to consider sometimes the condition of the water; and though generally in all conditions fishing up is the most profitable, there are one or two cases in which good sport may be obtained by fishing down.

The angler may adopt this method with some success when the water is black, or when full and heavy though clear. In a full black water, with a strong current, fish are to be got only at the bank or channel,[1] and not in mid-stream. In this case, should the angler be on the channel side, it is advisable to fish the water from that side, casting across and slightly down-stream towards the bank, and allowing the current to bring the flies slowly round. When on the bank-side of a full water, black or clear, fish up only those banks where fish are rising and where the current is easy. Fishing down here would disturb the water below too much. If the river be heavy, fish down and across, selecting the gentler runs and ebb-waters. To fish up in these circumstances might bring the flies down too rapidly for the trout to be able to see them, for their vision is not so acute in a heavy water as in a low clear one. Another consideration that determines the angler to fish down here is, that thereby he is enabled to cover more water and catch more trout in a day's fishing than would be possible were he to adopt the slower and more fatiguing process of wading up a heavy stream; while, the water being full and heavy, there is not to the same extent that disturbance to the fish below which would follow on fishing down a low clear water.

[1] This word, in the angler's vocabulary, signifies the shelving gravelly side of the stream, as opposed to the higher grassy bank.

But I promised to take the beginner to the water and give him his first lesson in fly-fishing with the loop-line and spliced rod. On arriving at the riverside with all the implements of your craft, the first act in the day's drama is to place the loop-line, with the cast of flies attached, in the water, so that it may be thoroughly soaked, for the purpose of straightening the line and rendering it more tough and pliable. Never fish with dry gut; it is always brittle, and apt to snap when subjected to any strain. With a length of shoemaker's thread, well-rosined and doubled to make it sufficiently strong, tie together firmly the pieces of the rod, beginning with the spliced ends of the middle and top, and finishing off with the butt. By the time this is completed the line will have been sufficiently steeped, when you may connect it with the rod by passing the loop of the line through the corresponding loop at the point of the rod; and then, with the rod in your right hand, carefully unwind the line with your left till the trail-fly is reached.

At first sight it might seem that the operation of tying the rod would be both slow and tedious. In reality, however, it is neither. With properly prepared lengths of thread, a few turns only are necessary to make all fast; and as the line and cast are all in one, no time is lost in making connections between them. With a little practice, the whole process may be accomplished almost as quickly as any angler could fit up a jointed rod with its reel and attach his fly-cast.

The fisher is now fully armed for the fray—unless, indeed, in view of catastrophes, he requires to be fortified internally as well,—in which case, of course, the "pocket-pistol," with the regulation number of barrels, will be in urgent request. It is not advisable, however, at any time to discount a catastrophe; and I should not recommend the angler to vote urgency till he has either *landed* a two-pounder or *lost* one. In the former case "death and glory" may well go hand in hand; in the latter, thus may grief most fittingly be "crowned with consolation." And yet, when the "take is on," the fisher will find it perhaps more profitable not to spend much time in either exulting over his gains or wailing over his losses, but to draw from both alike, instead of from the flask, the incentive to redoubled efforts, till the lull of battle leave him space to count the slain and celebrate the triumph.

Until he attains to some degree of expertness in casting, the beginner should use a short rod of ten or eleven feet, with a hair-line of twelve or fifteen feet, and a length of gut in proportion, carrying not more than half-a-dozen flies. To simplify matters a little at first, let him select for practice an open stretch of water, free from bushes, trees, or whatever else would endanger his tackle or wreck his hopes; and, getting the wind in his favour, endeavour to cast out from the channel side towards the bank.

His efforts at this stage are more likely to be successful if directed to the gently running streams. For, although Mr Stewart is of a different opinion, it is much more difficult to cast with nicety and effect over pools than over streams. The trout detect the deception more readily on a calm, unruffled surface,—which is often, moreover, as clear as glass,—so readily, indeed, that fishing a pool is generally an unprofitable employment, unless the angler be aided in his efforts by a breeze. Here no current imparts to his flies their natural motion; this must be left for his skill to supply. Here he must cast with greater frequency to keep his flies afloat, with extreme delicacy lest he disturb the placid surface of the pool, and with consummate art to allure the trout from its haunts below. It may be true, as Mr Stewart says, that "on account of the roughness of the water in streams, it is not so easy to see a trout rise." But there are other indications of a trout's "rise" besides the appearance of his fin; and the "very roughness of the water," which is said to render it difficult to detect the "rise," is just that which will aid the young angler in getting a rise at all. For here the artificial character of his fly is not so readily discovered; and even should he not get a "rise" when his fly alights, his chances of success are often just as good when the stream is carrying his flies gently and naturally down. Hence it is that I recommend the beginner to take his first lessons in the gently running streams, and leave the pools till he has acquired an amount of facility and precision in casting to which a tyro may not reasonably lay claim.

In casting, the rod should be grasped with both hands—the left near the butt, and the right about eight or nine inches higher up. There being no reel on the rod, the hands can be so placed as to secure the amount of leverage necessary for a good cast. The upper parts of the arms are kept close to the body, and only the wrists and forearms are brought into play; so that anything like "thrashing" the water is avoided. Having made his first cast over the water mainly to get his line out in front of him, the young angler must now raise the point of his rod a little to bring the line round in a curve sufficiently near him, and so much under command as will enable him to lift it gently from the water and to make the next cast. This movement is effected by raising the rod gradually towards the perpendicular, and causing the point of it to describe something of a horse-shoe curve, when the line will be brought gently round in a corresponding sweep overhead, and derive, from this motion and its own weight, sufficient momentum to urge it forward to its full length. The point of the rod should not be carried much behind the body, and the line should not be sent out to its full length behind, but brought round in a curve, following the motion of the rod until fairly on the forward movement, when a slightly quickened action is imparted, and the rod is brought nearly to the horizontal. The line is thus gradually straightened in its forward course until it measures its full length over the stream—first touching the water near the middle point of the hair-line, when the droppers will fall gently, and almost simultaneously, with the trail-fly. When the line is fully extended on the water and no fish rises, the rod begins the return movement. As the stream carries the flies down, the point of the rod is gradually raised so as to keep the line perfectly under control in case of a "rise," otherwise the angler will soon find the whole cast in the most "admired disorder" at his feet. When the line has been carried down two or three yards towards him, this cast may be considered spent; and he should then prepare for the next by bringing the flies gently towards him, previous to raising them from the water, in the same manner as before.

I am aware that, in much of what has been said here, I am running counter to the expressed opinions of many anglers—perhaps of most anglers—who use the ordinary rod and reel line. Mr Stewart, for instance, advises the angler to "make the line go to its full length behind, and then pausing for a moment till it has done so, urge the rod forward;" and again, "not to urge the flies forward till they have gone the full length behind, or he will be apt to crack them off;" and again, "to employ considerable force in casting, and never allow the rod to make a lower angle with the water than from 40° to 45°;" and lastly, to "let the flies fall *first* upon the water, and as little of the line with them as possible."

Now I am not greatly concerned at present either to support these statements or to controvert them, but simply to point out that, whether correct or not as regards the ordinary rod angling, in fly-fishing with the loop-line they are not applicable. With a light untapered line on a reel greater force is required to cast than with a loop-line, and this, as has been urged, is one of the disadvantages of the reel-line in a long day's fishing. The effort necessary to extend the loop-line over the water will depend very much on the strength and direction of the wind, an opposing wind necessitating greater effort, a favouring one scarcely any; but certainly in all cases much less than a reel-line would require. Indeed, in an adverse wind, even the greatest efforts would fail to extend an ordinary reel-line, and consequently there would be loss, both of much good water and valuable time, in getting into the most favourable positions for its use. Moreover, with a reel-line there is greater danger of "cracking off the flies" from the greater force employed in urging them forward; and with *any* line this undesirable result is just as likely to follow from making the sweep too rapidly, and "after a pause impelling the line" forward too suddenly, as from allowing it to double behind. The motion imparted to the loop-line is continuous, but it is gentle; the flies in this motion lag somewhat behind the thicker portion of the cast, but there is no pause and no doubling back; and the line from its greater weight and better taper is gradually extended to its full length as it is brought round to the front by the forward motion of the rod, and this, too, without the employment of any "considerable force." And so I rather advise, with Mr Francis, that this forward motion should be eased half-way, than with Mr Stewart, that it should cease suddenly and altogether, when the rod is at an angle of 45° from the water. In the latter case, the line would fall in folds, and the flies in a swarm, to the terror of all the fish in the neighbourhood. The forward motion given to the rod is altogether a little swifter than the backward one, simply because the line is to be extended in front and not behind; but if the force employed in urging it forward be too great, the result, though different, will be just as disastrous as if a less force be suddenly arrested half-way. It will be an assistance to the angler in determining the amount of force necessary for the cast, if he direct his aim to an imaginary point two feet or so above the surface of the stream. The line will then reach the water without disturbing it, and the flies will alight gently and naturally thereon.

The precise angle—always a small one—which the rod makes with the water when the flies alight, will depend on the amount of wind-pressure which has to be overcome; the stronger the wind the lower do we hold the point of the rod, and consequently the greater length and weight of line will reach the water to bring down the flies upon the surface and keep them there. Mr Stewart's object in "never allowing the rod to make a lower angle with the water than from 40° to 45°," is, he says, to secure "that the flies shall alight first upon the water, and as little of the line with them as possible." But it will never secure that they alight at the proper place, or, in wind, that they even alight at all. Too much of the line is in such a case suspended over the stream to impart to the light cast sufficient steadying power, or ensure promptness and precision in the fall of the flies; and even if the angle vanished altogether, the lightness of the ordinary line might still quite effectually prevent this. Whereas, in my style of casting, the heavy hair-line promptly responds to the action of the rod, and brings down the lighter portion fully extended on the surface of the water; the tapering line falls gently and more gently till the gut is reached; and the trail and droppers alight almost simultaneously, with all the delicacy of gossamer.

The beginner will probably find it easier to cast from the right shoulder than from the left; but with increasing practice he will be able to cast from either side, according to circumstances of wind or position. Success in angling will demand from him much more than this; but nothing will minister more to such success than a masterly style of handling the rod. The angler of to-day, compared with his brother of thirty or forty years ago, has so many disadvantages in over-fished, polluted, and impoverished streams, and in highly educated trout, that he cannot afford to dispense with any benefit which improved skill in casting is calculated to bring him. The primitive "clothes-prop-and-line" style will not do now; and it has often been questioned whether Izaak himself, were he to revisit his former haunts and fight his battles o'er again with his own old weapons, would be able to kill one fish now where he was wont then to kill twenty. To meet the exigencies of the case now, the fly-fisher must learn to cast at any angle to the wind, and at any angle to the bank, to cover a rising fish with certainty in stream or pool; to cast under banks and overhanging trees, from pebbly channels and from ledges of shelving rook. In a word, he must be emphatically the man of resources, able from his knowledge and his skill to adapt himself and his style to the circumstances of the moment, and to meet with prompt and proper action every varying condition and sudden emergency. For his increased experience will have taught him that trout are to be found in other spots than those which he can reach with ease, that the biggest fish often lie in seemingly unlikely quarters, and that many a pounder breathes unmolested in waters passed over by most anglers in the belief that casting there would be impracticable.

But I have advised the beginner to try his skill first in the most favourable conditions of water and weather, on a gently running stream, with the wind blowing up. Let him wade in from the channel side and fish up, casting out towards the opposite bank. His object being to lay his flies as near the bank as possible, where the fish are lying in wait, the angle at which he should cast will depend very much on the width and depth of the stream. If the stream be both wide and deep, and the water at the bank can only be commanded with difficulty from the channel, the angler may make the first cast nearly straight across—say at an angle of 10° from the right angle, and allow his flies to sail down as much below that angle. His next cast should cover fresh water a few yards farther upstream at about 60° from the channel, and should cease at the point where the first cast commenced. In this second cast the flies will not, of course, fall so near the bank as in the first; but still they will cover water that may yield a fish. A third cast might be made at about 40° from the channel, and spent where the second began. Though in such a condition of the stream the beginner may thus make the most of his position on the channel side, he is not likely to make the most of the water. For when, from the depth of the stream or the strength of the current, the angler is unable perfectly to command the bank where the trout are rising, his best plan is to cross to the opposite side somewhere farther down, and fish up from the bank.

If the river is not so wide or deep as in the former case, and the bank can be reached more easily, the casts are made at more acute angles upstream—the first at about 60° from the channel, the second at 45°, and the third still higher up, at say 33°. The first cast must be considered spent before the line makes a right angle with the bank, the second when it has reached a point a short distance below that at which the first began, and the third a little below the starting-point of the second. In the best style of fishing up-stream the flies are never allowed to sail down opposite the angler, but are raised from the water while the line is yet well in hand, so as to command the next cast.

When the nature of the stream will admit, the angler should always endeavour, when fishing from the channel, to get nearer the bank than we have supposed possible in the two previous cases,—so near, indeed, as will enable him to reach it by casting at a more acute angle than before—that is, the more truly to *fish up* stream. Before entering the water, and as a preliminary venture, he should make a cast right up-stream over that part of the water which will be disturbed by wading, to secure any fish that may be lying there. Then let him wade well in towards the bank to command it with greater facility and success, and take his first cast at an angle of 28° or so with the channel. Considering it spent when it has reached 45°, he may make his second cast at 18° or so with the channel. In his third, which is made still more directly up-stream — almost straight up, in fact—the rod must be skilfully handled as the flies sail towards him, or disaster will be the only result. Since the line cannot come round with a sweep as in the other cases, but will bear almost directly down upon him, he should not allow the flies to cover more than two or tree yards of water before moving farther up to cast afresh.

If the trout are rising close to the bank, and cannot be readily covered from the channel, the most deadly mode of fishing is, as I have said, to cast up-stream from the bank. In this case the first cast is made about a foot or so from the side— it may even be straight up-stream within an inch of the bank, if fish are rising there; the second cast a yard or two farther out; and a third cast still farther into the stream, should a rising trout suggest it.

Acting on these hints the angler may, from one position or another, sweep every yard of the stream where fish are likely to be, his line radiating out from him at varying angles to bank or channel, and covering fresh and undisturbed water at each cast. If he be a novice, however, ignorant alike of the nature of the stream and of the habitats of the trout at the season, he may waste valuable time by fishing water that after all may prove unremunerative, if not utterly barren, unless he take a hint from the fish as well as from a brother fisher; for, if the trout are rising at all, they themselves will afford him sufficient indications of the proper spots over which he should cast. As a general rule, the moderately deep water near the banks, and the stream from its tail to its head, are the favourite haunts of trout; but they will also be found throughout the season in water where the shallow merges into the deep, in reaches where the stream is divided by an island or other obstruction, in quiet water beyond a stream or between two streams, in eddies behind stones, and in the main current itself.

The season of the year and the condition of the water will determine very much where trout will be found. But another and very important consideration is the direction of the wind. With the wind *from* the channel the angler may rely on finding the trout at the bank side, feeding on the flies which have been wafted thither; but if the wind blow *towards* the channel, he need not fish that portion of the water, but should pass on, and fish the bends where the wind blows towards the bank. There will always be reaches in the river where the angler will get the wind in this most favourable direction. A wind blowing directly up stream will be greatly to his advantage; for then the flies, acted on by the two opposing forces of wind and current, remain almost stationary on the surface and tempt the trout to rise at them. On the other hand, a strong wind blowing down-stream will combine with the current to hurry them along too rapidly for fish to seize them as they pass. In the former case, the flies will be wafted into the eddies, banks, and necks of pools, and it is over these that the casts ought to be made. In the latter case, it can only be in sheltered reaches where any flies will be found; the most of them indeed will be blown off the water altogether. In the absence of wind, and in a "small" water, the angler should fish the streams off the channel side, passing up from stream to stream, and casting to the bank where all the large trout are then lying. To fish from a high bank in such circumstances would endanger his success by exposing him more to the view of the fish than by wading from the channel; but if the bank is low, I fish as frequently from it as from the other side.

The angler will thus see that the direction of the wind is a most important consideration in determining where he should fish, since it determines very much where the fish lie. Where the wind has carried the flies, there will the trout be found feeding on them, and there may the angler most reasonably expect success. So important do I consider this, that I should lay down as the first canon of artificial fly-fishing—*Wherever the wind blows towards the bank, fish off the bank, provided it cannot be commanded from the channel; but if it can be, fish from the channel, casting into the bank.*

When circumstances necessitate fishing down, and the angler is able to command the river, the cast should be made across stream and slightly down, and the flies allowed to sail gently and naturally with the current. To secure this gentle and natural motion in a heavy stream, it is necessary from the moment the flies alight to give the line way a little by yielding the rod, instead of raising the point as in up-stream fishing. If the line be kept taut, the flies either hang against the stream and appear to breast it, or they sweep round with an alarming velocity. In both cases the appearance is unnatural, the surface of the water is unduly disturbed, the droppers come in contact with the line, and even should the trout manage to seize the fly in such unfavourable circumstances, the necessity of his breaking the surface to do so lessens the chance of his being firmly hooked. Hence we can account for the number of fish that are lost in angling down-stream.

Mr Stewart's advice to the angler when fishing down a heavy water, is to "throw the flies partly up and partly across, and never allow them to get

ANGLES AT WHICH TO CAST.

No. 1.—Fishing up-stream from Channel side.

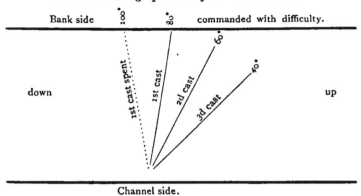

No. 2.—Fishing up-stream from Channel side.

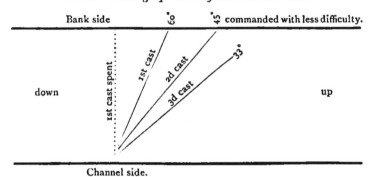

No. 3.—Fishing up-stream from Channel side.

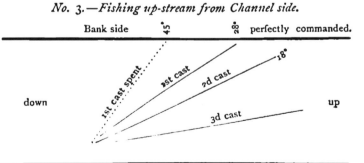

ANGLES AT WHICH TO CAST.

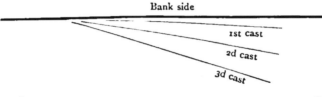

No. 4.—Fishing up-stream from Bank side.

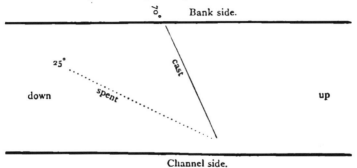

No. 5.—Fishing down from Channel side.

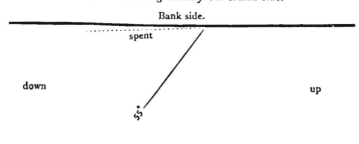

No. 6 —Fishing down from Bank side.

below that part of the stream opposite to him." Now this is nothing less than an attempt at a compromise between up-stream and down-stream fishing, and comes strangely from a fisherman of Mr Stewart's experience. According to this method the angler is going down-stream, first revealing himself and all his belongings to the fish, and then attempting to hoodwink and capture them by fishing up. I should call this the walking-down system of fishing up. To command a wide river when fishing down, one may sometimes require to cast right across, more generally across and down, but certainly never across and up. In fishing down an ordinary stream from the channel side, the angler should cast towards the bank at an angle of about 70° from his own side, and allow the current to bring the flies down and across until the line makes an angle of about 25° with the channel, when he may consider the cast spent. Then let him take a step or two down-stream, and repeat the process over another stretch of fresh water. If he is fishing down from the bank side, however, and casting towards the channel in a broad stream, he must give the line an angle of about 55° with the bank,—in smaller rivers a proportionally smaller angle, and in both cases allow the flies to sail down till they are extended in a straight line below him close into the bank. Covering in this way more water at each cast when fishing down from the bank than from the channel, he should walk down a yard or two before making the next venture.

I have already stated that fishing down from the bank is never very satisfactory in any circumstances, and should only be resorted to when no other method will suit. With a strong wind blowing down-stream, it is better to cross to the channel, cast towards the bank, and fish down; but if the wind be only moderate, it is better still to endeavour to fish up, by casting as near as possible to the wind and wading towards the bank; and where the water is too wide to be commanded from the channel, to cast up-stream from the bank.

In fishing such a stream as the Daer with a strong wind blowing down and the water low, I would work up-stream as far as I intended to fish, casting across if I could not cast up, rather than walk up two or three miles and fish down. In a large full water, where the sharp eye of the trout could not serve it so well, and where wading up would be difficult on account of the strength of the current, I would reverse the process by first walking up as far as time would permit and then fishing down. In the latter case the result might be fairly good, but it would certainly be better in the former.

Mr Francis advises the angler to "allow his fly

to sink some inches under water, even to mid-water if he pleases, and then *work* it gently by raising and lowering the point of the rod;" and many other English authors recommend that the natural motion of the fly should be "assisted," and a "life-like appearance" imparted to it by jerking it up, down, and across stream. I have considered these recommendations in a previous chapter, and have tried to show that they are at once antiquated and absurd, and utterly at variance with what every observer knows of the behaviour of the natural insect whose motions it is our intention to imitate. I have only to remind the angler that he should, so far as he can, follow nature in the motions of his flies quite as much as in their colour and form, and that, therefore, he should never "work" his flies, but make a skilful cast, dexterously keep his line well in hand as the flies sail down, and leave the stream to do the "working" business, and impart to them their "natural motion."

> "For thus at large I venture to support,
> Nature best followed best secures the sport."

I have already urged the beginner to be guided in his casting by the hints he receives from the rising trout. In endeavouring to cover a rising fish the angler should make the cast 2 or 3 feet above the precise spot where the fish rose, allowing the flies to sail over him, so as to permit of his seeing and seizing them if he feel inclined to do so. Should a trout not take his fly the first time he covers it, though then, certainly, the best chance of capturing it is gone, he may cast over it again, or even a third time if the fish continue rising. But on no account let him dally, as some anglers do, for hours over one fish in the hope of capturing it at last; for even should he not lose his labour altogether, he will certainly lose much of his time which might have been more profitably spent in catering for the wants of the less fastidious fish. Mr Francis tells us that he "stuck at a fish for three-quarters of an hour, casting without stopping as the fish kept rising." We are glad to be assured that he met with his reward at last—why, of course, had he not, we should never have heard of the exploit—and we cannot but admire his patient endurance in these literally trying circumstances; but no man who was not "playing" at angling would ever dream of spending as much as three-quarters of an hour over the best "kipper" in Tweed.

Mr Stewart says that, "as the moment the flies alight is the most deadly of the whole cast, the oftener it is repeated the better." This broad general statement must be taken with some reservation. It is undoubtedly sometimes perfectly true, but it is just as often not true. It is indeed quite possible for the angler to cast too frequently. If trout are rising *freely* at the natural insect, it can only be to satisfy the " keen demands of appetite;" and as these demands brook no delay, the first moment of the fly's appearance will most likely be the last of its existence. Clearly, therefore, in this case the most deadly moment of the angler's cast is the moment his flies alight. But fish, like folk, are not always at starvation-point; they are often shy and sometimes fickle; and so flies may alight and yet fish may not rise. But let the fly sail gently downstream, and make as though it would escape him, and then "the blessing brightens as it takes its flight," and the wayward, greedy trout leaps to secure it. For myself, I could not say whether, in the whole course of a season's fishing, I capture more fish with fly at Mr Stewart's "deadly moments," or during those which succeed. If trout, then, are taking well, it is a perfectly good system to cast frequently, and so multiply these critical and fateful times. But if otherwise, the angler's opportunities are not to be measured by the frequency of his casts; the imitation will offer a more attractive lure in its progress down-stream than at the instant when it alights; and therefore the angler should allow his flies to sail down two or three yards according to circumstances, before moving up to make the next cast.

The frequency, then, with which the angler should cast, will depend so far on the humour of the fish, but not on this altogether. It will be regulated, also, in great measure by the rapidity of the stream; a gentle current evidently requiring less frequent casting than a rapid one, and a pool more frequent casting than either. It is in this respect, as well as in the greater skill demanded in handling the rod, that the pool presents more difficulty to the young angler than the stream. For it is only by frequent and dexterous casting that he can at once conceal the artificial character of the flies, and prevent them from sinking too much to be attractive.

But a third consideration remains. If the angler is fishing up-stream, he must not allow his line to float so far down at each cast as when he is fishing down-stream, otherwise he would not be able to command the next throw. He must therefore, when fishing up, be content to cover less water at each venture than when fishing down—that is, he must cast more frequently.

Should a fish take the fly at the moment of its alighting, the angler, even if he do not perceive the rise, will receive indications of it in a slight tightening of the line. He must then strike instantly, but not too hard. For the fish, lying with its head up-stream, is in the most favourable position for hooking himself when the angler is below him; and the stroke being against him, the slightest twitch or turn of the wrist is generally sufficient to secure him. Alike in fishing up as in fishing down stream, one should strike gently, but more gently when fishing down than when fishing up, because the current is against him. In pools very gentle striking is needed. If the trout do not seize the fly when it alights, it is necessary to watch carefully the motion of the line as it floats down-stream; for should it stop for a moment, it is almost a certainty that a fish has interrupted its progress. Now is the time to strike, and in ten times out of a dozen the trout is hooked. The point of the rod is immediately raised, and the line kept tight while the fish is taken gently down-stream, the angler being careful to keep always below it, whether he is wading or on the bank.

If he be wading when he hooks a small fish, it is unnecessary to bring it to the side, as it can be much more expeditiously removed in the water. When trout are taking well, and time, therefore, is valuable, it is profitable in the long-run even to lose a small one now and again through some lack of courtesy than to be too nice in playing them down to the channel. When the "rise is on" I seldom spend more than a few seconds over a fish, unless, indeed, from his size he demands more attention. Large trout are always worthy of some care in landing, and should receive all the consideration which the angler can bestow, as it often requires more skill to kill a trout a couple of pounds in weight, with fine tackle on a loop-rod, than to land a lordly salmon ten times that weight with a hundred yards of eight-plait on a multiplying winch. For, as Cotton said to the young aspirant after piscatorial fame, "This, sir, is a war where you sometimes win, and must sometimes expect to lose." And though every angler knows that the cowardly fish that "fight and run away" are always bigger than the manlier ones that "stand and deliver," it is good policy, at least so long as the issue of the strife is doubtful, "to weigh the enemy more mighty than he seems." Up with the point of your rod, then, "muster your wits," and take him steadily down-stream to the nearest gravel-bed or easy landing-stage, and never let him get below you. Should he show "game," and throw himself out of the water, you must, to relieve the strain, lower the point of the rod as he drops back again, for

> "Now is it manhood, wisdom, and defence
> To give the enemy way;"

but the instant he reaches the water resume your advantage, and relax not your effort till in exhaustion and defeat he measures his scaly length upon the channel.

To take a smaller fish off the line while in the water, raise the rod as before and bring the fish towards you—moving down-stream, if necessary, so as to have him always above you. Thus is he sooner choked; while the pressure of the current, with you instead of against you, prevents undue straining of the line, and very often frustrates any attempt at a sudden bolt. Whenever he shows signs of distress, by turning over on his side, then is the time to seize hold of him in the water. With the rod thrown back from the butt, bring the line within your reach; and, keeping the rod in the right hand, slip the left as far as possible along the line, placing what you have thus secured in charge of the right, which, while still retaining its hold, throws the slackened portion clear into the water before the left intrusts it with any more. This process is repeated as the trout is approached. Should he make a sudden spring, the line is still free to respond, the fish is still under command, and the operation of "hauling in" has just to be begun again. When the fish is within reach, the left hand, while retaining the hold it has on the line at the time, also takes possession of the rod and sets free the right to seize the fish. Now, resting the rod on the left arm with the butt to the body, transfer the trout to the left hand and remove the hook with the right. Lastly, grasp the rod with the right hand, and with the left stow the fish in your creel, and you are ready for another cast. All this—which looks intricate enough, if not bewildering, at first sight—is really the work of a few seconds; and in an ordinary rise of trout you will kill three in this way in the time you would take one to the bank.

With heavier fish considerable tact and care are required; but practice will bring success here as elsewhere. The chief point to attend to is, Don't let the fish get down-stream before you. I have frequently, when angling with the loop-line, secured large trout very slightly hooked, simply by keeping below them till they were exhausted. Such trout generally struggle more or less in any circumstances of capture, and sometimes escape even under the best management; but the chances of their doing so are certainly minimised when they are taken down-stream. Whereas, if a large trout get below the angler, the chances are ten to one that he will escape, unless very securely hooked and on strong tackle—on such tackle, indeed, as few fly-fishers would care to use. Even in fishing down-stream, it is necessary to get below a big fish as soon as possible.

I admit that, in rivers where salmon and sea-trout are abundant, a reel-line is indispensable, otherwise the angler is in momentary peril of losing his cast; but in such a river as the Clyde, where it is the exception and not the rule to meet with trout or grayling over two or three pounds in weight, the loop-line and rod have immense advantages over the other. I have often killed trout upwards of five pounds with it, and generally I have no difficulty with fish of two or three pounds; but, unfortunately, it is not every day that it is subjected to such severe tests as these.

When the angler desires to pass over any reach of the stream where from barren or deep water, adverse wind, thick wood, or other obstruction, casting would be inconvenient or unadvisable, the rod is raised perpendicularly, and that part of the line which falls below the butt is wound round the left hand till the trail-fly is reached; and thus secured, the rod and line can be carried about with ease and without risk. When fishing is resumed the process is reversed—the line, as it is unwound from the trail-fly, sailing down-stream till all is liberated for another venture. It may also, of course, be unwound on the bank; and in either case the process is accomplished, with a little practice, in a few seconds.

Some anglers evince great preference for a thread-like line, in the belief that it enables them to cast with greater lightness and nicety. This is a mistake, if it is their intention to throw a long line;

for even in a dead calm some weight is necessary to carry it forward and cast with certainty, while in a strong wind it is perfectly useless. This light line, however, in the hands of those who recommend it, is generally a very short one, and is cast from a single-handed rod. To fish with it at all requires that the angler wades right up the centre of the stream; and, while securing a few trout by dint of great physical exertion and constant casting, he so disturbs the water for other anglers following in his wake as materially to affect their prospects of success. This method of fishing seems to me to savour a little of the selfish fish-for-self style, in which, moreover, the paltriness of the end cannot be urged as any justification of the questionable means. Fortunately, it is only in "small" clear water with a favouring breeze, that it can be practised at all, and even then the results bear no proportion to the labour.

The preceding remarks are more or less generally applicable to artificial-fly fishing at any time throughout the entire season. In what remains of this chapter, I shall offer a few hints, bearing more particularly on the special cast for each month, and the conditions of water and weather most favourable for its use.

April Fishing.—The following is the cast for this month: The teal-drake with black hackle forms

April Fishing.

the trail-fly, with March browns and blaes (starling-wing and black hackle) alternating for the other eight. The young angler will remember that though I use nine flies on the cast, I have recommended that he should begin with six on a correspondingly shorter line, until practice enables him to cast a gut-line of 16 feet, without a twist from end to end.

At this season warm genial days—if such there be—with wind and sunshine, are the most favourable for successful sport; but considerable execution is sometimes done on a black water, if the day be dull, with occasional showers. A leaden sky, however, with mist on the hills, a bluish appearance as of smoke in the atmosphere, or heavy rain-clouds looming to windward—the frequent harbingers of coming storm — are certainly not fraught with blessings for the angler.

The weather, of course, in this month, as in others, influences the development of the natural flies, and so far determines when the trout will take the imitation; but there are times when the conditions seem all that could be desired, and yet the results are admittedly and wonderfully poor. On such occasions, instead of attributing his non-success to the whims and caprices of the giddy trout, or to the loss of his own right hand's cunning, the angler will most probably find the explanation in some portending atmospheric disturbance. For trout, in the interests of science, may well be enrolled active members of the Meteorological Society; they are more sensitive to atmospheric influences than a barometer, and rarely take well when there is an impending change. This is especially the case when, after a long spell of fine weather, there are some indications of a coming storm. And even when no such indications present themselves to the weather prophet—nay, when Mercury himself brings no warning of the frowning face of Jove, the trout seem to have some instinctive premonition of what is approaching, and defy all art to tempt them to the surface. This occurs now and again all through the season. The "rise" may be "on," the fun most furious, and the hopes of the angler at the highest, when, all of a sudden, without hint or warning, the sport ceases, and not another fin is seen to move that day. The case is evidently hopeless, though the cause may be mysterious, and the angler gives up in disgust. But perhaps on the morrow, or, it may be, before he is fairly home, the rising wind and the blackening heavens convince him that some "wide area of depression" had o'erspread the stream, and abated the ardour of the rising fish.

In genial weather good sport is almost certain whether the water is black or not, as the March browns will then make their appearance on the stream and tempt the hungry trout to renew their acquaintance with their long-lost surface-food. If the morning be bright and warm, the flies will come out early, and consequently the trout will take an hour or two sooner than if it be dull and cold. The "rise" is usually "on" between 10 and 11 A.M., and may continue for twenty minutes or half an hour, after which the flies go off, and it may be half an hour, or even an hour, before they appear again. These golden opportunities may be offered to the angler three or four times during the day, according to the state of the weather. Should the morning dawn propitiously for the early appearance of the flies, this little "fitful fever" will generally be over for the day by 3 o'clock in the afternoon; but a cold morning, by delaying the advent of the flies till mid-day, or even 1 o'clock, will reduce the fishing time to a few hours of the afternoon; if, indeed, it do not altogether destroy the chances of sport that day. As a general rule, to a successful day's fishing at this season some progress towards filling the basket would require to be made in the forenoon. Good sport is sometimes obtained after 1 o'clock, but certainly the most hopeful sign is the appearance of the favourite March brown in the early hours of the day.

Though the angler thus earnestly looks for the appearance of the natural insect on the water, and from that predicts his fortune for the day, he will generally find that it is not during the presence of great swarms of March browns that he will obtain the best sport. In reality, it frequently happens that not a trout will take his flies in such circumstances. His main, if not his only, chance of success, lies in presenting his flies when the natural insects are passing off, or have already passed off, the water altogether. This I have shown to arise from the fact that the imitations he offers to the trout are as one in a thousand among the swarms of their natural competitors, and have therefore only one chance in a thousand of attracting the attention of the fish; and unless the artificial closely resembles the natural, it will be outweighed even in this one chance.

May Fishing.—May is unquestionably the best fly-fishing month in the year. With bright sunshine—and wind, if the water is "small"—the angler cannot fail to obtain sport. The weather is then less liable to sudden changes and alternations, and consequently success is more to be relied on than during

> "The uncertain glory of an April day,
> Which now shows all the beauty of the sun,
> And by-and-by a cloud takes all away."

Trout in most streams are now in fine condition,

and afford the angler rare play. In the full tide of lusty youth and vigour they are to be found in all parts of the water, breasting the strong currents as well as sporting in the gentle runs and eddies; and water which the angler would judiciously pass over a month earlier, may now be fished with success.

An alteration on the cast is now necessary, as the March browns will soon disappear, to be succeeded by those that are born of hotter days and brighter sun. Notable among such is the sand-fly, which makes its appearance about the 6th of the month. At the beginning of May, it is as well to substitute two sand-flies for two March browns, and after the natural insect appears, gradually to remove all the March browns and replace them by sand-flies. About the middle of the month I would recommend that two of the blaes, which have been doing duty since the beginning of April, be removed, and a green tail and a black blae substituted. This last fly takes splendidly in cold days during both May and June, and on such days two or three of them may profitably take the place of the sand-flies; but in bright sunshine this change would be undesirable, for it is then that the sand-fly is most effective.

When the sand-flies have come fairly on the water, which is generally about the middle of May, the cast should be composed and arranged thus: 1, the trail-fly—the teal-drake tied with black hackle; 2, the sand-fly; 3, the blae; 4, the sand-fly; 5, the green-tail; 6, the sand-fly; 7, the black blae; 8, the sand-fly; 9, the blae. This cast is serviceable during May and June, except that in the case of the trail-fly, the black hackle is changed for the red towards the end of May.

It will be observed that the sand-fly is the principal *entrée* in this bill of fare for the month, and the young angler may rest assured that it has not been inserted there without special regard to the aldermanic tastes and gastronomic predilections of those who are to dine and die. For, not only is it undoubtedly the most killing lure in a warm and dry May, but it remains longer in season than any other individual fly that appears on the water. The natural insects, as already shown, are not hatched in the water like most of the other flies, but in the dry, sandy, exposed channel of the stream; and whenever this becomes heated by the sun's rays, they flit in myriads over the water. Hence it is during heat and sunshine that this fly affords the best sport. In such favourable circumstances it may take as early as 7 or 8 o'clock in the morning, but in cold dull weather it will not appear at all; and the angler's mainstay then must be the black blae, which usually comes on the water about 11 or 12 o'clock.

Though the sand-fly generally disappears at the beginning of June, in the upper reaches of the river, where its development is delayed consequent upon the greater altitude, the artificial lure may prove very effective even as far on as the end of June. Some anglers hold that these flies never appear on the water unless blown there by the wind, but this is a mistake. Of course wind *will* blow them on the water, but they also find their way to their own destruction with quite as much certainty in its absence. I have scored some of my greatest successes with this fly in a "small" clear water during bright sunshine, and without a breath of wind. In such circumstances, the flies will be observed over the entire surface of the stream, "dancing merrily to their death," and the angler has only to select the most suitable streams and broken water to ensure a good "take." In wind, however, he will be guided by the general recommendation already given, and devote his attention to those reaches of the river where the wind blows from channel to bank, as it is only in such quarters that the flies can reach the water at all.

From what has been said of the hatching-ground of the sand-fly, it will readily be understood that all rivers, or even all parts of the same river, are not alike favourable for its development. Where the bed of the stream is rough and stony it is not found in abundance. At and above Thankerton, where the Clyde flows for miles over a sandy bed, the flies are plentiful, and the sport consequently good. Higher up, between Roberton and Elvanfoot, the channel is rough and rocky, and the sand-flies are less abundant. Above Elvanfoot, again, the sandy bed reappears, and again they find a congenial home. The Tweed, on the other hand, affords no such varieties of channel, but flows for the most part over a stony bed, and cannot therefore be compared to the Clyde as a sand-fly stream. But here the law of compensation comes in to save the lives of the trout and the sport of the anglers; for we find that those rivers, or portions of them, which are not naturally adapted for sand-fly fishing, are usually the best for the May-fly; and this because the latter is hatched under stones in the bed of the stream, where the sand-fly cannot exist.

A bright day with sunshine and wind is generally the best for angling during this month. But this rule is subject to several modifications. On a black water, for example, bright sunshine is desirable during the period of the sand-fly's existence; but, both before its advent and after its departure, a dull day is to be preferred; and then the angler who is possessed of any skill in his art, should never be content with anything less than a basket of from twelve to twenty pounds, either on Clyde or on Tweed. Again, on the lower reaches of these rivers, a dull cloudy day in May is most favourable for good sport; and towards the end of the month cold days are frequently red-letter days in the angler's calendar, for these furnish the best conditions for the appearance of the iron-blue dun. I remember one such day some years ago, when I secured a basket of twenty-five pounds with this fly in the course of a few hours' fishing at Thornilee towards the end of May when the hills lay white with snow; while the sport during several hot bright days which succeeded was poor in the extreme. Hot sultry days at this season are generally unlucky, for then the flies upon which the fish chiefly feed do not put in an appearance at all.

It is a curious fact that trout will not take well when the wind blows from the south during hot days in May, June, and July. In spring this does not hold; but as the season advances, a hot day, with a dry south wind, producing a sultry heat and throwing a haze over the hills, is the most unpropitious of any. Even an east wind,—that great bugbear of anglers—which blows up Clyde from Culter to its source, and up the greater part of Tweed,—is much to be preferred, and in all the fishing months frequently proves a blessing in disguise. There is no gainsaying the fact, that during the fishing season there are many sultry, inauspicious days—days when even the siren sand-fly fails to lure, and when the angler's tenantless basket speaks to him only of blighted hopes and fruitless toil. In these depressing circumstances, the creeper, the caddis-bait, very small worms, and even the minnow (fished up-stream), may help to retrieve the fortune of the day, and prove the man an angler still.

When the rivers are in flood, bait-fishing in some form or other must be resorted to; but in clear water I should confine myself to the artificial fly, the creeper, or the caddis, believing that, should these fail, there is little to be hoped for from any other lure until the appearance of the May-fly.

June Fishing.—The artificial flies best suited for this month are still the sand-fly and the blaes. The cast may be made up thus: 1, trail-fly—teal-drake, with red hackle; 2, blae, as in March and April; 3, sand-fly; 4, black, blae, or iron-blue dun; 5, hare's-ear dun or autumn dun; 6, sand-fly; 7, blae; 8, hare's-ear dun; 9, blae.

Success may still attend operations with the artificial fly during the early days of the month, especially in a black water after a small flood; and the sand-fly may be very effective in the upper reaches of the stream, where it is later in appearing. But as the May-fly is then at the height of its popularity with the trout, the angler must consult the prevailing taste, and offer the natural insect when the days are warm and sunny.

July Fishing.—From the end of June till the end of August, fly-fishing with the small artificial fly is not by any means a remunerative employment, unless on a cold stormy day, or in a black stream after heavy rains; and then the following will be found a good cast: 1, trail-fly—froghopper; 2, blae, as in spring; 3, sand-fly; 4, hare's-ear dun; 5, white tip; 6, sand-fly; 7, blae; 8, sand-fly; 9, blae.

The black mote makes its appearance during hot weather in June, and exists throughout July and August. In hot sultry days, when feeding on this fly, the trout will rise to nothing else; and when such is the case, the angler will do well to have the cast composed entirely of it.

August, September, and October Fishing.—1, Trail-fly—autumn red; 2, blae; 3, autumn musk-fly; 4, pale autumn dun, or willow-fly; 5, white tip; 6, blae; 7, hare's-ear dun; 8, blae; 9, autumn brown.

The above form a good selection for a cast in autumn, but the angler need not limit himself to these. Several of the flies already given in the list may be found more attractive than others on certain days; and whenever one or more particular flies are observed to be doing well, let the cast carry two or three good specimens of the favourites.

The months of July and August are the most unproductive of the season in artificial-fly fishing. Towards the end of August, however, when the heat begins to moderate, the fly will again do some execution, and in September it is frequently as effective as in the spring. With such weather as would be considered favourable in May, the angler will be able to make a capital basket on a September day after 11 o'clock in the forenoon.

In October trout begin to get out of condition, but in Clyde the grayling are just then coming to perfection—at least to such perfection as their poor capacity can ever hope to reach. They take the artificial fly freely; so freely, indeed, that they frequently fill up a large section of the creel, which the angler would rather see occupied by the more dainty trout. Towards the end of this month the natural flies do not come on the water till late in the day, and consequently, unless the weather be fine and "fresh," the entire day's fishing may be restricted to two hours or so after 1 o'clock.

General Remarks.

We have seen that the natural flies make their appearance in regular rotation from March to October, and that the artificial flies which the angler should use at any one time ought to be imitations of such flies as are then in existence. The dates already given for the appearance of the natural insects will hold good in ordinary seasons, but it must be remembered that the times of their development and the terms of their existence are alike subject to the influence of heat and cold. Speaking generally, and in view of the whole season, I may say that an early spring and a warm summer will accelerate their advent and shorten their stay; and that a backward season will retard their development and prolong the period of their existence. But all the flies of a particular month are not alike influenced by the same weather. What may be favourable for one class may be quite the reverse for another. The characteristic flies of spring and autumn come out with heat and sunshine, but this cannot be said for all the flies of summer. Some of them — including the whole family of duns—require a comparatively cold day for their appearance; while others, as the sand-fly, the black mote, the green-tail and May-fly, do not appear but on hot bright days; and even in the case of these latter there is a "distinction with a difference."

It is not enough, therefore, that the angler, in selecting his cast for the day, should merely consult his season's list of flies; he should ascertain for himself, by actual observation, what insects are then on the water, and so be guided in his choice. Now he may find several species in existence at the same time, but he will not find all equally in favour with the trout; and such as are for the nonce in high esteem should be largely represented on his cast, if he do not wish his pannier to present a sorry appearance even on a very favourable day.

Many anglers entertain the idea that when their flies, which may reasonably be expected to kill, do not succeed well, it is necessary to exchange them for others whose prototypes, it may be, are not then on the water—that, in fact, the want of success at any time is always to be attributed to a bad selection of flies, and that they must be changed till a happy issue confirm the choice. Even if we take no account of the waste of time which such a proceeding entails, and the loss of the opportunity when the "rise" does come on, it is tantamount to surrendering the position which they profess to maintain, and admitting that, after all, what the trout will take at any one season bears no relation to what nature has provided for it at that season, and that one fly is just as likely to kill as another at any season whatever. My advice is, select carefully good imitations of those flies which observation shows to be on the water and most in favour with the trout, and stick to them, in the assurance that if they fail, the fault may lie in the angler's want of skill, or in the trout's want of appetite, but certainly not in the flies themselves.

The weather, in so far as it regulates the appearance of the flies, will determine the "rise" of the fish. In cold days, especially in April, when there is not sufficient heat to bring out the flies, there is no inducement for the trout to come to the surface to feed. They must, in that case, content themselves with grub and larvæ at the bottom. Again, when the river is big with what is familiarly known in Scotland as " snaw-broo," the chances of success in any kind of fishing are of the remotest. Good baskets are often got during a snowstorm, but scarcely ever when the water is thoroughly saturated with snow, as it is then too cold to bring the flies to maturity.

But even when the season has brought round the flies, trout, as we have seen, do not always take advantage of their opportunities. They are a peculiarly impressionable tribe, and many of their seeming vagaries and whims are still unexplained. But indeed, in this respect, trout are not by any means alone. How many men can explain themselves even to themselves? and "Who is't can read a woman?" Why, then, need we grudge the trout a little oddity or a caprice? We know the fact— though we may not always be able to account for it—that flies may sport most temptingly on the surface, and yet trout may heed them not. We have alluded to their susceptibility to atmospheric influences, their decided and seemingly unreasonable aversion to certain winds with certain states of weather, and their equally decided and seemingly unreasonable preference for others. But there are many more peculiarities in their behaviour which we can reduce to no law, and for which we cannot find even a likely explanation. Some may call them mere freaks, and think that thereby they have solved the problem. But every angler who desires that he should fare the better for his experience, and the trout the worse, will use not only his powers of persuasion to allure the fish from their element, but likewise his faculty of observation to study their habits within it.

In very hot sultry weather, such as occurs as the season advances, trout become languid and disinclined to take the artificial fly, except during the night. Then they leave their usual haunts and come out to the shallows in search of food; and it is during those nights which succeed hot and oppressive days, when not a fish will stir, that the best sport is obtained with the artificial fly.

Given a showery April and a dry May, small floods in summer, and bright sunshine in autumn, and I predict for the angler a rare time of it.

Should April be mild and balmy, with occasional showers, heavy baskets will be the rule; but there is no doubt that May is the best month. The weather is then more settled, the trout feed more readily, and the sport is therefore more certain. September I should place next in order after April and May; indeed it is frequently not much inferior to either.

Up to the middle of June the angler may anticipate more or less sport with the artificial fly in ordinary conditions of the water; but during the next two months the most choice day for a great "take" is the one immediately following a flood, with the weather cool and the water still running black. Few practical anglers will agree with Mr Francis in his recommendation never to fish in a flooded water. Every one knows that splendid sport is to be had with the worm in such a water; and my heaviest "takes" with the artificial fly have been in a black water on the day following a "spate." Many years ago, when circumstances were altogether more favourable to the angler than now, when the river ran full and in capital fishing order for a week after a flood, the good days were not so few; but now the effective system of hill-drainage, which carries off to the sea all the rain nearly as fast as it falls, carries off also in one day the fortunes and the chances of many. And so to any angler who can devote only one day at a time to "the gentle art," I would unhesitatingly say, choose the day after a flood, and fish with the artificial fly.

On the upper reaches of the Clyde, when the water is "small" and clear, sunshine and wind are absolutely necessary to good sport. On Tweed, sun suits very well during April, but in the summer months a dull, cold, showery day is best. In the absence of wind, the streams and broken water only should be fished; nothing can come of fishing smooth water in a dead calm. Sunshine, however, is never desirable with a black water for the artificial fly, except in the case of the sand-fly, which must have heat as well as sunshine. All the other varieties of flies are more successful on a dull day, when the water is in this condition. Fish can see the angler much better when the day is dull than on a bright sunny day in "small" clear water; but in either case he should fish up-stream should wind permit. A warm, dull day is very unfavourable in either a clear or a black water for fly-fishing; and I should much prefer a hot day with bright sunshine.

It will thus be seen that in selecting a portion of water for the day's sport with the artificial fly, the angler has to take various circumstances into account. The season of the year and the flies then in existence, the habits as well as the habitats of the fish at that season, the state of the weather and the condition of the water, the nature of the channel and the direction and force of the wind, besides a host of minor considerations which experience may act upon, though it cannot always tabulate—all must enter into his calculations of the chances of success, quite apart from any practical skill in mere casting. The importance of the wind element has already been shown. In an appendix will be found a statement of the winds most favourable for up-stream fishing on all the main reaches of the Clyde and the Tweed. It may be found useful to the beginner. For, with a knowledge of the direction or set of the stream, and the quarter from which the wind is blowing in the morning, the angler may generally be able to map out mentally the section of the water he should select for the day, so as to reap the full benefit of fishing up-stream.

In bringing to a close these desultory remarks on artificial-fly fishing, I desire to record, as the conviction of a life-experience, that no other method of angling can at all compare with it, either in respect to the skill and knowledge required in its exercise, or the results which it is calculated to yield. A very moderate angler may soon become tolerably successful in the practice of minnow-fishing and worm-fishing down-stream, but it is in artificial-fly fishing that the difference between an expert and a novice is most apparent. And on no occasion is the difference more observable than on a day when trout are taking well. There are days —thoroughly hopeless days for sport—when fish are not inclined to rise, and when all anglers, good and bad, are placed very much on the same level. It is on such occasions that the adept, recognising the futility of exertion, is content to wait like Micawber till something "turns up," and to exclaim with Hermione—

> "There's some ill planet reigns :
> I must be patient till the heavens look
> With an aspect more favourable ; "

while the novice, in the eager enthusiasm of inexperience, perseveres to the end and possibly secures a few fish. But let the "rise" come "on" in a "small" clear water, and call into full play all the practical skill and resources of each, and it will not be long till the disparity of baskets will show who is the experienced fly-fisher.

CHAPTER V.

NATURAL-FLY FISHING.

The May-Fly.

"Away, be gone; the sport is at the best—
Ay, so I fear; the more is my unrest."
—*Romeo and Juliet.*

IF one is ever to be tempted to go a-fishing, it will surely be on a May morning. To such as have been "long in populous cities pent," the merry month will speak of open sky and healthful breeze; and from the "hum, the shock of men," the work and the worry, it will invite the toil-worn and the care-worn to enjoy "a respite, however brief," by mountain burn or meadow brook. The lover of nature will then hie forth to woo her and hold converse with her charms. Endeared to him through all her moods, she reveals "her blessed attributes, her balmy powers," in the first mantling blush of summer time. He sees the hills "with verdure clad," the rippling streams replete with life, the vale bespangled with the pastoral cowslips and "daisy stars whose firmament is green." O'er him steals the gentle zephyr, laden with the sweets of hawthorn and of brier-rose, and on his ear there falls

> "The raining music from a morning cloud,
> When vanished larks are carolling above."

And if he be an enthusiastic disciple of the rod to boot, happy is he in his hope. Possessed of even a modicum of skill, and blessed with the generally favourable weather of May, he will not return with empty creel. Of the "taking" character of the flies then on the wing there is no need to speak, and no cause to doubt: the May-fly as a lure has no compeer. Moreover, the trout captivated and captured by it are the biggest and best in the river. Then in the full tide of life and in the the joy of its fulness, they will not tamely yield up their liberty on demand, but will make a brave show, and fight a gallant fight, calling forth the skill and energies of the angler, and affording him the most genuine and exhilarating sport. At no other season do circumstances so combine to favour the gentle art, and crown its pursuit with such assured success. But, alas!

> "The hand of joy is ever at his lips
> Bidding adieu."

Still, if it cannot be said of angling as of love—that "its month is ever May," or of the angler as of the summer bird—that in his year he has no winter, we can derive from the rarity of good sport only the greater zest for its enjoyment; and when "May is in the sere," let the happy memories of the big baskets of the past colour our visions of the bigger baskets of the future, while

> "We dream the winter through,
> Then waken to the sun again
> To find our summer vision true!"

I have already considered the claims of the stone-fly to the title of the May-fly, and noted some points in its natural history. In ordinary seasons it appears about the 20th of May, and lasts till the 6th or 10th of June. The time of its development and the period of its existence will of course be influenced by the state of the weather and the nature of the district: on the lower reaches of the Clyde and the Tweed, it may be seen a week or ten days earlier than in the upper sections of those rivers. On some streams it is found in greater abundance than on others; and even on the same stream, as we have seen, all portions are not alike favourable. It is never plentiful on rivers which flow over a soft muddy bed, for a stony channel is its natural home. The eggs are deposited in the water; and when hatched, the young larvæ—the well-known creepers—manage to crawl underneath the stones, where they pass the long pupal term of their existence. When about to change into the perfect form, they come out of their retreats, the pupal cases split and the winged insects emerge, leaving their shed pellicles upon the channel.

Like most water-bred flies—with the exception of a few of the larger species, such as the green drake—the May-flies prefer the rippling stream to the silent pool, and will rarely be found in comparatively still water. "They love to remain near the water in which they were reared, and seldom travel to any distance from the familiar banks."[1] The angler, therefore, has not far to go to seek them; while, owing to their dull and sluggish habits, he has no difficulty in capturing them as they sit under the stones or banks at the side of the stream. Mr Stewart advises that they be collected the night before they are wanted for fishing, on the ground that the gathering of them consumes much time. If the angler is "up with the lark," however, he will not find it so. The insects are most readily obtained at daybreak, when as many can be gathered in half an hour as will suffice for the day's fishing. They are then to be found on the channel near the

[1] Wood's Insects at Home, p. 264.

heads of streams, or on the grassy banks, if there is no dew. Later on in the morning, under the heat of the sun, they disperse over the channel beds, and are not so readily found. There is another advantage (already alluded to) in gathering them at early dawn: the newly hatched insects are then of the bright yellow colour most in demand with the trout. As the day advances, they become more sombre in their hue, and consequently not so readily distinguishable from those hatched at an earlier period, which are too brittle for the angler's purpose.

In the full assurance of doing great execution with them, the angler should collect a supply sufficient for all that day's needs. With the battle all his own, it must be irritating in the extreme to run short of ammunition: so let him provide abundance. The insects are frequently carried in a tin-case, perforated to admit the air, and furnished with a lid, and a narrow aperture just sufficient to allow one fly to come out at a time. The tin, however, gets too readily heated with the sun, causing the flies to flutter about inside, to their certain injury or death. A very small wicker-basket of similar construction would answer better, and could be easily fitted with a strap, or borne as an appendage to the creel; but, for my part, I prefer to carry the insects in a cotton bag with a little clean moss.

The May-fly is fished either by floating the fly, or by partly sinking it, and the tackle used will depend on the method adopted. A floating fly may be fished either up or down, according to the direction of the wind; a partly sunk fly up-stream only. Mr Stewart does not speak of fishing with it down, and Mr Francis evidently does not know that it can be fished up; but both methods will be described here.

Four varieties of tackle may be given for fishing with a floating fly.

1. Two No. 5 hooks, tied back to back, and slightly bevelled. On each hook an insect is impaled by inserting the point in one shoulder at the root of the wing and bringing it out at the other. This kind of tackle is best in a rough full water whether black or clear.

2. A No. 3 and a No. 2 hook, tied similarly to the above. This is suited for one fly only, which is placed upon the hook in the same manner as the last, the smaller hook being left bare. This arrangement does well in a "small" clear water with a slight breeze.

3. Two No. 2 hooks, tied back to back, and half an inch farther up on the same gut two No. 3 hooks similarly tied. Two insects are required here. Insert the larger hook in the shoulder in each case, and running the fly down to the smaller hook, fix

The May-Fly.

it in the back. This is a deadly tackle. The two No. 2 hooks keep the flies in position, and prevent the trout from seizing and carrying off with impunity the bodies of the flies, minus the wings and heads.

4. An arrangement similar to the last, but single; one smaller (No. 2) and one larger hook (No. 3), tied with their barbs half an inch apart. This will be found very effective when fishing with one fly.

In floating the May-fly, use a long light rod with a very light line, carrying two or three yards of gut, the last two of which should be of the finest possible. A reel is essential in this, as in all kinds of fishing with a floating live insect. With a light line of this nature, the wind, as has been said, must determine whether it is to be fished up-stream or down. Raising the rod, the angler must allow the flies to be wafted on to the stream, so that they will in the most gentle, because most natural, manner alight upon its surface. On no account must he *cast* the line, for then the flies will be either injured or whipped off altogether. If the wind cease, the fisher has, without doubt, lost a good friend, but the sport need not stop for all that. Let him keep well out of sight, bring the point of the rod over the stream, skilfully allow his flies to drop in the most dainty fashion on its surface, and keep them there as they sail adown, adown. To do this with effect in a *gentle* stream in the absence of wind, he must be careful not to keep the line tight after the fly has reached the water, for if he do, the insect will be immediately immersed and rendered totally useless. Follow it as it is slowly borne along, guiding without checking its motion. In fishing *pools* with a good breeze blowing, keep the line entirely out of the water, and permit the fly only to touch the surface. This is advantageous, even in a gently flowing stream, when the wind is high. In *strong currents*, with the wind blowing down, do not attempt to keep pace with the stream, for you will certainly lose the race and deny the trout any chance of seizing the fly; but, holding the rod well up as you move slowly down, now raise the insect out of the water and now lower it again, and so retard its progress and keep it playing upon the surface. Always fish from the bank side of pools, whether working up or down; and when a trout seizes the fly, strike instantly.

It is as necessary in natural-fly fishing as it is in artificial, to keep out of sight of the fish; but, owing to the difference of tackle and method employed, it is more difficult to do so in the former case than in the latter, especially, as we have seen, in the absence of wind. And therefore, a black water is a desideratum at all times for a floating fly either up or down stream.

But the May-fly, as I have said, can be used under water as well as on the surface, and for this the ordinary fly-fishing rod will suit well enough. The line, however, including two yards of fine gut at the extremity, must not be more than a length and a half of the rod. The tackle consists either of one large hook or of two smaller ones. The larger hook is a No. 10, to the shank of which two bristles of horse-hair are lashed to prevent the flies from slipping down, and so destroying their appearance. Place two insects on the hook, in each case inserting the point at the head, and bringing it out at the tail. When a trout takes the flies on this tackle, the angler should allow it to run for a short distance before striking; and when he does strike, it should be gently and firmly down-stream.

In the second case, two No. 7 hooks, with short shanks, are placed back to back, the one fully a quarter of an inch above the other. A fly is impaled on each hook, the point being inserted at the head, the body threaded on the shank, and the point brought out at the tail. Prompt striking is necessary here, but in no case must it be too hard. I use both kinds of tackle; when the fish are taking freely, the single hook, I find, answers perfectly well; but when trout are shy, their advances are more likely to meet with a readier response from the double barb.

Before casting, moisten the wings of the flies with saliva. This will ensure that they sink to some extent below the surface, and so constitute a much more deadly bait than if they were floating. Note, too, that the same result will not be attained by merely soaking them, however thoroughly, in the stream.

Fishing with the natural fly below the surface is practised only up-stream, and in the absence of wind. In contrast to the method of fishing with a floating fly, all casts with the sunk fly should be made from the channel and towards the bank. This style of angling is most successful under a bright sun, when the water is "small" and clear. Indeed, whatever method may be adopted in fishing with the May-fly, and whatever the condition of water, the angler will invariably find that bright sunshine will bring him most sport. A dull cloudy day is unfavourable; and if the water be very full, it is better, even when there is no wind, to fish a floating fly down-stream than a sunk fly up.

The best period of the day for May-fly fishing is generally from about nine o'clock in the morning until three in the afternoon. In the lower reaches of the Clyde and the Tweed, where the rivers run over dark rocky beds, trout take it most readily in the early morning if the weather be fresh and warm, but not so well during a hot bright day. In the upper reaches, however, where the bed of the stream is gravelly and stony, the "takes" are best from nine to three, when the weather is warm and sunny, though a mild morning will not be entirely barren; but in no case is May-fly fishing ever successful in cold weather. In the early morning trout are to be found in thin ebb-water at the sides and near the heads of streams, as well as in the broken water; but as the day advances, they take to the deeper streams and pools. During the night, too, the angler may do great execution with this fly among the big fish that then frequent these pools.

Mr Stewart asserts, probably on the authority of Younger, that the first heavy flood which occurs after the May-flies come out carries them all away for the season. This is true only should the flood take place towards the close of the season. At any other period of their existence, a "spate" will work no such disastrous results. The morning thereafter will find them as numerous and as lively as ever; and if the angler do not make an extra good "take" that day with the water in such grand "ply," it will not be because he could find no flies.

Another remark of this excellent author calls for some notice. He states that the virtues of the

May-fly as a lure are little known elsewhere than on Tweedside. This is not so. On the contrary, it has been well known, and deservedly held in the highest estimation, on the Clyde and its tributaries by every experienced angler since ever I handled a rod. It is the lure to which I devote most attention during the limited period of the fly's existence, and I have frequently captured from 20 to 30 lb. of trout with it in the course of a few hours. Twelve years ago, on the lower reaches of the Clyde, I caught 20 lb. and upwards daily for six days in succession, and was home again before breakfast on each occasion; and during the summer of 1882, my son and I killed on the Clyde and one of its tributaries, by its means, 104 lb. of trout in three consecutive days.

When circumstances necessitate the use of the artificial fly, it should be fished either up or down stream as a floating live fly: but fished in any way, it will prove but a poor substitute for its natural prototype.

The Green Drake.

This fly is known in Scotland as the yellow fly, in England as the green drake. In ordinary seasons it makes its appearance in the beginning of June, and usually lasts from a fortnight to three weeks. Its development, habits, and home have already been described in the list of flies given in a previous chapter. What I have to do here is to note its value as a lure, and the method of its use.

I am again obliged to dissent from the remarks of Mr Stewart. He states that this fly "is almost as difficult to catch as the trout; so that, as far as angling at least in Scotland is concerned, it hardly deserves attention.". Why it should be more difficult of capture in Scotland than elsewhere, is left to the imagination of the reader to discover: and the only reason that is likely to suggest itself to him is, that the yellow fly of the North shares the characteristic shrewdness of the inhabitants, and has more nimbleness and cunning than its English appellation of "green drake" would lead one to suppose. But the truth is not so flattering. The green drake is certainly more commonly met with in England than in Scotland, because the more sluggish streams of the South, flanked by muddy banks, and bordered by rushes, are better suited to its habits than gravelly beds or pebbly channels. It is not the greater difficulty of its capture here, but the less favourable character of our more rapid rivers, that explains why it may be of more account elsewhere than in Scotland. But even in Scotland it is to be found abundantly on many of the rivers, lochs, and burns. It is easily captured close to the riverside if the day be dull and cloudy; but in bright sunshine it is tempted to try its wings and to take its flight over the fields, where, of course, it cannot so readily be found. To effect a capture in such circumstances, the angler should use a fine net stretched over a large hoop.

Though it may not rival the May-fly as a lure, the yellow fly is, as every practical angler knows, a very deadly fly. The trout taken with it are generally of a large size; and many a score of 20-lb. baskets have fallen to my green drakes. On one occasion I captured twenty-three trout, weighing $23\frac{1}{2}$ lb., and on the day following twelve trout, weighing 14 lb.

The flies are best carried in a wooden box, corresponding in length with the lid of the fishing-basket, to which it may be attached by means of a strap. It should be furnished with a sliding lid on the top, to allow one insect to come out at a time; and the sides must be perforated to admit the air. As it is most desirable to keep the insects dry, some provision should be made for covering the box in a heavy rain.

The usual method of fishing with the green drake is familiarly known in England as dibbing or daping. It requires a very light rod, from 16 to 18 feet in length. The line, which must be upon a reel, is composed of 30 or 40 yards of fine silk or cotton thread (the latter three-ply, and slightly twisted). To this is attached a gut cast of 10 or 12 feet, carrying two No. 5 hooks. The hooks are tied back to back, with their points turned somewhat towards each other, and a live fly is impaled on each. Insert the hook in the fly at one shoulder near the root of the wing, and bring it out at the other. Be careful that the fingers are dry when baiting the insect: the wings are extremely tender, and are speedily destroyed by water.

In fishing with this fly, it is essential to have the wind in your favour, whether it blows up, down, or across stream. From the fact that the wind is the main agent in floating the flies, this style of fishing is usually termed "blow-line" fishing. Choose, then, the bank where the wind is most likely to second your efforts and make success possible, and, holding the rod nearly erect, with a moderate length of line out, allow the wind to take it well over the river. When it has been wafted over the spot where you intend to make the descent, gently lower the point of the rod until the flies alight daintily upon the surface of the water, and then, by a skilful management of the rod and the favour of the breeze, you will succeed in keeping them there, flitting along with every appearance of natural motion. Care must be taken not to allow any part of the gut-line to touch the water, otherwise the flies will be soaked and rendered useless. When a trout seizes the fly, you cannot strike too quickly, though it is quite possible to strike too hard.

Unlike the May-fly, the green drake succeeds best on a rough, breezy day, with little or no sunshine. A showery day, or even a thoroughly wet one, will prove very profitable for sport; whether it accord with the angler's conception of outdoor enjoyment or not, is another question. To the enthusiastic angler, however, the ideas are by no means incompatible. In such conditions of weather, the condition of the water is of less importance; it may be either black or clear, and the "take" may be good. The fly, as I have said, is abundant on many of our burns; and when these are swollen after a flood, the drake is a wonderful killer.

When the day is fine and bright, the water "small" and clear, and the wind blows lightly over its surface, it is more advantageous to fish with one fly only. For this purpose use a No. 3 or No. 4 hook and a No. 2, tied in the same manner as in the larger tackle, and place the fly on the larger hook, leaving the smaller one uncovered. This does not make such a bulky appearance in clear water and weather as the double bait, and is consequently less likely to excite the suspicions of the ever-wary trout.

When the natural insect is not to be found during its season, I use the artificial, which may be fished either by dibbing, or by casting as any ordinary imitation. If the fly is to be cast, I use the form already given in the list of artificial lures. Two, and occasionally three, such flies are placed upon the line one yard apart. The casts may be made either up or down stream, according to the condition of the water and the direction of the wind. The artificial fly will be always most successful in a full, black water, or on a rough, stormy day. Even in these circumstances, however, it never equals the natural insect as a lure; while in a "small" clear water the trout have little difficulty in detecting the deception.

If the artificial fly is required for dibbing, I make one thus: A piece of very thin cork, wrapped once round, and ribbed with brown silk, forms the body. Dress each wing with the tip of a feather from the breast of a wild drake, dyed greenish-yellow. Take another feather from the breast, dye it yellow, strip off one side, raise the fibre on the other with the finger, and pare with scissors to the length required for the hackle. Two or three turns below the wings will be sufficient. Dress on two hooks; a No. 4 at the tail, and, rather more than half an inch from it, a No. 5 reversed, and placed underneath the wings.

This imitation is used in precisely the same conditions of water and weather as are necessary for dibbing with the live fly. It is occasionally successful, especially on a breezy day.

In the absence of the natural insect I prefer dibbing with the artificial fly to casting with it; but sometimes when the former method fails, the latter succeeds.

The Black Ant.

This insect, although neither so attractive in appearance, nor so well known to the average angler, as the May-fly or the green drake, deserves to take rank with them among the best lures in natural-fly fishing. It is a great favourite with the trout, and on that account alone should be prized by the angler; but it derives an additional value for him from the time of its advent, and thus

> " by season seasoned is
> To its right praise and true perfection."

It comes to his aid in August, when the May-fly and the drake have passed away, and when artificial-fly fishing is at its very worst. This species of ant is found on marshy ground near rivers, and may be picked up in thousands off the rushes when the day is hot and bright. From about the beginning of August on to September, baskets of from 10 to 20 lb. a-day frequently testify to its powers, and in some instances as many as 30 lb. in one day have been scored.

This fly is fished with either single or double tackle. In the former case two insects are impaled on a No. 6 hook, by inserting the point through the shoulder of each. Place them closely together, with their heads pointing in opposite directions, and their backs next the gut. The bodies of the insects will thus rest on the water in a natural position, their wings will be kept as much as possible from contact with it, and the fascination of the lure will be maintained till the angler's purposes have been served. In the double tackle two No. 3 hooks are tied back to back, and a fly is fixed on each in the same manner as in the single. With either tackle the angler must use a very light rod, from 16 to 18 feet in length, with a short line of light gut.

The ant is fished very much in the same way as the green drake, either up or down stream, according to the direction of the wind, and either in clear water, or in dark water after a flood. Unlike the green - drake fishing, however, which is always dependent on the wind, and cannot be enjoyed in its absence, black-ant fishing may be practised when there is not a breath of wind. In such a case the angler must fish down-stream only, direct his attention solely to the broken water, and eschew the quiet pools as likely to yield him nothing but abundance of disappointment. It is most advantageously cast from the bank side; but in fishing with such a short line, the angler must be specially careful lest the sight of his person destroy the chances of his success. The line should be kept entirely out of the water, and only the flies permitted to rest on its surface. A little dexterity will prevent them from sinking, and the stream will impart to them a natural motion. When a trout seizes the flies, strike instantly but gently.

All natural flies whose home is on the riverside may be used as lures in the same way as the ant, provided they are large enough to have some appearance on the water, and of sufficiently good report among the trout to render them acceptable. Of such are the down-looker, the night-hawk, and the many varieties of moths which appear at night, and which may be gathered in plenty under the banks. The March brown also is occasionally so employed; but the difficulty of finding a sufficient number, at the time when it would be of most service, proves a barrier to its general use. If this fly could be obtained on the banks in abundance in the early morning, before the water was alive with its myriads, it would doubtless far outshine in fame the already famous artificial, and deserve to be regarded as the " May-fly of spring."

CHAPTER VI.

INSECT-BAIT FISHING.

The Creeper.

"More matter for a May morning."
—*Twelfth Night.*

WE have seen that the vast majority of flies which, in perfect though ephemeral beauty, sport on the surface of the stream to the delight of the fish, are merely the fully developed forms of insects that have been bred underneath it. Many of these creatures, notwithstanding their marvellous adaptation to their surroundings, never attain to the crown and perfection of their existence, but in their immature and frequently helpless conditions of larva and pupa, fall an easy prey to the keen-eyed and rapacious fish. Possibly the principle of the "survival of the fittest" obtains in water as on land; but if so, in this case they survive only to be the better fitted to minister ere long in a daintier dress to more fastidious tastes. In their " happy hunting-grounds " below, the trout are wont to consider these aquatic larvæ as quite fair game, and doubtless find them remarkably good eating. This is more or less true regarding the larvæ of all flies at all seasons; but it is especially the case in winter and early spring, when, most of the flies being still undeveloped, the absence of winged life above compels the trout to seek their nourishment below.

With the knowledge of this fact before him, the angler will have himself to blame if he do not profit by it. The insects in these immature states are, it is true, neither so attractive to the sight nor so pleasant to handle as the winged flies; and their unsavoury nature, no less than an imperfect appreciation of their value as lures, induces many anglers to abjure them altogether. So long, however, as they constitute a perfectly legitimate bait in all open waters, and so long as they rank high in the estimation of the trout, they cannot be entirely neglected by the fisher who caters for the patronage of the fish, or makes provision for his own sport. Indeed, in their larval forms, many of these flies are as lures superior to all other ground-bait, and second in importance only to the winged insects themselves.

Of all such, perhaps the one best known to the

angler is the creeper or crab, the larva of the May or stone fly. Although found under the stones along the margin of rivers during most of the winter and spring months, it deserves little notice from the angler till about the 10th or 12th of May. At this season, if the water is low and clear, and the sun bright and hot, the creeper fisher will generally meet with his reward in a splendid basket. This is well known on the Clyde and the Tweed, where the creeper is a great favourite with many an angler; but the practical fly-fisher would consider these very conditions most favourable for the sand-fly, and would therefore be likely to prefer it as a more reliable lure. If the day be very sultry, however, the great heat will hurry on the development of all the sand-flies at one time: their lives may indeed be merry, but they will certainly be short; for in an hour or less they will all be gone, and the angler's sport will go with them. It is in these circumstances that the artificial fly must be discarded, and recourse had to the creeper, when it will prove itself a most worthy and acceptable substitute.

There need be no difficulty in procuring the insects in abundance. They will be found, as I have said, under the stones that lie embedded in sand near the edges of the streams where the water is a few inches in depth. In a dry season, when the river becomes low, the creepers retire with the stream, and always have their home near its margin. They are best carried in a small perforated tin-box, containing a little moss, and furnished with a sliding lid to permit one insect to come out at a time.

The rod and line recommended for May-fly fishing up-stream will answer admirably for creeper. The gut should be of the finest, and the tackle may be either single or double. In the single tackle a large hook, a No. 10, is employed. Two insects, threaded from mouth to tail on this hook, will be sufficient to cover the metal and form a tempting bait. Sinkers are unnecessary; a large hook thus baited sinks of itself. With this tackle do not strike on the first intimation that a trout has seized the bait, but allow the fish to run for a short distance before you respond. It is a large bait on a large hook, and possibly the trout, unable or unwilling to gulp it down all at once, is prolonging the delight by sucking it "smaller by degrees and beautifully less." So give him time to work his own destruction, or you'll lose him.

For a double tackle you may use two No. 5 or two No. 6 hooks, tied back to back, with their barbs about a quarter of an inch apart. Shorten the shank of the upper hook a little, so that the ends of both may nearly coincide on the gut; this makes a neater finish. File both at the back before tying, and they will be more likely to keep their position. An insect is impaled on each hook in the same manner as before. With such a tackle strike the instant you have reason to believe that a trout has taken your bait: do not wait for the tug at the rod-top, but let your eye guide you; for should the line be checked for a moment in its progress down-stream, it is almost certain that a trout has intercepted it, and then you cannot strike too soon. This tackle, as well as the double tackle given for fishing the May-fly under water, is specially recommended to the young angler, who in any kind of fishing is generally inclined to strike before he ought. Here his characteristic though pardonable haste will be more likely to issue in gain than in loss.

When using the creeper I always fish up with either of the tackles just described, casting into the eddies and edges of the roughish streams, as well as in the broken water. The method is the same as that employed in fishing with the May-fly or the worm up-stream; and the creeper possesses this advantage over the May-fly, that, being a more hardy bait, it will both last longer and be less likely to part company with the hook. The angler is thus able to cast with greater freedom, and is saved the necessity of renewing his bait so frequently.

Some anglers, however, fish the creeper downstream. The tackle they use consists of two No. 2 hooks tied in much the same way as in the Stewart tackle, but with the barbs only half an inch apart. Baiting with one creeper only, they pass the end or lower hook through the second segment in the back of the insect, and the upper hook through the body near the tail and at right angles to the lower hook. The hooks are thus almost entirely concealed, but great care is required to fix them without destroying the bait altogether. A small sinker-shot—No. 3 or No. 4—is placed on the line about nine inches from the hooks, to maintain the bait at a proper depth in the roughish streams, in which it is most successful. The experienced angler, indeed, selects this kind of water only, and passes over the heavier currents as well as the quiet unruffled pools. With a sinker, however, the hook is apt to get fixed on stones in the bed of the river; and the angler who uses one, must raise the point of his rod now and again to secure that his bait moves slowly down with the stream. Prompt striking, on the slightest interruption to the course of the line, is as necessary in this case as in the former.

The creeper may be fished with more or less success till about the end of May; but only in low clear water, and in bright sunshine, will it ever fill the creel. In other circumstances the angler will do better if he confine himself to the artificial fly until the season brings round the May-fly. Creepers are perhaps most deadly towards the end of the month, when they are just about to assume the winged state. I remember—'tis now many years ago—that in the Tweed, above its junction with Biggar Water, I captured with the creeper 29 lb. of splendid trout in the course of a day, or rather part of a day; for there were no railways in the district in those days, and on that occasion, as on many others, I walked in the morning from Lanark to the Tweed, fished till the evening, and then walked home again with my loaded creel. Creels of fish then, as every angler knows, were much better loaded than they are now, and the walk home was itself a task quite heavy enough; but possibly, though paradoxically, it would have been heavier had the creel been lighter.

The Caddis.

Caddis-bait or cod-bait is the name given to the immature form of various water-flies belonging to the Phryganidæ family. Some of these insects in their winged state, such as the musk-brown or cinnamon fly, and the green-tail or grannom, are familiar to all anglers; and notice has already been taken (Chapter II.) of their mode of development, and the strange habitations they construct for themselves in which to pass the larval and pupal stages of their existence. It was stated that some of these caddis-cases are carried about by the larvæ, and others are fixed to the under sides of stones in the water. It is the larvæ whose cases are constructed of sand and small stones, that constitute the fisher's bait. He will find them generally in the deep sides of streams and heads of pools. They are common enough in most rivers and burns.

In the hands of an experienced angler the caddis proves a very deadly bait, and well merits the attention of all brethren of the rod from the beginning of May till the end of July. The larvæ may be gathered at any time during the day. Some fishers lay in a stock the evening before they are wanted; but the fresher they are the better, as the insects then present the fine yellow appearance so very tempting to the trout. They are most conveniently carried about in a woollen bag. Before placing any one on the hook, the angler must, of course, break the shell and take out the insect by the head.

In fishing with the caddis, use an ordinary trout rod and line, with a yard and a half of gut. The tackle varies according to the taste of the angler.

Some use only one hook, a No. 5, and run it right through the insect from tail to head. This makes a very unsatisfactory bait; for after a few casts, the soft liquid contents of the body escape, and the sides collapse, leaving merely the skin on the hook. In a small burn, where the bait is merely dropped over the bank, it is not so easily destroyed, but in a river, where frequent casting is necessary, the insect is speedily rendered unrecognisable, and requires to be constantly renewed.

Another method of fishing is to use two No. 3 hooks, tied back to back, with their barbs slightly bevelled. An insect is impaled on each by inserting the point at one side close to the head and bringing it out at the other. As the head and shoulders are the only hard portions of the bait, an insect so placed will maintain its shape better, and serve the angler's purposes much longer, than if threaded on the hook from end to end.

The tackle I prefer is a modification of the latter. The hooks are the same, and placed back to back, but so that one is three-eighths of an inch above the other. The insects are put on each in the manner just described. The object of this arrangement is to give the bait a somewhat larger and more attractive appearance in the eye of the fish, and still to retain the double chance implied in the double hook.

The Caddis.

The season of caddis-fishing corresponds closely with that of worm-fishing, and the manner and conditions of operation are much the same in both. It is most successful when fished up-stream in a low clear water, with bright sunshine. When the morning is fine and warm, daybreak is the most favourable time for sport; and though on a good day the bait continues to "take" till about two o'clock in the afternoon, the angler who is "up in the morning early" will have the heaviest basket. If the weather be cold in the morning, and there be dew on the ground, he need not begin operations till the sun comes out. Fish from the channel side, casting cautiously into the streams and broken water, in precisely the same manner as with creeper and worm. If a sinker is used at all, it should be a very small one indeed. Though it succeeds well in clear water, the caddis, like the worm, is very effective in a black one, especially in flooded burns and smaller streams. In fishing down-stream, as he should in such circumstances, the angler must remember to keep always below his bait, as in worm-fishing, so that he may strike with the current and not against it.

Caddis is unknown to many fishers, and, I suspect, is much underrated, even by some who do know it. The angler who has any experience of its powers, however, will prefer it to the worm in a "small" clear water; and I am convinced that from May to July better sport may often be obtained with it than with any other lure, with the exceptions of the creeper and the May-fly.

The Grub.

Besides the aquatic larvæ already noticed, many imperfect insect forms bred of the earth, and even less prepossessing in appearance than the creeper, have long been known to the angler as very deadly baits. Walton recommends the "young brood of a wasp" and the "spawn of the beetle" as very good lures for roach and dace; Cotton gives the "ash-grub" and the "dock-worm" as great favourites with grayling; and almost all writers since their days have included these and other grubs in their list of generally accepted baits for river-fishing.

For myself, I never use grubs; but as many trout anglers on Tweed and Clyde set great store by them, it may be as well to give them a place here. Those chiefly used are the common earth-grubs. They will generally be found on turning up garden soil, turf, old coal-dross heaps, or old banks of earth. The roots of the common dock, too, are a favourite harbour. According to Mr Wood, in their larval state they remain in the ground for three years, increasing so much in size and fat that their tightened skin seems scarcely able to hold its contents. Big and burly of body as they are, however, they are extremely tender of heart, and cannot well be baited on a hook without some preparation to render them tough. Sometimes this is effected by steaming them in a jar, but Cotton advises that they be simply kept for a time in bran.

There is no doubt that this grub is a great killer during nearly the whole of the fishing season, especially in spring, when it will do great wonders in a muddy or a black water after a flood. It is generally fished on a double tackle, the hooks varying in size according to the size of the grub. Place two hooks on the same gut, either facing the same way, or back to back, at a distance of three-quarters of an inch—the larger and upper a No. 4, and the smaller a No. 3. Pass the upper hook through the shoulder and the other through the lower part of the body, taking care to keep the line tight between the hooks. The double tackle is to prevent, as far as possible, the soft, unshapely grub from slipping off the metal altogether, as well as to hook the fish better. If a single hook is used, as in the old style, a stiff horsehair must be warped to the shank before baiting; but in any case the insect is so easily injured that only gentle handling will make a presentable bait. A small sinker is attached to the line at the end of the first thread of gut, so that the bait may trundle along the bottom. Grub is fished in the same manner, places, and conditions of water as the worm.

Even to many anglers who are not too nice to foul their fingers, this bait presents such a forbidding appearance, that no assurance of its deadly nature, however well grounded, will ever overcome their disinclination to use it. Many fishers on the Clyde, however, have of late been in the habit of employing it, to the exclusion of every other kind of bait, but the difficulty of obtaining a sufficient supply pretty effectually prevents its general use. Indeed, to ensure a stock for a day's fishing, the angler would require to spend the previous day in collecting them. This, of course, is inconvenient, and would not suit every one.

And now, with the quaint and cautious remark of Cotton to his disciple, we may conclude all that need be said of insect-bait fishing: "There are several other baits besides these few I have named you, which also do very great execution at the bottom, and some that are peculiar to certain countries and rivers, of which every angler may in his own place make his own observation; and some others that I do not think fit to put you in mind of, because I would not corrupt you, but would have you, as in all things else I observe you to be, a very honest gentleman—a *fair* angler."

CHAPTER VII.

WORM-FISHING.

" Ay me! what perils do environ
The fish that meddles with cold iron!"
—*Hudibras,* adapted.

THE worm has always been a favourite lure. Most probably it was our first. Did we not, when schoolboys, betake ourselves on a holiday to the nearest burn, and there, with deepest cunning, lie in wait for simple minnows, behind a lob-worm on a bent pin? But though we have doubtless all got beyond the pin, many of the fraternity of anglers have not yet outgrown their first love for the worm, but still find in it their be-all and end-all. This reveals lamentable want of taste, and almost unpardonable ignorance of the surpassing charms of fly-fishing. While Stewart justly assigns the first place in scientific angling to the artificial fly, he is nevertheless a very valiant champion of the rights of the worm. He says that many of his brother anglers disparage it, because they consider it so simple that any one may succeed in it; and he proceeds to show that, if brought to a clear water on a warm sunny day, such anglers would speedily discover their mistake. Now I am not of those who ignore its claims, or decry its merits. I am, moreover, quite at one with Mr Stewart in his attempt to free worm-fishers from the charge of being unscientific, and to raise their favourite pastime to the rank of a sport. But while admitting that it is a branch of the art well calculated, when practised in clear water and sunny weather, to test the angler's dexterity in casting and his acquaintance with the habits of the fish, I should be disposed to say that Stewart had unduly extolled its powers as a lure, and attributed to it a pre-eminence which it does not possess. He tells us that "worm-fishing is the most certain and deadly of all fishing; and by it more trout may be captured in the month of July than by any other means in any other month of the year." I cannot say that such is my experience. The worm cannot for a moment compare with the May-fly in the certainty of its operation; and even the creeper and the caddis may fairly compete with it in power of execution. One might possibly kill more fish in July or August with worm than with fly, for these are the months when the flies are passing off; but employ each lure in its own appropriate season, and there is no question that the May-fly is "the most certain and deadly of all fishing."

No doubt trout were more plentiful in most of our streams when Mr Stewart affirmed that "he was not worthy of the name of angler who could not, in any day of the month of July, when the water was clear, kill from 15 lb. to 20 lb. weight of trout in any county in the south of Scotland;" but had such a test of skill been applied to members of the angling community, even in his days, whatever other good points may have distinguished the true disciples of old Izaak, I fear me that the one outstanding characteristic of the brotherhood must have been its selectness. After writing off a fair amount for deterioration of streams since then, as one old enough to have fished before Stewart, and to have experience both of the present and of the former days, I have no hesitation in saying that his test of discipleship would still remain much too high. For there are days—and many of them—in July, when all the arts of the worm-fisher, or of any other fisher, utterly fail to obtain a tithe of that weight of fish. This I say, not so much from any anxiety to be still considered, in the face of such poor results, "worthy of the name of angler," as from a conviction that any aspirant to angling fame, who starts with the expectation of reaching this high standard of excellence, will assuredly be doomed to disappointment. But whatever may be said for the deadly character of the worm-lure, all are agreed that worm-fishing cannot furnish occasion for the display of the angler's highest art. This is afforded by artificial-fly fishing alone. No angler "worthy of the name," who has once mastered its niceties in detail, and attained to such a degree of perfection in the art as to feel its charm, would, even with the seductive prospect of a big basket before him, ever think of resorting to the worm, except in such conditions and at such seasons as would scarcely admit of the use of the fly. What these conditions and seasons are, it will now be my aim to show.

The worm may be used with success in flooded waters from March to October, or for that matter, indeed, all the year round. In such waters the amount of skill required to do well is very considerable, and the "takes" of experts are oftentimes large; and if the experienced worm-fisher has come out mainly for a big basket, it is in a flooded water that he is most likely to get it: but if he desire the best opportunity for the test of his powers, let him choose a "small" clear water in the hot bright days of June and July. Then he must, as in fly-fishing in clear water, cast up-stream with some dexterity and precision, and exercise that nicety in handling his rod which fine tackle and observant trout demand. To a skilful worm-fisher, the results, though not so invariably good as Stewart affirms, will yet be sometimes excellent, and often sufficiently encouraging to lead him to regard the worm as the best lure in clear water when fly-fishing is at its worst.

In fishing with this, as with any other kind of bait, a reel-rod is essential. It should be both light and stiff; and the length need not be more than 13 feet. The double-handed 14 to 16 feet rod recommended by Stewart, and perhaps well suited to a man of his six-feet-two proportions, will—unless made of very light material, such as bamboo or white pine—in the hands of the average angler of ordinary stature, prove a most fatiguing and unwieldy implement, interfering at once with facility in casting and promptness in striking. As I have already urged in all kinds of up-stream fishing, the gut-line, for a yard or two next the hooks, should be of the finest. Indeed some anglers, when fishing in either a clear or a flooded water, use a line entirely composed of gut; and to obviate the objection that such a line might be nearly as invisible to the fisher as it is intended to be to the fish, they affix to it a small piece of red cloth, a few inches from the point of the rod, as a guide to the position of the line and an index of its movements. The tackle I use for a small water consists of three No. 2 hooks, tied on a fine hair of gut, in the same manner as in No. 1 minnow-tackle. In very low water some prefer No. 1 hooks with correspondingly smaller worms. Enter the upper hook through the worm near the head, the second through the middle, and the third a little above the tail. This must be done with as little injury to the creature as possible, and in such a way that it may hang loosely between the hooks, and be free to assume a position sufficiently natural to render it an object of interest and desire to the trout. Generally speaking, no sinkers are necessary in up-stream fishing; for the water being "small," the trout have no difficulty in seeing the bait, and seizing it too, if so disposed. Sinkers, in most cases, so far from keeping the bait waiting the leisure of the trout, merely impede the desirable motion which renders it attractive; and should they get fixed below stones, they may stop progress altogether. Those who consider sinkers indispensable in all waters, plead that thereby the worm will most surely reach or approach the bottom; but in a "small" water the bait is already sufficiently weighted with the hooks to secure that end, and anything additional will lead to delay, if not to disaster. In deep reaches of the river, however, where there is a heavy run, sinkers may be required even in such conditions of water.

Fishing up-stream with the worm possesses all the advantages of fishing up with the artificial fly, and these need not be again detailed here. The method of casting, however, is not the same in both. The angler must not send out his line behind him in the wide curve recommended in fly-fishing with the loop-line; neither must he urge his line forward in the same manner and with the same velocity as in casting with his fly; but bringing the bait to within a short distance of the spot where he is standing, let him endeavour to give the line more of a gentle swing than a decided cast, lowering the point of his rod at the moment of imparting to it the forward impetus, and continuing to lower it until the worm is in the water. The bait will thus be sent out to the full length of the line, and will alight with gentleness and in good condition. Any violent or jerking motion in casting should be avoided as certain to destroy the worm and alarm the trout. Practice only will enable the novice to surmount what may appear to him the insuperable difficulty of casting neatly and accurately without damage to the bait; but he will be guided in his efforts more by watching for a few moments an expert worm-fisher at work than by perusing pages of elaborate description. When the angler has reason to believe that his worm has reached the bottom, the point of the rod must be raised gently and gradually as the bait is carried down-stream. The length of line he should have in the water will depend on circumstances, but, in general, more danger is to be apprehended from a long line than from a short one. In a rapid current there should be just as much as will allow the worm to reach the bottom, for a greater length of line exposed to the action of such a stream would result in bringing the bait at once to the surface. If to fish an eddy the angler requires to cast across a stream, he must keep his line out of the rapid run, and allow the worm to be acted on only by the quieter water in which it is cast. There is less risk in permitting more of the line to touch the water when fishing an open gentle stream, as a short line is more likely to withdraw the bait from the natural action of the current. In wind it is imperative to have some length of line in the stream, and the reason is obvious. In determining, therefore, the amount to be immersed at any time, the angler must be guided by the nature of the current in which the cast is to be made; and the considerations that will weigh with him in every case are—that the worm should trundle along the bottom, that it should maintain the motion imparted to it by the stream only, and be neither accelerated nor retarded by any action of the line. He will do much to secure these ends if he remember the rule given in fly-fishing upstream, and never allow his lure to get below him. Ere it has reached a point opposite to him, and in the absence of any response from the trout, he should take another step up-stream and cast again.

When using this tackle—commonly called "Stewart's tackle," but employed long before his time—it is best to strike the moment you have cause to think the fish has taken the bait. You are generally advised of this important fact by the stoppage of the line. This is the first indication, but not the only one. It is unwise, however, to wait for the further proof of the trout's presence which is afforded by the tremulous motion of the line. Though this is certainly a surer indication of an attack upon the bait than the mere interruption of the line (which may be caused by an obstruction at the bottom), still, the angler who hesitates to strike in the hope of thereby making "assurance doubly sure," will almost to a certainty lose his fish. His eye must detect the bite before his hand does so, for his chances of success with this tackle lie altogether in the keenness of his perception and his readiness for action. In using the single-hook tackle, on the other hand, it is hardly ever safe to strike at once. Indeed it is difficult to say when to strike. The chances of catching the trout being in this case limited to one hook, which, moreover, only part of the bait conceals, while a large portion remains innocent of steel, there would seem to be the same uncertainty of knowing when to strike, as of knowing what part of the bait has been seized. If feeding greedily, the trout may bolt the whole of it; if shy, he may simply seize and nibble either end. In the former case, prompt striking will be most deadly; in the latter, though a quick stroke might prove a lucky one, it were better to give him a second or two to manifest his intentions. But sometimes he carries the worm bodily off to his retreat, and then the line runs rapidly out. The moment this is observed is the moment to strike, and generally you will not fail to astonish him. Whether the angler strike quickly with the Stewart tackle, or less smartly with the single, he must in any case be careful to strike down-stream, and never up.

In wading up the water, select for bait-fishing all spots where trout are most likely to lie—such as the margin of a swift stream, the eddies behind rough stones or rocks, streams in communication with pools, the recesses underneath the banks, and all broken streamy water of moderate depth. As it is of the first importance that the learner should know where to fish as well as how, let him from the beginning carefully observe the nature and condition of the water in all places where he hooks a fish. He will thus gain a practical—the only useful—knowledge of their habitats, which will save him both much time and needless trouble in his future efforts: for an experienced angler can tell to a certainty where he ought to catch a fish.

During June and July the worm takes very well in the early hours of the morning, if the weather be fine, and trout will then be found in shallow streams and gentle runs. If the morning is cold, they do not take freely; and in this respect worm-fishing resembles May-fly fishing, as neither usually succeeds well until the sun comes out. From that time on to one or three o'clock in the afternoon, good sport may be had in both. Where worm has done well in the early part of the day, there is frequently a lull during the later hours. In June I have often caught heavy baskets with the worm before eight o'clock in the morning when the weather was mild and warm, and it was no unusual occurrence for the "take" to go off after that hour for the rest of the day. Trout often take during a moonlight night in June, if the weather be fine and warm; and the angler who is enthusiastic enough to continue the sport then, will meet with them in the thin water at the edges of gentle currents on the channel side. After July the worm does not do so well unless in flooded waters, or in burns where the fish, being but poorly fed, are always on the outlook for something to eat, and so fall an easy prey at almost any time of the year.

In *flooded waters* fine gut is still desirable, although certainly not so necessary as in clear water. The line should be weighted to some extent, but only so much as will keep the bait on the bottom, and permit it to move slowly with the current. This is the main point to be attended to in worm-fishing down-stream during floods. The line must be loaded less or more in proportion to the strength of the current; and the angler has often to increase or diminish the number of sinkers on his line while fishing even a very short reach of water. The sinkers employed are No. 2 and No. 3 split shot. They are placed on the line about 8 or 9 inches from the bait, and if more than one be necessary, they should be set close together, so as to lessen the risk of any interruption to the line through their becoming fixed on obstructions at the bottom. A good way of getting the worm to move more smoothly on the bottom, with less chance of entangling among stones, is to fix the leads on a bobber of gut, about $2\frac{1}{2}$ inches long, attached to the line at the first knot above the worm, or about 8 or more inches from the hooks. A knot may be put on the bobber to prevent the leads slipping off. This arrangement is more suitable for Stewart tackle.

Many anglers prefer to use a single hook when worm-fishing in flooded water. The size varies from No. 8 to No. 10, and the mode of baiting is simple enough. Entering the hook a little below the head, thread the worm on the shank till the point of the hook approaches the tail; and in order to accomplish this more expeditiously, wet the finger and thumb slightly, and take a little sand between them before commencing operations. Though this single and common hook undoubtedly gets many good baskets in a full water, I always prefer the Stewart tackle, made up of No. 2 or No. 3 hooks, according to the size and condition of the stream. Slightly larger worms are used with the larger hooks. With this tackle the worm is kept longer alive, it is allowed to assume a more natural appearance and position, and when fish are biting shy, there is more likelihood of hooking them. Some anglers fish with two sets of Stewart tackle, the second at a distance of from 2 to $2\frac{1}{2}$ feet above the lead. In a heavy water this arrangement is sometimes very effective.

It is not necessary to fish up when the water is flooded: its turbid condition is quite sufficient to screen the angler from view. Nor must he expect to find fish where he found them when the water was clear. When a river comes down in flood, the trout leave the main current and betake themselves to the shallows and eddies for shelter, where they await whatever food the stream brings down to them. Even large trout do so; and during a flood I have frequently got big fish at the shallow sides of streams, in water not more than a few inches in depth. Large trout seldom quit the deep pools for such places at any other time, unless, indeed, during the night. In flooded water, then, the places most likely to yield sport are the ebb portion of the deep pools where there is an easy run, and at the edges of the streams and eddies. As the number of such spots in a flooded water is limited, the angler should make the most of a lucky place when he finds one.

In such a condition of water it is best to use a short line. Though the size of the stream and the nature of the particular reach of it where the cast is to be made, ought in some measure to regulate the length of the line, it will be found that, in most cases, a line of 2 yards, or one little more than half the length of the rod, will amply suffice for all the angler's need; for it is not necessary to cast far off, seeing that the fish are lying near. The channel side is the proper one to fish from, especially if there is a deep run. Should the water on this side be very shallow, it will be necessary to cast more towards the bank. As examples of what are meant by deep channel runs—the choicest portions of water to fish during a flood—I may instance the channel at the wire bridge below Peebles, and Neidpath Castle Pool, on the Tweed; and on the Clyde, Thankerton Bridge Pool above the bridge, the Heather Brae Pool, and the Rock Pool above Thankerton. Such places are always of most account when the water is clayey and red.

As the water falls and begins to get black, fewer pellets and smaller worms must be employed, and casts must now be made more into the runs where there is a good flow of water than into the shallows. Should the day be dull, with the water in this condition, it may be better to change to the minnow; but if there be bright sunshine, it is advisable to keep to the worm or to try the fly. Trout take the worm in flooded waters in all states of the weather—not even excepting a thunderstorm —and at all times of the day; but in a "small" clear water, although they may take when the day is coarse and blustering, we have seen that the most favourable conditions are heat and bright sunshine, and the most favourable time the earlier part of the day.

In small or partial floods, sufficient only to render the water muddy, worm-fishing is never very successful, as the worms are washed into the stream only during full floods, when trout are on the outlook for them. It is when the fish are expecting a supply of their natural food that good baskets are got with this or with any lure. Trout seldom take worm until they have been satiated with surface-food; and hence worm-fishing is best during June and July, when the flies, having served their end, are passing off. Should there be a long period of dry weather during these months, the trout are ready to welcome with eagerness the ground-bait which the first flood brings down to them. A succession of floods, on the other hand, is unfavourable to sport, as the fish, now gorged with worms and grub, can afford to play the epicure.

Trout take for a short time at the beginning of a flood; but after the water has risen considerably, and while it continues rising, there is generally a complete cessation of sport. If the flood be a full one, and the river run thick and muddy, the fish seek the eddies and shallows near the sides, and the angler will meet with little success until the water has to some extent subsided. Should he live at some distance from the stream, he would do well, if he be a worm-fisher, to start as soon as possible after the rain has ceased, so as to reach the riverside ere the favourable opportunity has passed; for in these days of hill-drainage and improved farming, a few hours may suffice to reduce a swollen and highly flooded stream to the condition which the worm-fisher loves. If the flood occur during the season of artificial-fly fishing, the angler need not be in such haste to reach the scene of operations, for the successful use of the fly requires that the turbid water shall in large measure have passed off, and the brown colour given place to the black.

An important factor in the worm-fisher's calculations of success is his supply of well-scoured worms. Though, in a flooded water, trout will frequently take a large and freshly dug worm, being then attracted by its powerful odour rather than by its portly appearance, yet in ordinary circumstances a small reddish worm, when properly prepared, will prove the most alluring. The small blue-headed worm, and what is called the common marsh-worm, I prefer to all others. If kept for a few days in moss, which has been previously washed and left slightly damp, they assume a fine pinkish colour which seems to possess great charms in the eyes of the trout. For their further cleansing, I usually wash the worms before placing them in the moss; and should they be kept for more than a week, the moss requires to be renewed from time to time. The brandling, so much lauded by many anglers, I have little esteem for. It is extremely soft, is difficult to bait, and even when baited, is useless after one or two casts. The worms should be of the same kind, and equally well scoured, whether for fishing in clear or in flooded waters—the only difference being that they should be smaller for a clear water and larger for a discoloured one. They are most convenient for use at the water-side, when carried in a flannel bag. The angler should never start on a day's bait-fishing without seeing that his worms are perfect in condition and abundant in quantity. Better carry too many than too few. Next to having none at all when the water is suitable, there is nothing so tantalising to the expectant angler as to possess an insufficient or a badly prepared supply. It will not only prove a source of much worry and discontent every time a fresh bait is required—and that may be pretty often—but it will likewise destroy every chance of a heavy basket, even should the trout be in a "taking" mood.

Burns often furnish abundant sport to the worm-fisher when they are clear, but more often when they are flooded. The amount of skill required to fish them with effect is even less than would be deemed sufficient for successful worm-fishing in a flooded river. In most cases the angler has simply to keep himself well out of sight, drop his bait gently in, and leave the trout to complete the business: and generally said trout won't be long about it; for his straitened circumstances necessitating a scanty board, he is almost always in a chronic state of hunger, and consequently not inclined to be too fastidious in his tastes. The larger burns, that run over a stony channel, and have more open banks, may require a little more caution, especially if the water be low and clear; but even in their case the "keen demands of appetite" in the trout will be found to go far towards meeting any lack of skill in the angler. Besides, trout in burns are more unsophisticated than their brethren of the rivers; their comparative immunity from disturbance renders them less wary, and so they fall an easier prey.

Several of the lures that obtain in rivers will generally be found effective in burns, and their efficiency is most marked after a flood. The artificial fly is then often very successful; but the favourite baits are worm and caddis. In well-stocked burns a capital basket can almost invariably be obtained with either, and this, too, when the angler would often fail in the larger streams.

As in rivers, so in burns, the best time for sport is during the months of June and July, when the water is clear and the weather warm and bright. At this season, let the angler start at daybreak and fish the burn up. And though, possibly more from lack of imagination than of piscatorial power, his tale of trout may not equal that of the Shepherd in the 'Noctes,' who "ane day, in the Megget, caucht a cartfu', which, as it gaed doun the road, the kintra folk thocht was a cartfu' o' herrins, being a' preceesely o' ae size to an unce,"—still he may capture sufficient to satisfy his ambition, and more than fill his creel. He will find that the earlier hours of the day are the best; the "takes" are fewer after one or two o'clock in the afternoon; but it is no uncommon occurrence for twelve or eighteen dozen to be picked up before that time in a well-stocked burn. A day's "take" of burn-trout looks better when stated in dozens than in pounds. They are more numerous than large; and as they generally pay promptly for what they get, and are rarely credited with a worm, the angler must be content to conduct this branch of his "silent business" on the admirable principle of "small profits and quick returns."

If the water be clear, the angler must of course fish up. Using an ordinary trout-rod and a short fine line, a small Stewart tackle, and a tiny lively worm, let him drop his bait gently into the pools or into the streams, behind stones and below banks, in ripples and in eddies, remembering that wherever there is sufficient—and sometimes even where there is scarcely sufficient—water to cover a fish, the chances are that he may raise one. But he must keep well out of sight, and take care lest his own shadow or that of his rod fall athwart the stream. Much caution and some creeping may be necessary, and not unfrequently indeed, in this as in other matters of finesse, he must "stoop to conquer." If any sinker be used at all in such waters, a No. 3 shot will be found quite heavy enough. With caddis-bait, sinkers are unnecessary. In floods, burns, like rivers, are best fished downstream, the angler adapting the quantity of lead to the strength of the current.

The trout of what are properly called *hill-burns* are the most easily caught, and the most worthless when caught. They are small and wofully ill-fed; black they are too, without the extenuating qualification of comeliness. In most cases such burns are mere drains through the peat-moss, and yet they often contain large numbers of greedy trout, lurking under the bank or half-stranded in holes in the heather. Their well-known and unattractive characteristics are enormously developed heads and jaws, long attenuated bodies, and alarmingly ravenous dispositions. Really I should not advise any angler to waste his time or shock his sensibilities by hauling out such miserable caricatures of the genus *Salmo*.

My remarks on burn-fishing apply to the larger and more open burns that drain a wide area of rich pasture or meadow land. The trout in them may be small, but they are generally in much better condition, and present a more inviting appearance, than those of the hill-drains. They have bright yellow sides and crimson-spotted backs, while their flesh is sometimes more delicate than that of larger river-trout. All burns are not alike plentifully stocked with trout, any more than all rivers are. In accounting for this, regard must be had to a variety of circumstances, such as the character of the district through which they run, and the mode in which it is drained; the nature of their channels as affording food-supplies, shelter, and spawning-ground; and last, though not least, the extent to which they are fished. The extensive system of land-drainage now in operation has very materially affected the number of trout, not only in our burns but also in our larger rivers. Burns are important spawning-grounds of the fish, and therefore may in every sense be called feeders of the streams. Whatever, then, acts injuriously on the young of trout in burns, must tend to their diminution in the rivers. The drains carry the rain too hastily from the hills—a very short time indeed suffices to run it all off. The burns rise both higher and more quickly than formerly during floods, and fall more speedily and to a much lower level during a long period of drought. The result in both cases may be equally disastrous: in the former, the spawning-beds are frequently torn up, and the ova washed away by the swollen waters; in the latter, they are often left high and dry, and exposed to almost certain destruction ere the waters cover them again.

Though burn-fishing does not demand so much scientific skill as river-fishing, it calls for a more vigorous exercise of the physical powers. This exercise is of the most beneficial and exhilarating kind. Well-stocked burns are not to be found at every railway station. Were this so, one might safely predict that they would not long be well stocked. While the angler has therefore generally some miles to cover before he can reach the scene of his sport, he must also traverse a greater distance, and expend more effort while engaged in it, than if he plied his craft by casting his flies over the parent stream. But even with this prospect of unwonted exertion before him, the angler is to be congratulated, if not envied, who finds himself at the foot of the Megget or other well-stored burn, at early dawn of a June morning, just as the mists are passing off the mountain-tops, and Nature wakes to greet the sun. He has come, let us hope, to cool his fevered brow, to "dodge dull care," and throw off, for one day at least, its galling yoke, to reinvigorate his limbs, and revive his jaded spirit. Not a soul is near him, but the everlasting hills are around him, and eloquent in their silence they tell of patience, endurance, and strength. Yet are they "lovely in their strength," for on this glad morning have they thrown around their native ruggedness the brightest robe of summer green. Far above dull earth and its clouded day, they rear their summits in the sunlight, and hope is there, and calm. Down the peaceful valley, from rock to rock, skips in its mad delight the prattling child of the mountain, laughing to the day, and hasting to be free. From out its dewy bed the lark upsprings, and soars aloft to pay its orisons at the very gate of heaven. What heart is there but would beat in full accord with Nature's own life-pulse, partake her calm and joy, and inhale the spirit of her freedom? Up the glen the angler blithely strides, with a glistening trophy from every pool, and fresh heart from every trophy. And if he be not dull of sense or soul, he may bear thence other treasures richer far,—treasures revealed in contemplation of the wondrous world of life that teems in water and in air, of storied records in splintered rock or ice-worn boulder, of beauty's forms in mountain-daisy or in blue harebell, whose modest graces cannot hide the touch of "an unrivalled pencil." Yes,

"The poetry of earth is never dead,"

but to the lover of Nature is ever an inspiration

and a joy. Now he tracks the burnie to the upland solitudes—its cradle in the mountain's lap, where, though its sweet infant babbling awakes no murmured response save the distant bleating of the fold or the whistle of the wild curlew, its bright and yet unsullied face is kissed into rippling smiles by the gentle breath of heaven. There, far above the sordid atmosphere of mart or shop,

> "the fretful stir
> Unprofitable, and the fever of the world,"

the scorn of selfish men and the mockery of friendship insincere, his spirit is soothed and chastened in presence of that calm beauty and restful peace that link earth with the sky. His thoughts are won from cares below and rise to loftier heights with wider range, for now his soul has caught the glow of heaven, and his heart beats high with fuller life. And when the shadows are lengthening in the vale below, exulting in the consciousness of renovated strength, he turns his steps towards home, "owing no man hate, envying no man's happiness"; and even if fortune have denied him a heavy basket, she has at least granted him serenity unclouded, a mind ennobled, and a frame invigorated. In thankfulness and hope and high resolve he returns to dreary daily toil, physically, intellectually, and morally, a stronger and better man.

CHAPTER VIII.

MINNOW-FISHING.

"*First Fisherman.*—Master, I marvel how the fishes live in the sea.
"*Second Fisherman.*—Why, as men do a-land; the great ones eat up the little ones."
—*Pericles.*

THOUGH "from the finny subject of the sea these fishers tell the infirmities of men," the observant angler, were he disposed so to moralise, would find enough to give point to his satire in the characteristic rapacity of the lords of the streams. Pigmies as they are in comparison with the tyrants of the brine, many of them, in their own way, domineer, if not to the content of their hearts, at least to the extent of their stomachs, over the smaller fry not only of their own class but even of their own species, and do not scruple, when tempting subject and fitting opportunity offer, to appropriate the persons of others to fatten their own. The trout is not the least voracious of such in this respect, nor is the voracity a peculiar endowment of the "great ones" only: it is an attribute of the entire species. The possession of a capacity for receiving gives title sufficient to any usurper, however diminutive, to constitute itself the recipient. Might is right in all cases here, and the only principle that seems to obtain any recognition in the carrying out of "the good old rule, the simple plan," is the selection of the fittest. It is not my province to inveigh against that sad proclivity which prompts one fish to show such distinguishing — or extinguishing — marks of its regard for another, but rather to point out how the angler may so take advantage of the ravenous instinct as to endanger its possessor and lure it to destruction. Besides swallowing the younger members of its own species, the trout indulges its rapacious propensities at the expense of other representatives of the finny tribe, such as the parr, the loach, and the stickle-back; but the only victim with which our angler need concern himself at present, as with a legitimate and attractive lure, is the minnow.

Though, as an art, minnow-fishing may not demand that dexterity and nicety in casting, nor that consummate delicacy in handling the rod, which we are prepared to grant to successful fishing with the artificial fly, there can be no question that it calls for the constant exercise of close observation, of cool judgment, of decided action, and of no small degree of manipulative skill; while, as a sport, it exerts that enlivening and captivating influence over its votaries which constitutes one great charm of all good and true fishing, evoking in its pursuit feelings now of earnestness and enthusiasm, now of uncertainty and fear, now of hope and exultation. And when I add that the trout captured with this lure are generally the best which the stream contains—not even excepting those taken with the May-fly—I think I have said enough to convince the novice that minnow-fishing, in the hands of an adept, must prove an exhilarating pastime, a scientific sport, and an " art worth his learning."

But we must first catch the minnows, if ever we are to catch the trout in the act of devouring them; and happily this is, in general, not very difficult to do. In flooded waters they will be found in the easy shallow eddies near the banks, at the mouths of burns or the outlets of field-drains, at the shallow edges of pools, and amongst grass or aquatic plants at the river-side. In low clear water they are not confined to these retreats; they venture farther into the open stream, and may be taken almost anywhere. Many methods of capture have been suggested, and sometimes one may answer, and sometimes another. Minnow-traps, of a convenient size to fit the pocket, may now be obtained at the tackle-maker's, and are usually effective enough. They are especially useful when the water is clear; but a small hand-net, made to screw into the butt of the rod, is a ready means of capturing a supply, if worked at the eddies and among the weeds at the banks of flooded streams. When both these contrivances fail, the hook and line must be resorted to. On a fine gut place two No. 4 hooks, 12 inches apart, bait with small pieces of worm, and cast into the little bays and sheltered places near the margin of the river. Only the small or medium-sized minnows of a bright silvery hue on the under side should be selected; the greenish-coloured or the spawning are useless.

However expeditious the angler may be in securing his bait, the process occupies time—and often the best time of the day. Let him, then, whenever he has a chance at the beginning of the season, or at other times, lay in a stock of them at home for future use. They are easily kept, out of doors or within, in any roomy vessel; and if the water be changed occasionally, and always kept cool, they will continue in good condition for months. When this arrangement is inconvenient, they may be preserved for some time by placing them when alive in spirits of wine. When kept in this way, however, they assume a yellowish colour, which deprives them considerably of the attractive appearance on which so much of their effectiveness depends. Nor do they look much better when salted. They are then both dull in hue and easily destroyed in baiting. I never use a salted minnow when it is possible to get a fresh one; still, as there is sometimes a difficulty in finding minnows when the rivers are much flooded, salted specimens at such a time are not to be despised, as their frequent success fully proves. They will be all the better if they have not been kept more than four or five days. Live minnows are most conveniently carried to the river in a small pickle-bottle, fully half-filled with water, and well corked. By changing the water at intervals, whenever they show signs of becoming languid, they may be kept alive during the whole day. From two to three dozen of them would be necessary for a successful raid upon their natural enemies.

For fishing with the minnow a stiffish double-handed rod about 14 feet long will be found the most suitable. On this point Mr Blaine, in 'The Encyclopædia of Rural Sports,' says: "The minnow-spinning rod requires length and strength, combined with lightness, which requisites appear best obtained by having it made of cane, except the last joint. It must be neither too flexible nor too stubborn, as either extreme will impair its utility: if too stiff, the hook or the hold will be endangered when striking; if too pliant, it will yield to the resistance of the water too much to allow a ready stroke to be made when a bite occurs, and the fish will escape ere the effect of the stroke reaches him." The length of line must be in proportion to the size of the stream; but for ordinary purposes the entire length, including the cast of gut, need not exceed a half more than the rod. The gut itself should measure two yards or more, and for clear water it is absolutely necessary that it should be of the finest quality. On this cast two swivels are fixed; one of small size at the end of the second strand of gut from the hooks, and another slightly larger near the point of its connection with the hairline. The purpose of the swivels is not so much to assist the spinning of the bait—which would spin without them—as to prevent the spinning from twisting the line. And here I should recommend the use of the spring swivel, as by it nothing is easier than to effect, when desirable, a change of tackle from spinning-minnow to any other kind of minnow or to worm, or to substitute one size of hook for another.

The varieties of tackle given by authorities and used by anglers are almost endless. Some, furnished with as many as eleven hooks, literally bristle with steel, and seem to challenge an attack rather than to court one, presenting so many points of death to the fish, that even if it were willing to die, it might let slip many a glorious opportunity of so doing, ere it could finally decide in favour of any. Without entering into the merits or demerits of the tackle employed by others, I give a representation of the various kinds which I consider the best; and probably most anglers will be inclined to think that the appearance they present, when thus undraped, is sufficiently alarming. Nevertheless they are devised to suit all waters and conditions of water, all times during day or night and all seasons; and my experience of their virtues enables me to predict that they will be found equally adapted to all the varying moods and appetites of fish inclined to prey on their little neighbours. The principle is the same in all, and has its simplest illustration in Nos. 1 and 2. These differ merely in the size of the hook to suit the different sizes of bait which different conditions of water demand. The other numbers, 3 to 6, are modifications of the first two, in so far as they are furnished with small drag-hooks in strategic positions on flank or in rear, where they are most likely to give efficient support to the main ones, on which alone in every case the minnow is baited.

In fishing up-stream, with the water clear and the sun bright, I use No. 1 tackle, composed of

PL. II. MINNOW TACKLES page 196.

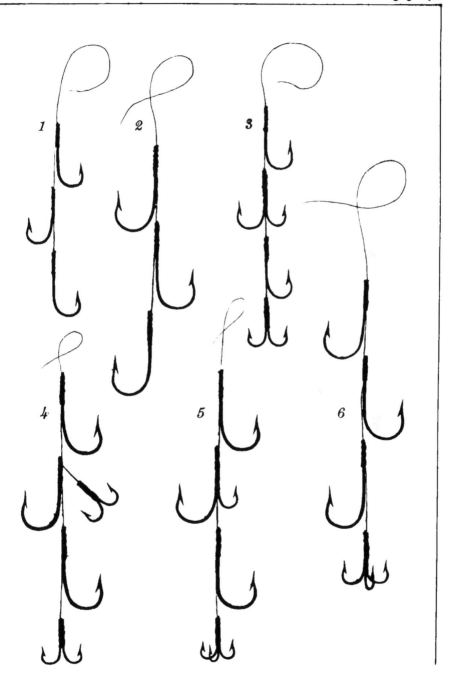

No. 8 hooks, baited with a very small minnow. If in making up this flight the second hook be placed a very little nearer to the head hook than to the tail one, the minnow will spin better than if it be placed exactly in the centre. The hooks should not be cut short in the shank, as some anglers recommend, because a good length of steel in each gives rigidity to the whole tackle, and takes and keeps a secure hold of every fish that bites. Enter the lowest hook about the root of the dorsal fin, and bring it out a little above the tail.
The exact point, however, at which to fix this hook will depend on the size of the minnow. The upper hook is put through both eyes, and the middle one through the back in an opposite direction. In all the kinds of tackle I give, the minnow is baited in precisely the same way, and the barbs of the hooks are allowed to protrude freely.

I am opposed to the almost universal style of running the minnow like a worm upon one of the hooks, and imparting to it a curve at the tail, as if it were itself a fish-hook. This arrangement is said, by those who adopt it, to make the minnow spin. No doubt it does, but it does more. It not only distorts the natural appearance of the bait, but causes it to revolve in the water with all the energy of a mill-wheel. The angler should see, then, that the hooks are inserted in such a manner as to leave the minnow as straight as he found it, and one condition of a good bait will be secured. The spinning is sufficiently provided for in the position of the middle hook, which, if placed through the minnow as directed, is well fitted to give it all the motion which is desirable. It will also be noticed that the upper hook is not passed through the lips, as is invariably advised, but through the eyes. The reason is, that as in my tackle this hook does not regulate the spinning, I am free to place it where it will interfere least with the preservation of the minnow, and be just as effective in the destruction of the trout. For this No. 1 tackle, the minnow should not exceed one inch and a half in length. A tackle, tied to suit a large minnow, may be accommodated to a smaller one by giving the gut a turn over the middle and upper hooks before inserting the latter.

For a large-flooded water, flight No. 2 is of the same simple description, but is made up of No. 10 hooks instead of No. 8, in order to carry a somewhat larger bait. In either of its two forms, this triple-hook tackle spins much better than any other; and were trout always taking well, I should not desire any change. But unfortunately trout are capricious in their tastes as well as voracious in their feeding; and if we cannot attract them at times with a daintier bait, we must endeavour to meet, so far as we can, any disposition on their part to toy with the good things already provided for them. Hence the necessity for the other tackle.

In fishing a low clear water up-stream, with the trout biting shyly and holding feebly, try flight No. 3 (hooks Nos. 8 and 3), and use small minnows to correspond. In a full black water, where the trout are equally coy, I recommend tackle No. 5 or 6, dressed with hooks Nos. 4 and 10, and baited with a larger minnow. No. 4, composed of hooks Nos. 10 and 6, is also very serviceable in flooded waters, and should carry a good-sized minnow. It, and Nos. 5 and 6, are well adapted for night as well as for day fishing. In all these varieties the smaller hooks act as drag or flying hooks, to secure, if possible, in some way or other those fish which bite shyly and short, and evince an inclination simply for a little flirtation with the gamesome lure—a state of affairs defined, by those who know, as "attention without intention." But the result—in low life as in high—often turns out more serious than was contemplated, for coquetry may end in capture. The mode of action of these flying-hooks is not always uniform. Usually they get hold of some part of the fish's head—the seat of giddiness; sometimes they catch him in the ordinary way, in the act of biting; while occasionally they play the part of grappling-irons, and seize him without much discrimination as to the precise locality. So much for the operation of the drag-hooks on shy or playful fish.

When, however, trout go boldly at the bait, how is the capture usually effected? At what point do they make the attack? Mr Stewart states that they generally seize the minnow by the tail, and he does not stand alone in this view. Captain Williamson, in a passage quoted by "Ephemera,"[1] says —"*All* fish, in seizing a spinning-bait, direct their attacks towards its tail, viewing it as an object of pursuit;" and then, with strange inconsistency, he adds—" *Many* a very large trout has, however, been taken merely by the lip-hook." "Ephemera's" own position is that "fish generally seize their prey by the middle,"[2] and that it is only when they run short at the spinning-bait that they are caught by the fly-hook at the tail. This seems nearer the truth. At all events, through the day, trout almost invariably seize the minnow by the head or shoulder. All my experience goes to prove this, for in any day's fishing with this lure I have caught nearly all my trout with the uppermost hook; and I have no reason to believe that mine is an excep-

---

[1] Handbook of Angling, p. 213.
[2] Ibid., p. 205.

tional case. In night-fishing, no doubt, it is somewhat different. Then the large trout often attack the minnow from behind, and are caught by tail or drag hooks.

I find myself compelled to differ from almost all writers on angling in regard to the use of lead in spinning for trout with the minnow. I never have sinkers on a spinning-trace, either when fishing up-stream or down, and this may fairly be considered as a point in favour of the tackle which I advocate. In Stoddart's 'Companion'[1] we are told that "the advantages of leading heavily consist of improved spinning, greater likelihood of attracting the eye of the fish, and a much better chance of hooking them." And Stewart says that "split shot are necessary to the minnow-fisher, and should be placed above the first swivel: if placed below, they interfere very much with the spinning." Now, if placed in any position whatever on my tackle, they will not only "interfere very much with the spinning," but in a low water will effectually bring it to a speedy termination. Why, even in the absence of sinkers, it requires very smart and skilful movements when fishing up-stream to prevent the minnow from reaching the bottom and abiding there permanently. But the tackle I recommend is adapted to make the minnow spin, even when drawn *slowly* through

[1] P. 109.

the water; and its weight, together with that of the bait, is quite sufficient in slow spinning to sink the minnow, and secure all those advantages of attracting and hooking which Stoddart claims for shotting.

In spinning a minnow, the angler can scarcely be said to be simulating the appearances and movements of a free and healthy fish, and yet it is undoubted that the trout take it as readily as, and sometimes more readily than, if it were in a sound and natural condition. The experiment has often been made (though I have never tried it) of drawing the minnow-bait through a shoal of live minnows, and watching how a big trout would dash through the host, single out the spinner, and make after it, to the neglect of all the others. The unusual motions of the minnow did not deter, much less alarm it; rather did they seem to indicate a disabled condition, and suggest an easier prey. At all events, I am inclined to think that, in attacking and taking a baited minnow, the trout makes its calculations under a distinct impression that it is a weak or injured specimen of its favourite game, and therefore one more likely to succumb to its rapacity. That the spinning is not simply a means of disguising the tackle, but a fair simulation of the action of a disabled minnow, I have often proved when catching minnows with the worm. On such occasions, a minnow which managed to escape after receiving a wound from the hook, would go whirling through the water in gyrations closely resembling those produced by the spinning-minnow.

No one should experience much difficulty in casting the line. The action may be fairly described as an overhand sweep, in which the bait, starting from a point near to the angler's own position, marks out a semicircle in its forward movement, and, through the gradual lowering of the point of the rod, as a check upon the impulsive swing, falls without noise or splash at the spot desired. The great desideratum in this, as in all bait-fishing, is gentleness in casting, so as to avoid injury to the bait and alarm to the fish; and the angler will attain to this the more readily, if in throwing the line, he can manage to keep the minnow from getting behind him. It is true that this is not always possible without spoiling the cast altogether. In stormy weather, with a contrary wind, for instance, it may be necessary to cast more from the shoulder in order to give the line an impetus sufficient to send it forward; but in ordinary circumstances there need be no call for the backward movement.

The minnow, like the worm, is fished both up-stream in a clear water and down-stream in a full one. In a flooded river with a heavy current, the cast, whether from bank or channel, is made somewhat down-stream, at an angle of about 60° with the side. Where the stream runs more smoothly and easily, the line is thrown more across than down—say at an angle of 75°. With the minnow in the water, the point of the rod is held only a short distance above the surface—and the more rapid the current the lower it must be—so as to keep the bait at a proper depth. What depth that may be will depend on the condition of the water, and is less for up-stream than for down, but if sunk 12 inches at any time it is enough. To work the minnow it must be drawn across stream and down in a series of movements, by which, in down-stream fishing, it spins about 2 feet each time, until it is brought gradually round to the side on which the angler is stationed. Those movements are not always uniform in their rate; they vary with the depth and strength of the current. But the object aimed at is the same in all, and that is to maintain the bait at the required distance below the surface. In down-stream fishing, the faster and heavier the current, the slower must the minnow be worked; while, on the other hand, a smooth and gentle current demands a more rapid motion. And even in one given cast there may be, and often is, a difference in the rate of the movements, according as the minnow is spinning through an easy part of the stream, or through one more rapid.

The cast may be considered spent when the bait has been brought close to the side, or parallel with the stream. The angler must be specially careful not to lift it until it has gained this position, for the last movement is sometimes the most deadly of the whole cast. Trout most frequently make a dash at the minnow at the second or third movement; but they occasionally follow it across to the side, whether channel or bank, closely eyeing its motions all the while, as though watching for a more favourable opportunity for pouncing on their wounded prey, and then, when it has reached the quieter water, and seems likely to elude their grasp, they end the chase by a determined gulp. And if the last section of the cast be in deep water close to the bank, the minnow will be brought within range and reach of the large trout which generally lurk there, like spiders watching for the flies which chance or fate may send. If, during the working of the cast, a fish make a rush at the minnow, but fail to seize it, the angler must spin steadily on, as though it had not done so, and he may allure it again. To alter the spinning, or interrupt the cast in mid-water, or even to withdraw it suddenly when it has reached the side, is to frighten off and lose many a good trout, which, having had the minnow in its eye, would, had circumstances only favoured its temerity, have made vigorous endeavours to get it also in its mouth. When the angler has exhausted his cast, the minnow, as we have seen, will be a good way below him. Let him then gently bring it to the surface and near to the spot where he is standing, before he attempts to give the next cast, which should, of course, be made a step or two farther on, so as to cover a fresh portion of water.

My opinions on striking with the spinning-minnow, as on shotting, do not coincide with those of many anglers; and probably the explanation in both cases is to be found in the difference of tackle. If, in fishing down-stream, the angler observe the trout take his bait, he should allow it merely time to turn before striking. But he must be sure that it *has* actually taken it; for an inexperienced fisher, seeing a trout following his minnow, is very apt to strike before the fish has, by seizing the bait, fully disclosed its intentions. Recommending, as I do, the angler to fish without sinkers, I find this caution all the more necessary, because, were the bait so heavily shotted as to be always out of his sight, the risk of striking too soon would in great measure be removed. Why I do not shot the line to avoid this risk is, as I have already shown, simply to avoid another and greater. But frequently in a flooded and discoloured water the first and only indication of a seizure of the bait is conveyed to the hand, and not to the eye, and then the angler cannot strike too soon. In up-stream fishing this is not so likely to be the case, for the condition of water is more favourable for seeing the trout actually make an attack upon the minnow, and a quick stroke down-stream should be the response. In any case, where a trout has not been *observed* to take the minnow, it is safest to strike the moment it is *felt*.

Down-stream fishing with the spinning-minnow, as with the worm, may be practised for a short time at the beginning of a flood. The trout then leave their retreats, to which they had retired when the waters were low, and venture out to the sides of the pools and the tails of the streams, on the outlook for food. It is in such places that the angler will find them; and if he be wise, he will make the most of his opportunities while they last, for when the river is in full flood, all fishing may as well be suspended. The best time, however, for the minnow is just after a flood, when the waters are subsiding and beginning to pass from a clayey to a dark porter colour, and when the day is dull, cold, and stormy. In this climate it is not a matter of great difficulty, even in the month of June to obtain the latter essential, but such a happy conspiracy of favourable conditions is rare. For before the time of extensive hill-drainage, of which I have already spoken, the rivers continued to run in splendid "ply" for several days together, and gave the minnow-fisher a chance of finding some occasions when all the conditions would be realised for enjoying himself to the top of his bent; but now he must consider himself highly favoured if he obtain a few hours' sport when the state of the water will permit, be the weather what it may. Nevertheless, if the heavens look so kindly on him as to send the cold and the storm-cloud, his time of good sport may end only with the day.

With the stream of a dark porter colour—that is, when the muddy stage is almost over—it is best to fish down the channel side, where the trout, under cover of the discoloured water, are still roaming over the shallows. As the river continues to fall, and becomes somewhat clearer on the ebb portions of the pools, the angler should direct his attention to the deeper water of both pools and streams, where, from the depth, the darker colour is longer maintained, and the deceptive nature of the lure less easily detected. Whether fishing from bank or channel, let him endeavour, if possible, to cover the whole expanse of water within range below, so as to bring the minnow round to his own side of the stream.

This lure, like others, is fished up-stream in clear water and bright sunshine. The weather here is an important factor, for with the water low, trout do not "take" well on a dull day, probably for the reason that when there is a play of sunlight on the surface, they are not so able to discern the snares that are laid for them below. The same necessity for sunshine exists when fishing with the artificial fly up a stream with a gravelly bed, as in the upper reaches of the Clyde; but where the river has a dark rocky channel, sunshine is not desirable.

Trouting up-stream with minnow, as with worm, in clear water, requires more skill than fishing down. The angler has to exercise more judgment in the selection of his water, and a greater vigilance in playing his lure. He must keep the minnow spinning more rapidly, to prevent it from sinking too far, and be ever on the alert to watch for, and respond to, the attack of the fish. These results will be attained by practice, and little need be added to what has been already said on the subjects of spinning and striking. As in spinning up-stream, the minnow is drawn more rapidly than in spinning down—and the faster the current, the quicker is it drawn—at each movement of the wrist it will spin farther, and allow of fewer such movements in the cast, some three or four being sufficient to exhaust it. Besides, since it is not desirable when fishing up to cover the whole of the water within reach, more frequent casting is necessary. In reference to striking, I have before remarked that, as in up-stream fishing the angler has a better chance of seeing the trout take his minnow, he has likewise a better chance of striking at the proper time.

Commencing at the tail of a stream, let him fish it up to its neck, casting into the rough broken water on the deepest side. If he be on the channel side, and there be deep water on the other, he should cast towards the bank up and across, at an angle, varying, of course, with the width of the stream; but if on the bank, let him cast up close to that side, and spin the minnow quickly down at an angle of about 10° from the bank. The main currents of streams will afford good sport, and even the pools, if there is a breeze to ruffle the surface. With a good strong wind, the angler may fish wherever there is a sufficient depth of water to sink the minnow; but in its absence he cannot do better than confine himself to the streams, which he should fish up from tail to neck, seeking out diligently all places to which large trout may be expected to resort. Even in flooded waters the minnow may be most successfully fished up-stream from the bank side of deep pools, by casting right up close to the margin and bringing it rapidly down. Indeed, I prefer fishing up to fishing down wherever it is possible in any stream, because it is much the more deadly method of the two; and in small rivers and burns, when in flood, I always adopt it, casting up and across over all places where fish are likely to lie.

In flooded waters the minnow may take less or more during the whole season; but the most favourable time, if not also the most legitimate, is from early spring till the end of June. In these months it is even a more profitable lure in full water than the worm; but from July to the end of the fishing season trout take it more shyly, even when the water is apparently quite suitable. Only occasionally, indeed, is a good basket got then, and that when the water is very dark. October is the worst month for minnow-fishing, and the sport with this or with any lure may well be discontinued from that time on to the 1st of March. For fishing upstream in a clear water, May and June are the favourite months, though then the "takes" may not be so large as in a falling water after a flood. Out of the whole year, June is unquestionably the best time for minnow-fishing, in either a black water or a clear one.

There is another method of fishing with the natural minnow which is often found most successful in floods. The tackle required is similar to that used in trolling for pike, and consists of two hooks (Nos. 4, 5, or 6, according to the size of the bait) tied back to back at one end of a gut-cast of some two yards long, fitted with a loop at the other. This loop is passed through a spring swivel, fastened to the hair-line. If you have not the ordinary baiting-needle at hand, you can make one easily enough. Take a darning-needle, attach it to the loop by means of a thread, and entering the point at the mouth of the minnow, slip it up to the tail, and run the bait on the gut until the hooks are left protruding slightly on each side of the mouth. Remove the needle and fix the loop on the swivel. A small piece of steel—sharpened to a point at one end, and notched with a file near the other, in order to carry the loop—makes a good baiting apparatus, and requires no thread; but a crochet-needle, if pointed at the plain end, is the readiest means of any. This tackle ought to be leaded more or less according to the strength of the current and the depth of water; and the sinkers are put on the line a little above the swivel, which is added not because we wish the minnow to spin, but for convenience in baiting. Fish down-stream in the same way as with the worm; and though, as I have said, its greatest use is during a flood, it is sometimes very effective in a low clear water during the cold days of early spring, and indeed till the end of June. The dead minnow is sometimes also baited as a worm on a single hook, and used in streams during summer; but none who have tried its merits have much to say in its favour.

Some fish with minnow as a live bait after much the same style as we adopt in pike-fishing. Only one hook—No. 6—is necessary, and it is fixed into the back of the minnow at the dorsal fin, or passed through the upper lip alone. The gut-line, which requires to be two or three yards long, is shotted twelve inches or so above the bait to keep it sunk perpendicularly. This tackle requires a float, which should be placed on the gut a yard or more from the hook, according to the depth of the river. A ready one may be made out of a common cork, either by boring a hole through it in the line of its axis, through which the gut is passed, and in which it is fixed by a wooden pin, or by making an incision of half an inch or so in the cork in a similar direction to receive the line, which is then kept in position by giving it one or two turns round to the other side. The proper places to fish with this lure are the deep pools. An advantage which it possesses over the spinning bait is that, from the way it is fixed on the hook, the minnow lives for a considerable time, swims about vigorously, and forms an object of attraction to hungry eyes. But on the whole, it is vastly inferior to the spinning minnow, inasmuch as the amount of water fished in any given cast is comparatively small, and consequently the loss of time is needlessly great. This style of angling is adapted for all seasons, and sometimes results in the capture of big fish. When the water is black, it is advisable in this, as in all other methods of minnow-fishing, to use large baits.

Tackle-makers have exercised great ingenuity in devising substitutes for the natural minnow, and it cannot be denied that they have often been tolerably successful. These artificial baits are of various materials, and all the kingdoms of nature have been laid under contribution to produce them. We have them of gutta-percha and india-rubber, of horn and bone, of zinc and tin, of glass and canvas. Those commonly in use are much too large, and in any case they are not nearly so valuable a bait as the natural minnow. When the river has subsided to some extent after a flood, and just as it is becoming black—the favourite time for all minnow-fishing—the phantom may do some execution for a few hours. Success may sometimes attend its use in "small" clear water on sunny days with a strong breeze, and it may then be fished either up-stream or down. The swivels I fix twenty-eight inches apart, but find no place for sinkers on this, any more than on the other spinning-tackle. Indeed, if there was little necessity for them on the natural minnow-line, there is even less for them on this; for most of the materials employed in its manufacture are in themselves heavy enough to sink it farther than is desirable; and even where it is lighter than the natural, it wants the animal buoyancy of the latter, and so of itself tends to maintain a lower level. Thus it is that, in fishing with any kind of artificial minnow, we must work the bait more rapidly than with the natural, in order to prevent it from sinking too low; and those anglers who shot the line must just exert themselves more than those who don't: and after all, the results will be much in favour of the slow spinner. In other respects the artificial minnow is fished very much in the same way as in up-stream fishing with its prototype, the only difference being that with it a greater variety of movement, up, down, or across stream, is admissible in spinning the bait. In up-stream fishing, the smaller the imitation the better. Trout, when hooked by it, do not hold so well; and the larger fish are not so easily deceived by any imitation, however perfect, which may have all the show without "the seal of nature's truth." For myself, I never use the artificial when I can get the real bait, and my largest baskets with the minnow have always fallen to the natural lure. Fishing in the Clyde one cold and stormy day in April, when the March brown was on the water, and when the stream was black and heavy, I caught with it 24 lb. of trout between Clyde Bridge End, below Abington, and "Johnstone's Pool" at Garf Burn; and on another occasion, with the same lure, in Tweed, I killed 25 lb. between Biggar Water Foot and Stobo.

In treating of the minnow, I have confined my remarks entirely to day-fishing. The conditions of successful angling with it and with other lures during the night will be set forth in the next chapter.

CHAPTER IX.

NIGHT-FISHING.

> "I must become a borrower of the night
> For a dark hour or twain."
> —*Macbeth.*

IT is no unwonted experience for the hardy fishermen of our shores to leave the light and warmth of home, and go forth to toil upon the unresting sea in the gloom and dangers of the night,

> "Darkling as they face the billows,
> A' to fill the woven willows."

And the professional angler, too, who plies his craft by river-side in happier scenes, recognising a necessity not laid upon the mere sportsman, "forbears at times to sleep the nights," and makes them "fellow-labourers with the days." But for the average angler, to whom the idea of fishing is mainly suggestive of an escape for the nonce from the anxieties of life, much of the charm of fishing lies in its association with open day, and sunny skies, and the glad voices and green vales of earth. Still the enthusiasm of a sportsman for his sport exists independently of much that enhances the pleasure of its exercise; and if that enthusiasm be genuine, it will not only often inspire him to seek the stream under frowning skies and in biting blasts, but will sometimes prove superior to his natural inclination for repose.

The sport which is to be had during many of the sultry days of June and July is not always such as either to tax the energies of the angler, or to fill his basket; for at this season artificial-fly fishing is on the wane, and in the "small" clear water his main hope lies in angling up-stream with the minnow, the worm, or the caddis. As it is precisely after such days that night-fishing promises greatest success, even the ordinary angler, possessed of ordinary love for his sport, may now and again be induced to "trust the opportunity of night" to supplement the meagre honours of the day.

Those writers who take exception to the exercise of the sport at night, because under the cloak of darkness much that is illegal is frequently practised, have to be reminded that that is most sadly true of more things than angling, and that it is tyrannous to interdict the lawful enjoyment of a sport on the ground that the ill-disposed have been known to take counsel of the night for its illegal exercise. Besides, an enactment against night-fishing, based on such a plea, would be as futile in restraining the poacher as it would be unjust to the legitimate angler; for to those bent on evil courses

> "How oft the sight of means to do ill deeds
> Makes ill deeds done!"

While I'am inclined to believe that pollution of rivers in the light has killed more fish than poaching in them in the dark, it is not in the spirit of the creed which says—

> "Who dares not stir by day must walk by night,
> And have is have, however men do catch,"

that I plead for a few hours' fishing under the silent gaze of stars, but solely out of enthusiastic devotion to a legitimate sport, most loved when most legitimately followed.

Not that my zeal for "the gentle art" would lead me in all circumstances to echo the transport of the poet, and exclaim—

> "Most glorious night!
> Thou wert not sent for slumber!"

but in fitting season I am not loath occasionally to forego my enchanting night-visions of big fish and glorious runs in a laudable endeavour to realise them. And when the feverish heat of the summer day is o'er, and a delicious coolness fills the air;

when the face of nature is so lightly veiled in shadow as yet to betray a winning charm in every feature; when the distracting hum of busy life is hushed, and there is

> "No whispering but of leaves on which the breath
> Of heaven plays music to the birds that slumber;"

the "honest" angler need not hesitate to trust himself and his fortunes under the wide canopy of sky, with no talisman but his fishing-rod, and no companion but his thoughts.

It is not said that angling by night will be invariably profitable, any more than it may be by day. For the magic wand may be raised o'er darkening stream and pool, the night may be propitious, and the twinkling stars in league with cunning, and yet not a fin may stir the depths in tribute to the witchery of art. In such circumstances night-fishing, if it do no more, will at least afford an admirable test of the angler's devotion to his pastime, and a splendid opportunity of giving effect to the advice of Father Walton when he cautioned his disciple to "be patient and forbear swearing, lest he be heard and catch no fish." But if his experiences of the fitful favours of even day-fishing have already taught him to sing with all his heart the old song—

> "If patience be a virtue, then
> How happy are we fishermen!"—

his mind will be all the more open to the potent influences of the night, which can invest his sport with a little halo of romance, and give new zest to its pursuit. For, once abroad by river-side under starry skies prophetic, it needs no "Midsummer Night's Dream" to people the brooks with naiads and the meads with "dapper elves" in order to entrance the fancy and disguise the gloom. To the thought that wakes when Nature sleeps, there come from out her passionless calm and rest the deeper revelations of her spirit, and the "voices of the night" are ever wafted to the listening ear. The rich hues that bloom in summer's prime are born of the light, and in the garish day enchain the eye; but the veiled and pensive beauty of the sombre night is for the contemplative soul which finds mystery in shadow, and "gathers magic thoughts in night's cool clime." And when the moon in queenly grace leads forth her glittering starry train through cloudless skies, the imaginative angler may fondly deem with Hood that, from off the fairy mantle of her silver sheen there fall

"In winding streams
Sparkles and midnight gleams,
For fishes to new gloss their argent scales."

Now there is silently lifted from the sleeping vale the dark shadow as of her sorrow, and through her glistering dewy tears she smiles serenely as she dreams of the warmer blush of a rosy dawn that shall kiss these tears away. But the stream sleeps not, sleeps never. Now shimmering 'neath the glance of heaven, now hurrying through the gloom which earth hath cast, yet ever to the music of its own glad heart, it rolls its ceaseless course to ocean, fraught with blessing, and rich in lessons to the wise, who can read the "books in the running brooks," no less by night than day. But to our angling.

The lures that obtain in night-fishing are fly, minnow, and worm. As the methods of using them at night do not materially differ from those already given for day-fishing, little more remains to be done here than to indicate the circumstances of time and place most favourable for good results. But I must premise that, although all these lures may be, and often are, resorted to in turn during the same night, still, seeing that the main reliance is upon the artificial fly in some of its forms, I always find it most convenient to employ the loop-rod and line throughout.

The night cast is made up of pretty strong gut, and the flies, six or seven in number, are placed thereon, about twenty-eight inches apart. The flies being fewer, this wider interval between them does not necessitate a longer cast than I use during the day; nor is there any difference in the length of line employed. Nothing is gained by using very fine gut at night. A stronger quality will be equally invisible to the fish, and of greater service to the angler. For it will not only save him many perplexing difficulties of the twists and tangles peculiar to fine gut, to the solution of which the darkness of night is never eminently favourable, but it will also enable him to make short work with even heavy fish, and so to take full advantage of the "rise" when it comes on.

Mr Francis recommends the night-fisher "never to use more than two flies in any circumstances," and assures him that he will find " one better than two, as the slightest hitch becomes fatal in the dark." Now there might be exceptional cases even in day-fishing, when there would be more than humour in the remark of the facetious author of 'Maxims and Hints,'—"I am humbly of opinion that your chance of *hooking* fish is much increased by your using two flies; but I think that, by using only one, you increase your chance of *landing* the fish." And it is readily acknowledged that there is greater risk of mishap or disaster attending the angler's operations in the night than in the day— and I have just hinted how it may be to some extent reduced; but what if, in his anxiety to avoid such risk altogether, he deprive himself of every chance of catching any fish? In a previous chapter I endeavoured to show that trout exercise a wonderful discrimination in their choice of flies no less by night than day; that one night they are fascinated by a fly of a particular hue, which next night may prove to possess no attractions for them; and that times without number a heavy basket has fallen to one individual fly, to the almost complete exclusion of its compeers on the line. Unless, therefore, the angler knows for a certainty which fly is in demand by the trout on any occasion, or unless he believes that one fly will kill as well as another, he will take care that his cast carries a fair and representative collection of those most in favour with night-feeding fish. They are either large or small as circumstances require: the latter have already been given in the list of "Gloamin' Flies"; the former, chiefly of the night-moth species, will be found under the distinctive heading of "Night Flies."

The best season for night-fishing is unquestionably from about the 20th of May till the end of June, but more or less success may attend its exercise until the close of July. Even in August, if the weather be dry and warm, the small artificial fly will sometimes reap a fair harvest in a moonlight night. Although wet nights are often very productive of sport, especially in June, the angler will be more likely to gain a substantial reward for his exertions, as he will certainly the better consult his personal comfort, if he select, for his first nocturnal venture, the night succeeding a hot sultry day, when the sky is clear and a balmy breeze blows softly from the west, and when no dew drenches the grass and no mist enshrouds the stream.

If he have come to the water early in the evening, he may suitably open the ball with the dance of the gloamin' flies, whose airy grace seldom fails to turn the heads of even the least impressionable of the finny fellows below. And after night-fall, what then? why, "on with the dance!"—only be careful to change the dancers; for in the darkened hours and till the moon appears, the portlier persons of the night-born moths are best devised to fascinate the fickle. And when the moon deigns to look down from on high and honour the sports with her gracious presence, if she find that you have again led forth the smaller flies of graceful mien to dance beneath her gaze, hers will be no merely passive patronage and formal recognition. A recipient of light herself, she will, in the gratitude of indebtedness, freely and playfully shed her lustre on the stream, and bring gleaming life to its surface. Indeed, so far as the pleasures of small-fly fishing are concerned, it is then that there "comes in the sweetest morsel of the night." Well may we anglers exclaim—

"Still shine, thou soul of rivers, as they run!"

and prolong our sports till "civil-suited morn" appears to warn night's revellers home. With such favourable omens these little light coquettes may ensnare in measured dance many a big fish, even at times far beyond the witching hour, in all the months of the night-fishing season.

Their place is taken by the large flies when the night is wet, dark, or cloudy, and when no moon appears. These flies are selected for such nights, not because the fish could not then see the small ones, but simply because their prototypes—the large moths—though abroad at night, do not go on the water during moonlight. Their imitations are therefore successful only in the entire absence of the moon, or in such reaches of the river as are for the time in shadow. If in such a dark and benighted condition the tyro be catching no fish, and be wellnigh despairing of success, let him consider whether he has done everything to merit it, and recall the words written by the humorous Penn: "You will not have good sport if you continue throwing after you have whipped your flies off. Pay attention to this; and if you have any doubt after dusk, you may easily ascertain the point by drawing the end of the line quickly through your hand,—particularly if you do not wear gloves." It is scarcely necessary to add that, if the result of such an experiment sufficiently explain the cause of failure, you will have no cause to regret having made it; if it do not, it will at all events tend much to enliven the dull intervals of no sport.

Night-flies, whether large or small, should be fished in gently flowing streams, in the necks and tails of pools, and at the channel as well as at the bank side of pools of moderate depth; but no rapid water will yield sport to the artificial fly after dusk. The angler must always fish down-stream at night, casting down and across; the necessity for fishing up does not exist when daylight is gone: and as trout take the lure more leisurely at night than during the day, the fisher should allow the flies to be carried gently and slowly round to his own side of the stream. He will generally fish from the bank side when the river is low and clear; the channel and the shallow stretches are best when the water is black: but large trout are often found at night roaming about at both sides, and circumstances must therefore determine very much the angler's mode of action.

If I hook a small trout when fishing from the bank, and if I cannot get down to the margin of the water, I bring him close to the side, and taking advantage of the moment when his first struggle is over, I lift him straight up on to the grass by the gut. To take him down to the tail of the pool would of course be safer, but his size may not demand such caution. For a fish of 2 or 3 lb., however, more consideration must be shown; and accordingly, I would have him down to a good landing-place ere we came to closer quarters. Though I might lose some time by this operation, I should not cause that disturbance among the other tenants of the pool which the same course of action would be sure to produce if adopted during the day.

Should no satisfactory gains fall to the small fly on a cool moonlight night, or to the large fly on a wet or dull one, the proceedings may be agreeably diversified by an appeal to the minnow, for it may suit well whether the moon appears or not; but the happiest augury for the success of this lure is a clear starry night, inclining to frost, or one in which there is a heavy fall of dew. Fish it during moonlight in the rough heavy streams, and in the absence of the moon, both in the pools and in the streams.

The method, given in last chapter, of baiting the natural minnow on two hooks placed back to back, frequently answers very well at night. If this tackle be cast from the channel into deep pools, and the bait allowed to lie at the bottom, the fisher will often be rewarded with very large fish. Like the fly, the spinning-minnow is always fished downstream at night, and worked more slowly through the water than in daylight. It will thus not only move at a pace more in keeping with the slower movements of the fish at night, but as the result of this leisurely spinning is to sink the bait, it will be brought within their notice and their reach when they are not feeding on the surface, while at the same time a better hold will be obtained of those that honour it with their regard. In deep quiet pools, the bait, though still worked slowly, must nevertheless be kept from fixing itself on the bottom by more frequent movements of the wrist during each cast. The artificial minnow cannot be recommended for good night-fishing.

In its own season the May-fly is sometimes a killing bait at night, but even then the other lures may share the sport with it. The most favourable conditions obtain when the night is calm and dull, but not cold. The natural insect is then fished with a light line so as to keep it floating on the surface, not after the manner of daping in which the wind carries the fly, but by leaving it entirely to the action of the current. Cast in comparatively still water, in pools and tails of pools, and in shallow reaches of the river where the trout are wont to roam at night in search of food.

The only other expedient of the night-fisher is the

worm, and recourse may be had to its agency in the eddies of streams on the channel side. It yields best sport on a moonlight night in the month of June.

Night-fishing, up till the end of June, is generally most profitable when prosecuted in a "small" black water after a small flood; but during the remainder of its season a low clear water is often productive of excellent sport. For minnow-fishing a "small" clear water is to be preferred in May, but a black water will not be without gain in June. The small artificial fly, however, will be of no avail in a black water under moonlight. During the month of June, trout may take at all hours of the night, with the proper lure, whether there be moonlight or not. As the season advances and the darkness deepens towards midnight, in the absence of the moon there is generally a lull in the sport from about half-past eleven till one o'clock in the morning, when the "take" may come on again and be continued till dawn. This holds good in July both with fly and minnow; but if the moon shine out, there may be uninterrupted success to both lures all night long.

In the early morning, when the sun is bright and warm, the May-fly in its season frequently proves very deadly. If the angler find the fly fruitless during June and July, let him at once resort to the minnow or the worm. The latter, should the morning be fine and warm, not unfrequently does considerable execution in rough broken water. Caddis-bait is also of good service from daybreak till eight or nine o'clock; in fact it succeeds better at that time than during any other portion of the twenty-four hours. August is the best month in the year for early-morning fishing with the small artificial fly, and its fortunes are brightest when the weather is so.

If the attraction of night-fishing be measured by its success alone, it has very considerable claims on the attention of even the average angler; for in the best part of the season, during the few hours which intervene between dusk and dawn, it is no uncommon occurrence to capture a basket of 15 or 20 lb. and upwards. The largest takes may be those secured during the day; but I have often, with various lures, scored 22 lb. during the night, and on very many occasions upwards of 20 lb. with minnow alone. But of course such baskets are not to be reckoned on every night. It may be, indeed, as I have said, that even in apparently favourable circumstances the sport will flag and the fish will not bite, and that all the resources both of philosophy and of flask will be taxed to their utmost to maintain that serenity of mind that has ever been such a distinctive and praiseworthy trait in the character of the angler. But he knows that a big "take" is not the only element in a fisher's happy lot. 'Tis a sweetening and soothing influence truly, and we have nothing but compassion for the angler who is one only in name; but he merits reprobation as well as pity whose whole heart is in his creel, and whose joy dies with his sport. The true angler is a lover of Nature as well as a lover of fish; and alike in the golden sunlight that gladdens her children and in the silent night that lulls them to repose—in the "gowan gem that spangles the lea," no less than in the far-off stars that stud the blue—he finds a charm to win and a call to adore. If his experience of the night make him no keener a fisher, it will at least leave him no worse a man. Poacher of an "honest" angler it cannot make; poet it may. And as he "feeds reflection in the dusky shade," his glowing thoughts will find a tongue to reach night's ear, and his serenade of love will wake her from her sleep to blush her thanks in day.

CHAPTER X.

GRAYLING-FISHING.

"Bait the hook well; this fish will bite."
—*Much Ado about Nothing.*

THOUGH several well-known authors have attributed to the grayling many, if not all, of the qualities for which the trout ranks so deservedly high with all sportsmen, what I have to say of it here will be brief, and more in the way of protest than of praise.

Mr Francis, in his 'Book on Angling' says, "I have a very high opinion of this fish;" and the author of the most recent work on 'Fly-Fishing' subscribes to this view, and impatiently adds,[1] "Every grayling-fisher who knows anything about it has the same." If to have caught thousands of grayling be sufficient to elevate one to the rank of

[1] Recollections of Fly-Fishing for Salmon, Trout, and Grayling. By Dr Edward Hamilton. P. 177.

a "grayling-fisher who knows anything about it," then I may be permitted to disclaim, for myself at least, any share in this opinion; and I am convinced that, among those entitled to the doubtful honour, I am not alone in my low estimate of the fish. But perhaps neither my opinion, nor my title to give it, will be regarded as quite admissible by a writer who, in the year of grace 1884, assures us that "the grayling is not found in Scotland."[1]

Something perhaps may be allowed to it on the score of form, but I would assuredly never go so far as to hold with Mr Pennell, that "the grayling has the beauty of Apollo—light, delicate, and gracefully symmetrical;" or with Mr Ronalds, that it is "more elegantly formed than the trout;" or with Mr Bullock, in the 'Fishing Gazette,' that it is "the queenly grayling;" or even with Mr Francis, that "if the trout be the gentleman of the stream, the grayling is certainly the lady." True, the grayling has a smaller head than the trout, and an inviting delicacy of lip; but such admittedly feminine charms are more than counterbalanced by its broader shoulders, its Roman nose, and the sinister expression of its "lozenge-shaped" eye.

But even if we grant all the elegance and symmetry of form that are claimed for the grayling, much more is required ere we can regard its capture

[1] Recollections of Fly-Fishing for Salmon, &c., p. 189.

as an object worthy of the angler's wiles. Beauty alone may prompt desire to win, but not in the case of a sportsman's fish; for there at least "beauty must be saved by merit." And so Mr Francis hastens to chronicle the virtues of Lady Grayling, and heads the list with this one: she "seldom becomes so shy as the trout does," and is "free to rise to all comers." I stop not to inquire whether womankind in these days, in their hurried quest of "rights," have

"Left all reserve and all the sex behind,"

and relegated shyness to the bashful man. But I am quite of opinion that the fish that values its own reputation, whether it values its life or not, will be disposed to show that caution and circumspection which a first acquaintance might impose, if not also the artful coyness of the shepherdess who harangued her impatient suitor thus:—

"But ken ye, lad, gif we confess o'er soon,
Ye think us cheap, and syne the wooing's done."

Whatever it may be in folk, at least in fish the want of shyness will, in the estimation of a proper fisher, be no charm at all. But it appears—and I am sorry to know it—that many Southern anglers' *beau-idéal* of a good fish is one easily deceived and easily caught. It is not mine. I consider the wariness of the trout a strong point in its favour, and I hold that, other things being equal, just in proportion to the difficulty of its capture, is the worth of capturing it.

But when the grayling has readily yielded to the blandishments of the angler, and has taken his lure, how does it comport itself? Mr Francis will answer. "Its play is composed of a series of rolls and tumbles," and "too often it behaves as a trout might be imagined to do if he had been drinking success to the May-fly rather too freely." Precisely so; indeed I should say oftener than too often it does so; but is this not rather an ungallant admission for its champion to make? I do not envy our author his keen angler's eye, if it is sharp enough to see the graceful bearing of the "lady of the stream" in the ungainly gambols of a devotee of Bacchus. But I am glad to notice the concession, that though this "behaviour" is only too real in the case of the grayling, it is merely imaginary in the case of the trout; and I fancy we have here got the reason of the absence of shyness in the one, and of its presence in the other. Deep potations oft make prospective heroes.

> "Inspiring bold John Barleycorn!
> What dangers thou canst make us scorn!"

But what of those that thou dost create? More discretion in her cups, and there will be less danger in the toils. Now the trout, the "gentleman of the streams,"—"drink like a fish," though he may, and as he ought—has all his wits about him when he is most in need of them; and though his "chance may faint under our better cunning," when he finds he has been deceived, he manfully fights for liberty and life; while the grayling, shy in fight, but not of lure, tamely yields herself a reeling captive; and ere she measures her unhonoured length upon the strand, drowns what remains of her consciousness of cowardice in the self-gratulatory toast,

> " Doubtless the pleasure is as great
> Of being cheated as to cheat."

In such a case the pleasure of the angler must be small indeed, unless, of course, he considers everything as fair in fishing as it is said to be in love, and that will cover a good deal.

There are, we are told, some "trout that must be caught with tickling"—and there may be some folk too, for that matter,—but then I opine that though their feelings are thus literally played upon, they are at least pleasingly conscious of the titillation, and gratefully responsive thereto. Cupid is always blind, but he needn't be drunk as well. And yet we have all heard of the swain who, under the influence of mighty ale, was decoyed by his too fond Phillis before the parson to be united to her "for better or for worse." "Take him away," said the minister, shocked at the insensate condition of the candidate for matrimony,—" take him away, and return with him when he is sober." But the expectant bride, fearful lest with the morning there might come " calm reflection," recognised the crisis of her fate, and in a flood of tears exclaimed: " Oh sir, 'deed sir, we maun be coupled the now; for gin I bide till he's sober, he winna come!" Ladies fish at times, and at times, too, with double tackle:

> " At once victorious with their hooks and eyes,
> They make the fishes and the men their prize."

Still, even then, who can say that they are not " fair" anglers with a " gentle art"? But the doting maiden of our story had the true instincts of a grayling-fisher, and angled for as questionable a prize. If a fish that is " free to rise to all comers," and that is " too often" incapable when it does rise, be styled a " lady,"

> "The sex, as well as she, may chide you for't; "

but I will content myself with the remark that it is certainly no gentleman.

That the picture which Mr Francis has given us of his grayling is no caricature, I could prove from my own experience of the reception it has always accorded to any overtures which I made to it. If, however, my open hostility rule me out of court, let us hear the testimony of others. Old Izaak says, "The grayling is much more simple, and therefore much bolder than the trout. He is not so good to angle for." Bowlker testifies that "when fairly hooked it is easily subdued." Mr Francks quaintly tells us that "the mouth of the grayling waters after every wasp, as his fins flutter after every fly; for if it be but a fly, or the produce of an insect, out of a generous curiosity he is ready to entertain him." Mr Blaine's opinion is that "the grayling is an inanimate fish when hooked." Even "Ephemera," who acknowledges that the grayling is "a favourite fish" of his, is constrained to admit that "it takes a fly boldly, but does not show much boldness after having taken it and been hooked;" and that though "it is a gamesome fish, it is not a game one." To capture a brace of such creatures may by some of our Southern friends be esteemed a fine art and gentle; but, pray, let all anglers who are also sportsmen reserve, if possible, their tackle and their talent for a worthier fish.

Some consideration might be shown for the grayling if it possessed even that secondary qualification of a good fish—the power to evoke pleasurable anticipations when there rings out

"That tocsin of the soul, the dinner-bell."

Tastes differ, and there may be grayling and grayling; but if I am to judge from those that I have tried—and they were in their best season—

grayling are not to be named in the same breath with the most ordinary trout, St Ambrose, Sanctus, Cotton, and a host of other gastronomists to the contrary notwithstanding. Walton reminds us that Gesner says, "the French value him so highly that they say he feeds on gold;" but what of that, if the French of his day were as discriminating as those in ours who prefer bull-trout to salmon? In spite of all that is said of its "thymy" and its "cucumber" fragrance, and its "firm and flaky flesh," I consider even the much-derided pike immeasurably its superior in edible virtues. Walton says that "all that write of the umber (grayling) declare him very medicinable." Possibly—and, judging by his flavour, very probably; but if so, let him be treated as medicine and used as sparingly.

But I have other and graver charges against the grayling. The introduction of this fish into a trout-stream invariably tells most unfavourably on the number and size of the tenants already in possession. Were I disposed to accuse the grayling of worrying and harassing the trout, I could find ample support for my accusation in the experience of many authorities. To quote only the late Mr Frank Buckland:[1] "Grayling, I have observed in my museum at South Kensington, are great bullies, and are continually hunting the trout

[1] Natural History of British Fishes, p. 331.

about." It is not, however, on the plea that the "lady" is a scold that I found my case for a separation, nor even on the more than doubtful statement of Mr Francis that she devours the spawn of the trout, but simply on the undoubted and perfectly comprehensible fact that a river will support only a certain number of fish in good size and condition. An influx of grayling into a trout-stream will therefore result in a corresponding diminution of the number of the trout, as well as in a deterioration of their quality. Moreover, this struggle for existence is unequal, the grayling always getting the best of it. Their ova are much smaller and far more numerous than those of trout, and in their feeding, grayling not only burrow at the bottom to a much greater extent than trout do, but they can rise from below through many feet of water to seize their surface-food. So that, even if trout did not habitually devour their own fry—which they do—the tendency would be for grayling to preponderate in numbers, and outstrip them in the race for life. This they are now doing in the Clyde. Above Lanark grayling are to be seen at present swarming in thousands, especially during the autumn months; while trout, which in those reaches were wont to yield great sport before the advent of the alien, are yearly becoming fewer in number and poorer in quality. When grayling were unknown there, a basket of 23 or 24 lb. of trout was not uncommon; now one of 4 or 5 lb. is considered good.

But again, the presence of grayling in a trout-stream will add greatly to the difficulty of obtaining what we should long ago have had from the Legislature, and what we must ere long have if our rivers are to receive the protection they deserve, and that is a close-time for trout. Sir Humphry Davy tells us that grayling-fishing may be pursued at "all times of the year." Few, we suspect, even of the lovers of tame sport and poor fish, would subscribe to this. Cotton more correctly styles the grayling a "winter fish"; and though modern English authors consider it legitimate to take him any time between August and Christmas, the opinion is wellnigh unanimous that November is his best month. Grayling are therefore most "in season" when trout are most out of it; and Mr Francis adduces this fact as one of his strongest arguments for the introduction of grayling, inasmuch as he sees in it a chance of obtaining sport of some kind all the year round. Of course he would take each in its own season only. But though all scrupulous grayling-fishers would desire to return to the water any trout they might happen to catch in the winter months, the weaker virtue of others would be all the better of any assistance which a stringent enactment might afford; and to those evil-doers, against whose practices such an enactment would be specially framed, the presence of "winter fish" in the stream would furnish ample occasion for evading the law and rendering it virtually a dead letter. For if grayling were allowed to be taken during the period that trout were on the spawning-beds, fishers whose reputation for honour was no better than their reputation as sportsmen, would not hesitate to take ill-conditioned trout while ostensibly fishing for grayling. And during the months of March, April, and May, when grayling spawn and trout-fishing is good, would the ill-conditioned grayling fare any better at the hands of some trout-fishers? As a matter of fact they do not. They are very fond of worm; and throughout the trout-fishing season, from February to October, I should say that probably more than one-half of all the baskets taken from the Clyde are composed of grayling.

Seeing then that, whether regard be had to the natural struggle for life between the fish, or to the equally natural action of many who angle for them, the safety and full development of the trout are quite incompatible with the presence of the grayling, surely, in the interests of fish and fishers alike, it were well that a trout-stream be reserved for trout, and a grayling-stream for grayling. This I hold equally applicable to all rivers, no matter where; but I confess I urge it specially on behalf of Scottish anglers and Scottish streams. I feel most strongly that the introduction of grayling into our rivers, with the view of improving their condition as fishing streams, is the most unfortunate and ill-advised step that has been taken in recent years. From the nature of their channels, ours are capital trout-streams, and, under judicious legislation, could be vastly improved. But no legislation will attain that end so long as grayling are allowed to remain in them. Of course, should their ejectment be resolved upon, we shall expect to hear of "tenant-right" and "compensation for unexhausted improvements." But let us trust that the rights will be permitted to revert to the poor trout that have been so unwarrantably dispossessed of them; and since the removal of the present interlopers will in itself constitute the "unexhausted" and inexhaustible "improvement," the claim for compensation will be found to have been already much more than discounted in the calamity of their arrival. I fear, however, that it is rather early to look for the total expulsion of the grayling from the Clyde, where they seem to have got so long a lease to run; but it may reasonably be hoped that proprietors of trout-streams, when they have a mind to improve the waters, will attach some weight to the words of Mr Buckland when he says, "The introduction of grayling into trout rivers should not be undertaken without due consideration," and be warned by the mischief already done in the Clyde to take heed and let well alone. Without doubt many of our rivers are sadly depopulated, and require to be restocked, but not restocked with grayling; and we look forward to the time when a large system of artificial hatching, both of salmon and of trout, will go hand in hand with wise legislation to replenish and protect our much impoverished streams.

It will now be evident that it is not my high opinion of the merits of the grayling, but its presence in our rivers, that has called forth this chapter. The few notes that follow on the method of its capture are inserted to meet the views, not only of those who love grayling, but of those who don't; so that, hearing there are grayling in abundance in the Clyde, both alike may start forthwith for that sorely vexed water, and angle, by every legitimate means in their power, by night and by day, for grayling, and for grayling alone:—

"That those may fish who never fished before,
And those who always fished may fish the more."

And though their deeds be in the water, of a truth I will not "write their virtues" there: they shall ever live in grateful memory. English anglers are heartily welcome to preserve, and to multiply, their grayling in their own streams; but while it is their boast that in many of them there are

> "Here and there a lusty trout,
> And here and there a grayling;"

I for my part would infinitely prefer that the trout may be "here" and the grayling "there."

Anglers for trout need not provide any additional tackle or lures for the capture of grayling. Feeding —as we all know too well—on much the same food as trout, grayling may be taken with the same flies and baits, although it is true very few are caught with the minnow. They congregate, too, in precisely those parts of the water where trout are to be, or ought to be, met with; and so the fly-fisher and the bait-fisher, in a stream that unfortunately contains both fish, may be just as likely to hook a grayling as a trout. Indeed the grayling that I have caught — and they are many — were taken of *their own* choice, not of *mine*.

More of bottom than of surface feeders, grayling take particular delight in the worm; and after a flood in autumn, with the river either black or clear —for they do not take well in a muddy or clayey water—the quantity captured may outnumber, if not outweigh, the angler's take of trout. We have seen that trout are, as a rule, to be got with worm in flooded waters during the whole season, and that we need not look for great baskets of them from a clear water after the month of July; but grayling will continue to accept the bait freely in a low clear water during autumn, even when trout will have none of it. In spring, too, with the river in a similar condition, the worm will do great things among them by those who have trout to protect and grayling to kill; but the best baskets—and for the lover of grayling alone, the best policy—will be his who follows the "sport" in the later months. Another bait for which grayling show a decided liking is the caddis. When it is in season, from April to July, it is an almost unfailing recipe for a good creel. Nor must we forget the creeper, for the grayling ever look on it with favour; indeed —and this shows the fish—they prefer it to the May-fly.

Grayling will take trout-flies more or less during all the season, but, speaking generally, the autumn months are the best. If the sun shine at midday—but we give this hint for those only who, though they may not love grayling less, yet love trout more—grayling will rise freely to the fly even in the middle of December. Captain St John Dick tells us that "they do not feed at all at night." Well, they may be somnambulists for aught we know, or they may be oftener "drinking success to the May-fly" than Mr Francis suspects; but I can assure the Captain that I have caught hundreds of pounds' weight of living "tumbling" grayling with the artificial fly at night. Moonlight nights are the very best for this fishing with the small fly, especially in a low clear water. If it is neither to feed nor to drink that they are then out of bed, the reason of their midnight exploiting and consequent capture may be the same as that given by the Folkestone night-fisherman to account for his wonderful "take" of conger-eels. "You see, sir," said he, "the conger comes up to the top on a frosty night to look at the moon, gets nipped by the cold and can't get down again." Though this moonshine theory, as it stands, would, when applied to grayling, save only part of the Captain's statement —for in the *absence* of the moon the large flies kill grayling as well as trout—it could very well be extended so as to account fully for all the facts: thus,—on a moonlight night grayling come up to look *at* the moon, and on a dark night they come up to look *for* it.

The conditions of water in fly-fishing for grayling are the same as those for trout, and the fly may be fished either up stream or down. Many anglers— chiefly English — prefer to cast across and down stream, particularly in deep water, so that the consequently slower motion of the fly may meet the wishes of those grayling that rise from some depth to seize it. Should a grayling miss your fly on its first rise, it may make many more attempts to secure it than a trout would do. Give it no occasion to upbraid you with—

"Stay, my charmer! can you leave me?"

until you have given it just cause to complete the couplet—

"Cruel, cruel, to deceive me!"

Strike immediately on the rise, but, remembering the "lady" of the delicate lip, strike as gently as possible. I have already spoken of its fighting or non-fighting qualities, and I have only to add on this point that, notwithstanding the averments of others, my experience in the capture of thousands of grayling fully bears out the opinion expressed long ago by that practical authority, Cotton, that "the grayling is one of the deadest-hearted fish in the world, and the bigger he is the more easily taken."

In the Clyde grayling spawn in March and April, and occasionally in the early part of May, depositing their roe among gravel at the tails of streams. The ova are, like those of the herring, very small and very prolific. The young fish grow rather rapidly until they weigh 1 or $1\frac{1}{2}$ lb., and then their yearly increase is not so decided as in the case of trout. The maximum weight which they are supposed to reach is, according to Mr Pennell, "from 4 to 5 lb."; but although I know that they have been caught upwards of 3 lb., the heaviest that ever fell, unfortunately, to my rod, weighed only 2¼ lb.

These fish are more gregarious than trout, and migrate from one part of the river to another. Their general tendency, when introduced into a water, is to move down-stream. This is fortunate, and is about the only virtue with which we can credit them; but to grant even this much is to show "gratitude for favours to come," for it is given only in the hope that this decided downward tendency in the fish may gather strength as they go, until it develop into an irresistible longing to leave for good the land—or the water—of their adoption, and to return whence they came. Meantime we may considerably facilitate their progress by reducing their numbers. Seeing that the fish came to us from England, we might for once adopt the English mode of killing them, and advise all Clyde fishers to try the sportsman-like lure of the "artificial grasshopper." And they may do this with the less compunction, as Mr Francis, who loves grayling so much, after assuring us that he "hesitates to notice the method of killing with the grasshopper, since the grayling is such a sporting fish that it is a shame to treat him like a poacher with such abominations,"—so far overcomes his scruples as not only to describe the "abomination," but to inform us that he "killed many fine grayling with it at Leintwardine." Our author clears himself completely, the Clyde fisher will observe, by pleading that "this most destructive method ought only to be tolerated when the grayling get so far ahead as *to want thinning down* pretty freely." Presumably such was the condition of affairs when he was at Leintwardine; and that said grayling did get a thinning, though we cannot be so sure that they "*wanted*" it, we conclude from what we are further told of "instances where, by the use of it, large 25 or 30 lb. baskets have been filled and emptied three times over in one day's fishing by a single rod." Verily its success at Leintwardine tempts me to recommend its use on the Clyde, since, whether our grayling "want thinning down" or not, the trout-fisher most assuredly desires to see them thinned.

CHAPTER XI.

SALMON-FISHING.

"And mighty hearts are held in slender chains!"
—*Rape of the Lock.*

THIS lordly fish deserves a volume to itself. Though it has been treated in greater or less detail by many writers on angling, no work exclusively devoted to its claims[1] has appeared among us since "Ephemera" wrote his 'Book of the Salmon.' That is well-nigh forty years ago. Since then great advances have been made in our knowledge of the natural history of the fish; pisciculturists have improved the means for its almost limitless artificial propagation; and the Legislature, with a fuller recognition of its immense economic value, has now and again come to its aid with measures for its

[1] From an angling point of view. The volumes of Mr Russel and others deal chiefly with its natural history and commercial importance.

greater protection. In the light of recent discoveries, and in view of the results of his own lifelong labours, the late Mr Frank Buckland promised, in 1880, to give to the world what he quaintly styled 'A Memoir of his Friend the Salmon'; but, alas! the genial and facile pen was to write no more. The performance of this task is reserved for another, and fortunate indeed will the salmon be if it find as loving and as enthusiastic a biographer.

No one would hail such a work with greater delight than the true Waltonian. He is no mere pot-hunter. His sport, pleasing as it is at all times, derives for him a greater joy when he can take an intelligent interest in the natural history of the fish he seeks, and find in the study of its structure and its habits the surest guide to the principles of his art.

It does not fall within the scope of this chapter to do much more than give, in the briefest and most practical form, the results of my experience in the capture of salmon. "Sport for kings" it has been called, and yet I have not accorded it the post of honour. To the salmon himself, probably, the post of honour would, in this case, as in many more, seem the post of danger, and with the natural instinct of self-preservation he might very well be content to prefer his life to his laurels. It is not, however, from any desire to accommodate our love of sport to his love of life, still less to decry his pre-eminent claims on the angler's regard, that I have placed the princely salmon after the common trout and commoner grayling, but simply because salmon-fishing with the rod is a luxury enjoyed only by the few. It may be true, as Mr Francis says, "there are fifty salmon-fishers now for one of twenty years ago." But has not the number of trout-fishers increased in a very much larger proportion? At all events, it is undoubted that, while the love of regal sport and vigorous joys may have grown with the means for its indulgence, out of the whole fraternity of anglers the number of those who wield the salmon-rod is still exceedingly and lamentably small. For it is not given to all to become fishers of salmon, even should they possess the rod and the reel, the capacity and the desire; the vast majority are obliged, by the stern force of circumstances, to "repress that noble rage," and remain outside the charmed circle of privilege. But to the angler fortunate enough to have enjoyed it, the sport seems worthy of all that can be said in its praise, whether regard be had to the skill which it demands, or to the emotions which it excites. From the moment when the first proud dash of a salmon in the exuberance of its strength electrifies the nerves and sends the blood madly dancing through the veins, till the close of the fight when it lies "broad upon its breathless side," a rich and beauteous prize, there rages within the breast of the angler a wild conflict of hopes and fears, exultations and alarms, that rise and swell with the varying fortunes of the struggle without, and create such an intensity of delirious excitement as none but a salmon-fisher can ever know.

> "Now hope exalts the fisher's beating heart,
> Now he turns pale, and fears his dubious art."

And yet, amid all this tumult of emotions he must maintain the cool head and the steady hand, to realise every new situation, and be ready to guard against its attendant risks, to meet every change in the enemy's front by a change of tactics, and to make its every humour subservient to his ends; in short, to be ever fertile in resources, self-possessed in direst need.

But all anglers, as I have said, are not salmon-fishers—and there may be some kinds of salmon-fishing, too, where there is not much angling; and while I yield to none in my esteem for the royal sport, when followed in the spirit of a royal sportsman, I might still recognise the highest angling art in some mere trout-fisher whose hooks were never guilty of a salmon's blood. Indeed, many excellent salmon-fishers, although fully alive to the attractions of their sport, have yet admitted that the kind of angling which pleased them most was a day's fly-fishing for yellow trout. Whether this be true of all who angle in preserves or not, the average angler in the open stream has, at all events, to "teach his necessity to reason thus,"—ay, and proudly make a virtue of it. The fates may not have granted him to wield the salmon-rod, but, for all that, he can find abundant scope for the exercise of the angler's craft, and the fullest joy in the emotions it excites, in the pursuit of smaller game, content to know that

> "When he cannot make love to the lips that he loves,
> He can always make love to the lips that are near."

And he thanks his stars, too, for the chance.

To the widest circle of anglers this little book appeals. Should the lovers of salmon and the heroes of sport think that in this brief chapter I fail to give to the monarch of the streams that supreme consideration which is due to its exalted rank, and that I show the scantiest courtesy to a fish whose virtues have inspired the poet's lays and thrilled the angler's soul, I can assure these discriminating friends that I fully share in their appreciation of the salmon's charms, and join most cordially in their tribute of praise; but I trust that they in turn will bear with me in my necessarily slight treatment of their favourite, when they realise the rarity with which it ministers to the ordinary angler's sport, and recognise the bounden duty that is laid upon all in this utilitarian age to consult "the greatest happiness of the greatest number."

Walton's knowledge of the natural history of the salmon was extremely imperfect, and his views on many points in salmon-fishing are consequently erroneous. Indeed, so often are his statements opposed to fact, that it has been questioned if he ever saw the fish of which he professes to treat. Among other doubtful stories, he tells us that "salmon are very seldom observed to bite at a minnow, yet sometimes they will, and not usually at a fly, but more usually at a worm." And the Cromwellian Captain Francks, in his 'Northern Memoirs' (written only five years after 'The Complete Angler,' though not published till 1694), says, "The ground-bait for salmon was of old the general practice, and beyond dispute brought considerable profit." But Francks knew of another "general practice" in Scottish rivers, which, whether it brought greater profit or not to the fisher, was certainly more deadly to the fish, and vastly more picturesque in the eyes of the onlooker. For he says, "when the salmon goes to the shallows, that is the time the prejudicate native consults his opportunity to put in execution that barbarous practice of murdering fish by moonshine, or at other times to martyr them with the blaze of a wisp and a barbed spear." The practice of leistering is now happily illegal, and so the reader is saved an account of it; ground-bait may still bring "considerable profit" when used at suitable times and in suitable waters, and something will be said on it by-and-by; but as modern salmon-fishers set greater store by the artificial fly, I shall direct attention to it first.

The lures that are ranked under the title of salmon-flies can be called so only by courtesy. They have no resemblance whatever to any fly on earth or in air, although Sir Humphry Davy supposed that the salmon rises to a fly because it has a distinct recollection of what it used to feed upon when a parr. Trout, we are well assured, take the artificial for the natural fly to which it bears some likeness, and on which, as solely fresh-water fish, they are accustomed to feed; but salmon, properly denizens of the sea or the estuaries of rivers, find their main subsistence there in the shape of sand-eels, shrimps, and crustacea of various kinds, and seek the river-beds only at certain seasons to spawn, and not to feed. Indeed, during the months in which they inhabit the streams, they live upon very little; and, the purpose of their migration effected, they return to the sea poorer in condition than when they left it. The flies which sport upon the surface of the river—creatures to them almost unknown—do not constitute their usual food; and they can hardly be said to be on the outlook for what, if presented to them, they would fail to recognise. Salmon, according to Buckland and many other naturalists, take the so-called fly of the angler for a specimen of their own favourite shrimp; and certainly the action of the lure, as it is worked by the rod, maintains any illusion which may be created by its colouring and shape. Real shrimps are deadly bait for salmon in Galway, as prawns are in the North Tyne, though, strange to say, in both cases the fish prefer them boiled. Some anglers, however, consider that it is mere whim, or curiosity, or love of colour, which brings a salmon to the fisher's fly; that, in fact, if it has not an eye to "the true, the beautiful, and the good," it has at least one to the glittering and the gaudy. The poet of the 'Rural Sports,' who more than once confessed that he was an angler, thus instructs the salmon-fly dresser how to minister to the salmon's tastes:—

> "To frame the little animal, provide
> All the gay hues that wait on female pride."

In that case it will be no light task nowadays to provide even one costume for "the little animal";

but what if the fashion of the fly is to keep pace with the fancy of the "female"? Moreover, if "female pride" is to direct in the matter of colours, why not also in the matter of cut?

Stoddart tells us that in his day it was held that, "in the lower parts of Tweed, salmon were not to be allured with any degree of readiness by means of the same colours and descriptions of flies as those successfully employed against them twenty or thirty years before." But although he considered that in those former times salmon were, like our grey-haired forefathers, of sober tastes and simple habits, content with homely fare and scornful of new-fangled delicacies, he was disposed to think that the desire for change originated as much in the capriciousness of the angler as in the vagaries of the fish. I am inclined to believe with him that there must have been then "a great deal of prejudice, self-conceit, and humbug exhibited by salmon-fishers generally with respect to their flies—a monstrous mass of nonsense hoarded up by the best of them;" and were my own anxious fears allayed by the assurance that there might be honourable exceptions in the case of "the best of them," I should not hesitate to repeat in this year of grace the same charitably sweeping denunciation of "salmon-fishers generally." At all events, I have no confidence in the thousand and one salmon-flies of prismatic

Salmon Flies

hues, more likely to delude the angler than the fish; and though my flies are certainly not all of the old hodden-grey tint, I do not require to go far afield to find ready material for them; for they are all dressed with the feathers of our common native birds. So dressed, they have proved as attractive and deadly to the fish as those that

> "Borrow the pride of land, of sea, and air;"

while they do not cost a tithe of the expense.

The following is my list of salmon-flies :—

1. *The Mallard, with black hackle.*—*Wing:* a feather from the back of the wing of the wild drake. This feather is dull white and black spotted to about half-way up, shading off to black and brown at the tip. *Body:* pig's wool dyed dark mauve, with a little yellow mohair round the tail of the fly, which is formed of a few fibres of golden-pheasant toppings, silver tinsel, and black hackle, with dark-red mohair or pig's wool at the root of the wing.

2. *The Mallard, with golden-pheasant hackle.*—*Wing,* as above. *Body:* dark-brown pig's wool in the upper part, succeeded by yellow; silver tinsel and dark-mauve pig's wool close to the wing; heron's hackle rolled farther down. *Tail:* golden-pheasant hackle. In all salmon-flies the wool should be picked up with a needle or a pin, to give the body a rough appearance.

3. *Golden-Pheasant Tail, with black hackle.*—*Wing:* golden-pheasant tail-feather. *Body:* dark-mauve in the upper part, and a little yellow pig's wool or mohair in the lower. *Tail:* golden-pheasant toppings, black hackle, silver tinsel, and dark-red mohair for the shoulder.

4. *Golden-Pheasant Tail, with yellow hackle.*— Same dressing as for No. 3, except that the *body* is black mohair in the upper part instead of mauve, the hackle yellow, and the tinsel gold.

5. *Brown Turkey, with black hackle.*—*Wing:* dark-brown feather with white tip from tail of turkey. *Body:* dark mauve in the upper part, yellow mohair in the lower. Dark-red mohair or pig's wool for shoulder. *Tail:* golden-pheasant toppings, gold tinsel, and black hackle. This fly was at one time a great favourite on the Clyde. It is sometimes dressed with a red hackle, but a black is preferable in a clear water.

6. *Brown Turkey, with mauve hackle.*—*Wing* and *body* as in No. 5, except golden-pheasant hackle instead of toppings for tail, mauve hackle instead of black, silver tinsel instead of gold, and heron's hackle below the wing.

7. *Black Turkey.*—*Wing:* a black feather with white tip from the tail of the turkey. *Body:* black mohair in the upper part, succeeded by dark mauve; dark red at the shoulder. *Tail:* golden-pheasant

Pl. IV. SALMON FLIES

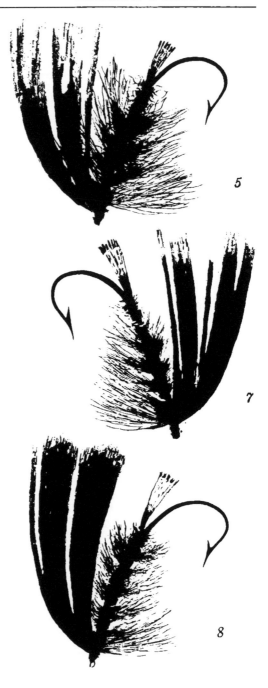

toppings, black hackle, and gold tinsel. The body may be varied by substituting dark-brown pig's wool for black and mauve. I always prefer pig's wool to mohair.

8. *Hen Pheasant.*—*Wing*: dark mottled feather from hen-pheasant tail. *Body*: black mohair in upper part, yellow farther down, dark mauve at the shoulder. *Tail*: golden-pheasant toppings, gold tinsel, and black hackle.

9. *Heron-Wing.*—*Wing*: feather from wing of heron. *Body*: yellow mohair, succeeded by dark mauve, dark red at the shoulder. *Tail*: golden-pheasant toppings, silver tinsel, and black hackle.

The size of the flies must in all cases be made to suit the size and condition of the water,—a low clear water demanding a small fly, and a dark heavy water a larger one.

The rod for salmon-fishing is generally made too long and too heavy. There is really no necessity for having one longer than 17 or 18 feet. The butt should be of ash, the middle of hickory, and the top of lancewood or greenheart. The middle piece should be somewhat stiff, but not clumsily turned. I prefer a brass ferrule between butt and middle, and a spliced connection between middle and top, both for greater security and additional advantage in casting. The reel contains from 60 to 100 yards of carefully prepared silk.

The eight-plait tapered silk lines are the best in use; they cast much better than hair, take up less room on the reel, are less liable to catch when running out, and do not absorb so much water. A triple gut casting-line of two yards or so, handmade, or machine-twisted and carefully tapered, connects the silk with the gut-line proper, which should itself measure three or four yards. The total length of gut must be a little less than that of the rod, so that when, on landing a fish, the reel-line is rolled up to its junction with the gut, the salmon will be quite within reach. For salmon-fishing one fly on the gut is sufficient; when, however, sea-trout may be expected, I use two of a smaller size. Before beginning operations let the angler see that all his tackle is in perfect order, that there is no weak strand of gut, and no false connections; for as the prize is great, so are the risks involved.

Salmon are always angled for down-stream. A good long line is required, especially in fishing with fly; but the precise length will, of course, depend on the size of the river. Many anglers boast of the distance to which they can cast their fly: but to cast out a line is one thing; to fish it properly when cast, and to recover it when spent, so as to effect a second throw, are other and very different things. Practice may do much to perfect skill, but only within the lever power which the angler has at command. If necessary, I can cast and control from 20 to 30 yards of line. It is only now and again, however, that there is any necessity to cover such a stretch of water. If it is desired on an occasion to send the fly to a spot which the length of line that can be cast and recalled would fail to reach, the angler may unwind a yard or so more, allowing it to hang loose at the reel, and cast as usual, when the slack portion will run out with the impetus of the cast; but this additional line has only to be taken in again before another venture can be made.

The mode of casting in fly-fishing is the same for salmon as for trout; but as the salmon-line is longer, it will, of course, be extended farther behind, and more effort will be required to cast it forward. In making the backward movement, however, the rod must not be allowed to get far behind, if the obvious dangers attendant on a long line are to be avoided. The cast is always made over the shoulder, and every angler should be able to make it either from right or left as circumstances require. When there are no obstacles in the way, I always cast from that shoulder which is next the river. In all fly-fishing, whether for salmon or for trout, see that the fly alights gently and invitingly on the surface.

In smooth water, cast well across and down stream, and allow the fly to come gradually round, alternately raising and lowering the point of the rod, until the line attains its natural tension, or reaches a point from which you can with facility make the next throw. By this working or plying of the line the wings of the fly are opened and closed, and the salmon is either deluded by this appearance of life in the lure, and is tempted to taste and try, or he is provoked by the vagaries of the fly to rise and sweep it from his sight. In fishing strong currents, it is necessary to cast farther down-stream than in fishing pools, in order that the fly may not be carried round so rapidly as to escape the notice of the fish. In this case, the point of the rod must be kept pretty well down, for the purpose of sinking the fly a little; and the working of the line should be performed more gently and less frequently than in quiet water, where the resistance to such movements is not so great. Where we have a pool with a current in the middle and a quiet eddy beyond, it may be proper to cast more nearly across, and to move the fly very gently, until it is swept into the current, when the ordinary working is resumed; but, in general, the casts for salmon are made much more down-stream with the current than those for trout. In all waters, the raising and lowering of the rod must be measured and gradual;

for salmon, as a rule, do not dash at the fly like trout, but are, at least in rivers, naturally more leisurely in their movements than smaller game, and require to be accommodated thus far, if the angler wish for sport. There are, indeed, instances in which salmon gulp the fly the moment it alights; but those are not common, and are generally confined to newly run fish, that show "the madness of the vexèd sea" from which they come.

From what depth or distance salmon may rise to a fly, is a question that does not readily admit of a solution, but I am inclined to believe that they can discern the lure much farther off than most anglers suppose. I have caught salmon in water twenty feet deep, where there were no rocky sides or sunken ledges on which they might rest; and as in such water the fish always keep near the bottom, I cannot doubt that they detected my fly from that depth. Again, in shallow water, I have seen a salmon, more than twenty feet distant from my fly, make boldly for the tempting morsel which had excited his cupidity. His aim was true; he met his fate; "he gulped the hidden hook, whereon he died." In all kinds of angling, a fruitless cast in good water does not always indicate that the angler has failed to attract the notice of the fish; rather is it a proof that, as a humorous writer puts it, "the fish has seen the line of invitation which you have kindly sent to him over the water, and does not intend to come." In the case of salmon that do not find their natural food on the surface of the water, it is, in most instances, mere caprice that leads them to rise to a fly at all; and we need not, therefore, attribute to defective vision the fact that they do not always leave their native depths, and make after every fanciful object that flits across the surface. Even when desire has prompted them to rise to what they see, their somewhat dignified movements may not bring them to the surface ere the lure has passed beyond their reach.

Salmon have their favourite haunts in a river, and these are not always of one character. In those rivers or parts of rivers over whose channels rocks and boulders are freely dispersed, harbours of refuge are numerous, and it would be a difficult matter for one previously unacquainted with the water to say where a fish might lie and where it might not. For salmon are very fastidious in their choice of an abode. They select retreats that seem to us to possess no special recommendation, and pass over others that we should consider peculiarly adapted for their purpose. But we need not complain that in this matter, as in many others, they exercise their own discretion. Doubtless, in their selection they study their own convenience, and not the angler's, and consider the questions of food, accommodation, and shelter, of more account than those of gaudy lures and deadly baits. With a very natural, though perhaps selfish, instinct,

> "They prize their lives for other ends
> Than merely to oblige their friends."

Though an experienced fisher, in a water to which he is a perfect stranger, should be able from the natural features of a pool to say where fish were likely to lie, it would be only the local angler who could with certainty tell where they *did* lie. But every angler knows that salmon are considerably influenced in their choice of a resting-place by the condition of the water; and that, when the river is full, he may fish with some confidence of success in places where he would never dream of casting a fly when the river is low. In a "small" clear water, salmon select the deeper runs, such as the throats of pools where the current is rough; and there they station themselves near large stones or rocks on the side next the stream. When the river is heavy, they retire into the quieter water of the pools, and may sometimes be found even in long deep reaches of the river, where no current at all is perceptible. In small rivers, when the water is low, the angler need not fish the necks of the streams beyond

> "The dubious point where with the pool
> Is mixed the trembling stream,"

unless the rest of the pool is sufficiently deep and rocky to afford shelter for fish, and there is wind enough to ruffle the surface. But in large rivers, there is every chance of finding salmon in the quieter parts of the pools, as well as in the necks, even when the water is low and clear.

A single cast in any one spot is generally sufficient to determine whether salmon are at hand and in the humour to take the fly, but a few more attempts must be made to allure a fish from any well-known favourite haunt; and all casts, wherever made, should be in the angler's best style. "Never," says Wheatley, "throw a fly without expecting a fish." Should the fish rise and fail to seize the fly, give him two or three more chances to impale himself; and, if he still decline the honour, tempt him with a different fly. It is true, you may not even then succeed; but do not give him up. Leave him to consider the matter for a while, and then renew your solicitations. It is possible that such a change may have "come o'er the spirit of his dream" as will give you cause for joy.

If you see a salmon rise and take the fly, let him turn before you strike. A young angler is very apt instinctively to tighten his line the moment he catches sight of the object of his ambition, with the almost inevitable result of snatching the fly from its mouth. A second will suffice for the salmon to turn, but that second must be given him. If, however, you are not sensible of his attack till you actually feel his weight on the line, give him not a moment's grace, but respond at once. In salmon-fishing, as usually practised with a long line in streams or rough water, it is not so easy to follow the fly with the eye as in trout-fishing, and in such cases the angler must needs depend more on feeling than on sight; but in fishing a pool or quiet reach of water with a short line, the same necessity is not laid upon him, and he should then watch for every indication of a rise. I am aware that my views on this point do not coincide with those of Stoddart, "Ephemera," and others, who say that one should never strike till he has actually felt the pull of the fish at the line. My practice has always been to strike the moment I saw the fish turn, although I had not felt his weight at all, and my reward has been the capture of many a hundred salmon. Strike gently in a heavy stream, and more firmly in a smooth water. In no case, however, does it involve any great exertion; a slight raising of the rod is generally sufficient to fix the hook. This accomplished, the contest for the mastery begins. If the fish be slightly hooked, he generally disports himself pretty freely out of the water, "impatient of the wound," or "indignant of the guile"; but he may be

> "Too sore enpiercèd with the shaft
> To soar with its light feathers,"

and then he seeks a refuge underneath. In any case, his first demand is usually for more rope; and the angler who would not that the first wild rush should bring the captive off scot-free must be ready to comply.

It is difficult at first for one to form an accurate idea of the size of the fish he has hooked, for the play and vigour are not always in direct proportion to the weight. A comparatively small fish, especially if newly run, may, at the first onset, afford quite an unexpected display of strength, and by his frantic efforts to escape, create a wrong impression of his bulk; while one of bigger frame may, for a time, be patient under the rod, and seem to acquiesce pleasantly in the arrangements made for his despatch, until, goaded by the barbed steel or exasperated by the incessant curb of the tackle, he rises in all the majesty of his might,

> "With such power
> As may hold sortance with his quality,"

threatening dire destruction to the weapons of war, and filling the angler's soul with wild alarm.

"Although," says "Ephemera," "a salmon or grilse, fresh run from the sea, is larger and in better condition than it will be after a few weeks' sojourn in fresh water, it is neither so strong nor so active—at all events, its strength and activity are not so enduring. One evident cause of this is, that fresh water hardens and renders tough and stiffly elastic the fins, which are soft and feebly pliant in fish fresh from the sea; and the natural consequence is that, aided by those whalebone fin-rays (for to the consistency, or very nearly so, of that substance fresh water reduces them), they are more capable of putting forth enduring effort, and strong and rapid motion, than the obese fresh-run fish with its limber fins. This will explain why the angler finds it frequently more difficult to tire out a small fish than a larger one. For myself, I have had, over and over again, an easier task in capturing with rod and line a fresh-run salmon of 15 lb. in weight, than a grilse half the size, which had been for a few weeks' training, as it were, in short but strengthening commons in fresh water. At all times a grilse will be found more powerful than a salmon of the same weight, because the fins of grilse are larger, in proportion to the size of their bodies, than the fins of adult salmon. Grilse possess, consequently, easier and greater powers of locomotion than salmon."[1]

After hooking your fish, endeavour to keep well up with him. Do not let him have all his own

[1] Book of the Salmon, p. 201 *et seq.*

way, but be sparing of the line, and maintain a good strain on the rod. Should he be a salmon of very decided and erroneous views, he may take at once across stream. Scruple not to remonstrate with him on the error of his ways by presenting him unreservedly with the butt. Show him that you and he are "linked together by the invisible gut of destiny," and that as he chose his own time and place to form the tie, so you will choose yours to dissolve it. If he plunge wildly and throw somersaults in the air, there is danger to the tackle, unless you speedily let him have the line; but wind up the moment the burst is over, and stand on your guard for the next. This is a losing game for the fish, if you play well, for every leap betrays the dimensions of the enemy, and tends to exhaust his strength. Never allow him to get down-stream before you, if you can at all prevent it: the result is pretty certain to be a lost fish, and a bitter repentance;

> "For when the fight becomes a chase,
> He wins the day that wins the race."

If he boldly steer right up the stream, "straight and steady as a bridegroom riding to the kirk," follow him up closely, but take care to keep always a little below. This has a wonderful effect in preventing him from "sulking" under big stones—a trick he is almost certain to resort to if he gets below you—and so wearing both your tackle and your patience. Whenever he shows an inclination to make for "foul" spots, such as roots of trees, narrow rushing rapids, or dangerous places, whither you cannot follow him, butt him severely, and turn his head down the water. For, as Mr Penn says, "if you can prevail upon him to walk a little way down-stream with you, you will have no difficulty afterwards in persuading him to let you have the pleasure of seeing him at dinner."

When the fish is well played out and exhibits evident signs of defeat, select a gravelly channel or level spot for a good landing, and winding close up, bring him cautiously to the strand, then, with the rod held well back in the left hand, seize him tightly above the tail with the right, and drag him on the bank. Do not consider him safe, however, till he is beyond all reach of his native element, and do not lay down the rod till then; for just as he is nearing the channel, or even when on it, he has a trick sometimes of remembering that he has forgot something, and of suddenly disappearing to fetch it. Though, of course, he "won't be absent a moment," it is as well to keep firm hold of the rod as the only pledge of his return. Let him have the line with him, however, and recover as before whenever his little game is over; and as soon as you conveniently can, "by a well-regulated exercise of gentle violence," land him comfortably, and take him into custody. In removing the fly, use great caution, else you may rob it both of its power to lure and its power to hold; and overhaul all the tackle before you hazard another throw.

For good fly-fishing for salmon in small rivers, consisting chiefly of streams and pools, I prefer a full water after a flood, whether it be clear or black; but in rivers, or parts of rivers, having long deep reaches, where scarcely any current can be detected, the water is in the best condition when it is "small" and clear. We may say, then, that in the upper reaches of such rivers as the Tweed, circumstances are favourable when the water is full, but in the lower portions there is always a sufficient body of water for salmon-angling, even if it be too low and clear higher up. It must be borne in mind that in order to fish with any chance of success in still water, it is absolutely necessary that there be a good breeze. In regard to the time of day best suited for fly-fishing, no rigid rule can be prescribed—so much depends upon the weather and the season. But it cannot be far amiss to say that, in the spring months, the business hours of the salmon are from 10 A.M. till 4 P.M.; and that if the morning be fine, the angler who loves despatch may come early. In summer, the salmon usually takes his siesta at mid-day, and had better be consulted in the morning or evening. Nothing can be done with him at all on hot fiery days; but when the weather is cool or windy at this season, you may "get a rise" out of him at any hour. Indeed, in summer, such days are the best for capturing all kinds of fish, if we except the perch and the minnow.

The observations made in a previous chapter on minnow-fishing for trout, may be taken as applying equally well to minnow-fishing for salmon. Almost the only points of difference have regard to the size of the hooks and the weighting of the line. I use three No. 13 hooks, and make up the tackle in the way already described, baiting with larger minnows to suit the larger hooks. To fish this bait properly, sinkers are necessary. In a low clear water two No. 2 shot will suffice, but more are needed if the water be heavy. They are generally placed about 18 inches from the hooks. Unless the line be well weighted, the angler runs very little chance of success; for salmon, unlike trout, rarely rise to the surface to seize the minnow. Besides keeping the bait well sunk, a few leads materially assist the slow spinning which is needed to suit the slower movements of the salmon, and to tempt him to take a bite. But such a style of fishing is not without its risks; for, plying his lure thus slowly and near the bottom, the angler is very apt to run foul of rocks and other obstructions, and get anchored in mid-stream. In all untoward circumstances, however, nothing is gained by fretting and fuming. The situation is unpleasant, perhaps, but do not be rash, for even in apparently hopeless cases a slight exercise of patience and perseverance will often free the lure, though it may indeed spoil the pool.

Salmon sometimes take the artificial minnow, the best form of which is perhaps the phantom; but when the natural can be got, let not the angler think of any other. The only excuse for the use of the artificial is the difficulty, sometimes experienced in spring, of procuring live minnows of a suitable size. This difficulty is the more to be regretted, for spring is without doubt the best season for salmon-fishing with this lure, as autumn is the most deadly with the fly. Stoddart recommends a bright day for the minnow in spring, when the river is low and clear; but my experience has always been that, in such conditions of water, the luckiest days at this season are certainly the dull cloudy ones. Indeed, a thoroughly wet day is sometimes fraught with excellent sport, especially if it occur after a prolonged drought.

Fish the minnow, as you do the fly, in rocky pools and heavy rough streams; and when you feel a fish, let him go a short way with the bait before you strike. If you see a salmon take the minnow—a rare occurrence, since the lure is well sunk—just let him turn ere you call him to account. Do not dally so long over a fish rising short at the minnow as you would do over one that missed your fly; after one or two ineffectual casts move on to "fresh fields and pastures new," before you have created alarm where you wished to allure, and return after a time to tempt him yet again.

And now let me add a word or two on salmon-fishing with the worm. The tackle required is of the simplest description, and consists of a single hook, No. 16, tied upon the same kind of gut as is used in minnow-spinning, and well weighted, so that there may be both slow motion and deep fishing. Three well-scoured worms, each about four inches long, of the kind already referred to in the chapter on "Worm-fishing," are required to form one good bait. Enter the hook about the upper third of the first worm, and bringing it out about the lower third, run the bait up the gut to make way for the others. Repeat the process with the second worm, reserving the third to cover the barb of the hook; bring down the others to meet it, and you will thus completely conceal shank, bend, and point, while the loose portions will hang over and form a tempting bait. If the worms are small, four may be necessary. I have said the line must be well loaded. This is imperative, both because we fish the worm in heavier water for salmon than for trout, and because salmon are somewhat deliberate in their mode of attack.

Having drawn off from the reel a yard or two more of line than you will need in casting, so that a fish on seizing the bait may run out without check, throw the worm up the heavy current, and allow it to move slowly round the deepest part of the pool where salmon lie; and, when it gets a little below you, walk down-stream with it till it leaves the best of the water. Then you may cast again. It is better to fish from the channel side than from the bank, not only because the worm is then carried along more naturally with the current, but also because the risk of its fixing on the bottom is considerably diminished.

The salmon may attack the bait several times before he finally "takes" it, and no restraint whatever must be placed upon him during these preliminary operations. Should he feel the slightest check on his movements his suspicions will be aroused, he will instantly drop the bait, and it must be a very tempting worm indeed that will induce him to renew the attack. If unresisted, he goes off with the bait in a lurching manner, like a cat with a mouse, now running for a short distance as though to find a convenient spot to devour his prize, now pausing as though he had found one; and only after, it may be, two or three successive freaks of this kind, does he settle down to enjoy it. When he comes to a final "stand," strike by sharply raising the rod. This will send the hook well home, when nothing remains to be done but to play him in the usual manner till he is exhausted. During its progress down-stream, the line may of course be arrested by some obstruction at the bottom; but the fact must be ascertained only by its subsequent movements, and no attempt should be made to interfere with its free motion, until sufficient time has elapsed for a fish to reveal his presence.

Though salmon sometimes take the fly in a pretty heavy water—even in one passing from the clayey condition to the black — they are seldom allured by either the minnow or the worm in such circumstances. Worm-fishing is always best in a low clear water. It should be practised during the summer and autumn months; and the most favourable hours are in the early morning before the sun comes forth in his strength, and in the evening after the heat of the day is over. In its proper season the worm in the morning, when the water is "small" and clear, often proves a greater success than any other lure throughout the day.

As a frequenter of most of our salmon-rivers, the sea-trout cannot be passed over without some little recognition. Its scientific name is the *Salmo trutta*, or salmon-trout, but its local names are very many and very confusing. It is the same as the white trout of Ireland, and the peal of Cornwall and Devonshire; and although often confounded with the bull-trout, is, in the opinion of many naturalists and most practical anglers, quite a distinct species from it.[1] Dr Günther, however, in his Report to the Tweed Fishery Commissioners, considers the bull-trout only a variety of the *Salmo trutta*. The bull-trout is often—perhaps too often—seen in the Tweed, where it is known simply as "The Trout"; and in the Coquet and other rivers in the north-east of England, where it commonly goes by the name of "The Salmon." It feeds more readily and voraciously than the salmon, and sometimes rivals that monarch himself both in size and weight. Moreover, the two are not unlike in appearance: indeed there is such an apparent resemblance between them, that in England, fishwives have been known to clip the round tail of the bull-trout quite square, and sell it for true salmon. But grilse and salmon on the one hand, can be readily distinguished from salmon-trout and bull-trout on the other, by the spots, which in these latter fish, after the smolt stage, invariably appear below the lateral line. Salmon and grilse, in some very few cases, have one or two

[1] Buckland's British Fishes, p. 322.

such spots, but the vast majority of the species have none at all. The bull-trout itself is marked out from all the allied species by the greater thickness of its neck, the more angular form of its gill-covers, the somewhat smaller size of its scales, and, in the full-grown fish, the more convex formation of the tail-fin.[1] Distinctions between it and its friends will also be found both in the shape and in the relative position of the other fins; but as these vary more or less in different stages of growth, they afford a less certain test of the species. The teeth, however, offer a ready means of distinguishing the sea-trout—at least in the earlier period of its existence—from the bull-trout and the salmon. All the three species have only a single series of vomerine teeth, or teeth on the central bone in the roof of the mouth (and in this lies the difference between them and the common river-trout, which has a double row), but they are most numerous in the sea-trout; and though these teeth are gradually lost in all the migratory species as the fish approaches mature age, in the sea-trout they are always retained for a longer period than in either the bull-trout or the salmon.[2] If, after an ex-

---

[1] Pennell's Angler Naturalist, p. 244 *et seq.*

[2] Many points in the history of the Salmonoids still remain very obscure. Dr Günther, in his 'Study of Fishes,' says : " We know of no group of fishes which offers so many difficulties to the

haustive examination of all these external characteristics, one should still be at a loss to say whether the fish he has caught be a salmon, a bull-trout, or a sea-trout, nothing remains but to adopt the method Josh Billings suggests for settling, at once and for ever, whether a certain fungus is a mushroom or a toad-stool—let him eat it and he will see. Though the result of the experiment with the fish would certainly not be so serious as that with the fungus, it would be quite as conclusive; for no one would fail to detect the bull-trout, when cooked, by its markedly inferior taste. Nevertheless, they are

ichthyologist with regard to the distinction of the species, as well as to certain points in their life-history." Some naturalists, such as Couch, reckon a vast number of species; but it is more than probable that many of these so-called species are merely varieties of the same fish, arising from changes in the external conditions of its existence. Dr Day, in his 'Fishes of Great Britain and Ireland' (vol. ii. p. 59), is clearly of this opinion; and, with special reference to the *Salmo trutta*, says: "It is evident that our anadromous sea-trout may take on a fresh-water state of existence, and breed there (as in the Lismore experiments), irrespective of which, by imperceptible changes, we find it in every country passing from one form to another."

Hybridism, too, has no inconsiderable share in increasing the varieties. According to Günther, "Abundant evidence has accumulated, showing the frequent occurrence of hybrids between the *S. fario* (common river-trout) and the *S. trutta* (sea-trout);" and "it is characteristic of hybrids that their characters are very variable, the degrees of affinity to one or other of the parents being inconstant; and as these hybrids are known readily to breed with either of the parent race, the variations of form, structure, and colour, are infinite."

sent in great quantities to the Parisian markets, where they seem to be held in high esteem.

Both sea-trout and bull-trout may be captured near the mouths of rivers more or less during the spring and summer; but it is in autumn that they ascend to spawn, and then they run, not only to the upper waters of the main stream, but even to the small hill-burns. One or two floods in March will take the most of them down again; but should the rivers continue low at that season, the angler in the Tweed, especially between Peebles and Thornilee, may expect to come across a few good fish in the course of a day's fishing for yellow trout. Though the bull-trout fights valiantly when hooked, and generally "dies game," the sea-trout is much his superior both in sporting and in edible qualities, and is consequently a more desirable object of pursuit. Indeed, if all were known, I fear the bull-trout would be even less of a favourite with some anglers than he is. For it was stated in evidence before the Salmon Disease Commission of 1880, that bull-trout feed largely on the young salmon-fry; that, as they ascend the river later than salmon, they benefit most by the close season; and that, being then consequently overcrowded in small pools, they are predisposed to disease. The late Mr Buckland, one of the Commissioners, went even further, and said: "I am convinced that the time is not far distant when serious steps must be taken to counteract the great predominance of bull-trout;" and again, "The superabundance of bull-trout in the Tweed is, in my opinion, one of the great causes of the salmon-disease in that river."

Indigenous in almost all salmon-rivers, sea-trout abound also in many streams where salmon are never seen; and even certain tributaries of the rivers which salmon frequent are inhabited by sea-trout alone. This is especially the case in the Whitadder, into which salmon never enter. Sea-trout may be looked for in all kinds of water—in pools, in eddies, and in rapid streams—and may be taken with fly, worm, or minnow, though they cannot be said to be particularly fond of the last.

A light salmon or grilse rod of 16 or 17 feet, with a line to correspond, will be found the most suitable for this kind of fishing. A reel is generally indispensable; nevertheless I have, when angling for yellow trout with the loop-rod, killed sea-trout upwards of 5 lb. in weight. The ordinary artificial trout-flies are great favourites with this fish during the whole season; the night-flies already given are also quite suitable, and the smaller salmon-flies are often greedily taken. The colours and varieties recommended by some anglers are almost endless, but are quite unnecessary, the fact being that equally in sea-trout flies as in salmon-flies, a very few of the more subdued colours are all that are needed for any river in the kingdom. They are dressed upon hooks varying in size from No. 4 to No. 10, according to the condition of the stream, large flies being required for heavy water. The cast may carry three if the flies are large, and five or six if small. The salmon-flies are most deadly when the water is heavy.

There is nothing in the method of sea-trout fishing that has not been already said under salmon-fishing. Fish down-stream. In summer and autumn, after or during a flood, large numbers are caught with the worm at the mouths of rivers, and in the sea they often take the spinning-minnow; but the fly is the best lure when the waters have subsided. When hooked, sea-trout give rare play. If fresh run, they are, in proportion to their size, stronger and wilder than any salmon, and fight with the greatest pertinacity to the end — the bitter end often for them indeed, but sometimes for the angler. In the small tidal streams in the west of Scotland I have known sea-trout of not more than 2 lb. in weight, on feeling the hook, dash impetuously up the water, surmounting three considerable falls in succession, and running out more than forty yards of line. They always require to be carefully played, if the fisher wish to maintain the connection with the fish, and bring them safely to bank.

The importance of the salmon as a food-fish was early recognised by the Legislature of this country. Even before Magna Charta, the common law of England prohibited the monopoly of salmon-fisheries by the Crown or its grantees, and ordered the suppression of all weirs or other devices interfering with the passage of the fish. Scotland, pre-eminently the land of salmon as well as "the land o' cakes," was not much behind in salmon law-making. From the time of Robert the Bruce until the union of the Parliaments, "Acts anent the Preservation of Salmonde" again and again found a place, and no mean place, in the statute-book. The Act of the first Parliament of James I. (1424) shows the spirit of the legislation and the "rigour of the law": "Quha sa ever be convict of slauchter of salmonde in time forbidden be the law, he sall pay fourtie shillings for the unlaw; and at the third time, gif he be convict of sik trespasse, he sall tyne his life, or then bye it."[1] Under such rigorous measures the poachers must have had a hard time of it. After the union of the Parliaments, however, the love for salmon among legislators grew cold, and their vigilance for its preservation relaxed. Till quite recent times, indeed, there was little attempt to

[1] The Salmon, by A. Russel, p. 136 *et seq*.

make the law for saving the salmon keep pace with the improvement and extension of the means for killing it; and had there not been a revival of interest in the good work, salmon would ere long have only been seen in the cases of museums.

The Legislature awaked to the necessity for action in 1857. Since that time various measures, notably those passed between 1861 and 1878, dealt stringently with illegal fishing, close-time, and other important matters ; and for the redress which these Acts have afforded, proprietors and anglers have always been grateful. Satisfied, however, they cannot be: the questions of netting, weirs, and pollutions, remain in a most unsatisfactory state, as the yearly Reports of the Fishery Inspectors continue to prove.

Since the killing of spawning fish was prohibited, there has naturally been an increase in the number of salmon that come to the adult stage. But though bigger fish may now be caught in the rivers, clean fish, especially in the upper waters, are few and far between. In spring, when a river opens, many salmon are undoubtedly to be met with ; but these are, for the most part, spawned fish making their way to sea: nearly the whole harvest of clean fish ascending the river is reaped by the tacksmen and the nets, and comparatively few reach the upper proprietors, until the season

T

when it is illegal to kill them. So long as the nets are spread — and that is from February to September — the only chance a salmon has of reaching the upper waters is during the weekly close-time from Saturday night till Monday morning, or during a flood, when net-fishing is impracticable.[1] In the Report of the Inspectors of Fisheries (England) for 1881, it is stated that the actual number of salmon taken with the rod in the Teify in Wales, during one season, was only 20, against 8700 captured with the nets. If this is so in what the Inspectors call "a river of great excellence," need we wonder at the miserable gleaning that is left for the proprietors on the upper reaches of the Tweed? The Inspectors admit the injustice which is thus done to the owners in the higher districts, and conclude their report thus: "We wish to repeat our strong opinion that the upper proprietors, in many cases, require more consideration than has hitherto been afforded to them. Owning, as they do, the most valuable breeding waters in each watershed, their influence is of the first importance in salmon preservation; and the

---

[1] Mr Young, in his First Report to the Fishery Board for Scotland, quotes the following from a Tay proprietor: "The weekly close-time must be admitted to be a *total failure*, as far as the interests of the upper proprietors are concerned, and necessarily so in a river of *such extent* as the Tay. The Saturday and Sunday fish, coming into the river, don't get *half-way* before they are caught by the *Monday morning* net."

measures adopted by Parliament in 1861, in 1865, and in 1873, to ensure a fairer distribution of fish, have not, in all cases, led to satisfactory results among the upper proprietors." In fact, the owners in the upper waters are still very much what Maxwell of Summertrees, in 'Redgauntlet,' styled them —" a sort of clocking-hens, to hatch the fish that folk below them are to catch and eat." Alike, then, on grounds of policy and equity, it is desirable that their grievances be removed.

It is undoubtedly true, as the lessees of the lower fisheries are never weary of saying, that salmon taken near the sea are most fit for the food of man, and that it is there the principal fisheries must be. But the upper owners never asked for an equal share with the lower. What they chiefly want, as pointed out by Mr Russel twenty years ago, " is not fish, but fishing—not gain, but sport. And the number of fish sufficient for sport, compared with what is necessary for profit, is utterly insignificant."

If the rights of these proprietors receive such scanty recognition, where shall the privileges of the sportsman angler appear? Under existing laws the angler is virtually excluded. This is unwisely done. Legitimate rod-fishing, under proper regulations, never yet injured a stream; and were some sections of the upper waters thrown open to the "honest" angler at a time when fish are in season, neither the sport of the proprietors nor the foodsupply of the community would be injured in the slightest degree. As a matter of fact, both would be undoubtedly and materially increased. At present, the number of clean fish killed by the legitimate rod-fisher during the short open season, amounts only to an infinitesimal fraction of the number of foul fish slaughtered by the poacher throughout the winter. The angler may be proverbially "honest" in the midst of strong temptation to be otherwise, when he conscientiously returns all unclean fish to the water whence they came; but he must be more than "honest" if he should manifest unwearied exertion to discountenance poaching in the upper waters, simply to provide fish for the people lower down. If even a small share of clean salmon fell to the rods of the legitimate anglers, a local interest in preserving the fish would be enlisted in the districts where it would most avail, and a practical guardianship would be established, which would do more to prevent the annual slaughter of tons of unclean fish than all the vigilance of all the bailiffs on the river, and would bring to the proprietors and the community at large a handsome return for the very small privilege accorded to the brethren of the rod.

Other grievances that still remain to be effectually dealt with by the Legislature are pollutions and obstructive weirs. Each alone is bad enough, but it is when in combination that their influence is most pernicious. Pollutions poison the river; weirs not only interfere with the free passage of the fish, but obstruct the natural flow of the water, which might have diminished the effects of the poison it contains. Prior to the passing of the Rivers Pollution Act of 1876, manufacturers and burgh commissioners alike—those with chemicals, these with sewage—scrupled not to turn what should have been, and had been, gladdening and life-giving streams, into very rivers of death. Though the evil has to some extent been mitigated, it has not yet by any means ceased. The Inspectors, in the report from which I have already quoted, "find it to be their duty to point out that the multiplication of salmon is seriously affected by pollution," and that, "in very few cases have steps been taken to render pollution harmless;" while Mr Young, the Inspector of Salmon-Fisheries for Scotland, is of opinion that "it is high time that stringent measures were taken to check the progress of pollution, for in one way, at least, the public health and the preservation of salmon are immediately connected." Although salmon, in their natural desire to reach the spawning-grounds in the upper reaches of a river, often "run the gauntlet" of chemical refuse, sewage, and other abominations at the mouth, it is the large volume of water there, or the floods at the time of their ascent, which dilute the poison and render it less deadly. But sometimes the impurities are too many — even for salmon. "Almost every year," says Dr Günther, "salmon and sea-trout in the grilse state make their appearance at the mouth of the Thames (where the migratory Salmonoids have been extinct for many years) ready to reascend and restock this river as soon as its poisoned water shall be sufficiently purified to allow them a passage."

In a paper on the Loch Lomond fishings, read before the Scotch Fisheries Improvement Association (26th September 1884), we find the following: "In dry weather hundreds of salmon and trout are found dead in the river Leven, poisoned by refuse from the dye-works—fat, healthy fish, quite fit for the table: in fact, the people collect them and sell them for food. Tens of thousands of young fry and smolts also die every year by this means on their way to the sea. Besides the actual death inflicted by these poisonous stuffs, they further injure the loch by keeping the fish in the cleaner waters of the tideway, pending a freshet to permit them to pass up; and when in that situation they fall a prey to the ever-watchful poacher, who nets the lower waters on the pretence of catching herring." Instances might be given of similar destruction in the Tay and many other rivers; but this is unnecessary: the facts are well known. It is encouraging to observe, however, that the importance of the subject is now so fully recognised, that Angling Associations and Fishery Boards are taking steps to obtain from the Government some remedy for the defects in the existing law; and that, in view of the wider interests to which the question appeals, a National Society has been recently formed in London, in order, as its prospectus bears, "to induce and secure immediate legislation for the prompt and effective suppression of the pollution of the streams of the country."

The evils attendant on weirs and pollutions are vastly increased by the excessive amount of land-drainage. This has been alluded to in a previous chapter as acting very prejudicially to the interests of the resident river-trout; but the migratory Salmonoids suffer from it even more severely. In the case of both fish, the changes caused by drainage tend to the destruction of the ova—the greater suddenness and violence of the flood washing away the spawn, and the greater height of the flooded water inducing the spawners (which always seek the shallows) to deposit their ova in higher situations, where they are, on the subsidence of the waters to a low level, exposed to imminent peril, if not to certain destruction. But if the drainage system is cruel to the ova, it is not kind to the ascending fish. Salmon do not incline to ascend a river either when it is very low or when it is in very high flood; they prefer a happy medium. Now we have seen that the effect of increased drainage is to bring down the water more quickly and in greater volume after rain, and to reduce it to a lower level during drought. The time favourable for the ascent of salmon is thus very considerably diminished, and the consequence is that they are often detained too long in the tidal waters, where they are either captured by the nets, devoured by their natural marine enemies, or poisoned by the pollutions of the river. Even should they escape these risks and enter the fresh water, the river, especially if it be obstructed by weirs, is no more favourable for their progress than it was for their entrance; and the result is overcrowding in the pools, with its attendant evils. A similar condition of affairs when the fish are on their passage to the sea can only lead to similar disastrous results. The increase of hill-drainage may, so far as the fish are concerned, be an irremediable evil; but all the more on that account should effective measures be speedily directed against those other evils, the removal of which is both practically possible and reasonably desired.

A new and more formidable enemy of the salmon has appeared in the form of what is now known as the fungus disease. It is not my purpose to enter upon the vexed question of its origin, nor am I prepared with any nostrum for its cure. Many and divers are the causes to which it has been attributed. It has been laid to the charge of pollution, of lowness of water caused by excessive land-drainage, of effects of frost and snow on the water, of overstocking or overcrowding of fish, of obstruction by weirs, of wounds caused by fish fighting on the spawning-beds, and many more. Whether the disease in its origin or in its development is to be attributed to any or to none of these, or whether this epidemic among the fish is simply Nature's method of thinning an overstocked community, are questions still unsolved. The Royal Commission of 1880 could do little more than submit a host of conflicting views; the Inspectors of Fisheries, though able in their most recent reports to record discoveries as to the propagation of the disease among various fish, are silent alike as to its cause and its cure; and science has been appealed to, but as yet has declined to reply.[1]

[1] The most recent contribution to this question is that contained in the Report of Professor Huxley, the Inspector of Fisheries (1883): "These experiments [of Mr George Murray] afford conclusive proof that the *saprolegnia* may attack a fish, the epidermis of which is entire and uninjured. They dispose of the theory that abrasions are a necessary precedent condition for the development of the disease; and as they show that perfectly

But pending the result of inquiry and experiment as to the cause of the distemper, much might be done to minimise its ravages, if not entirely to counteract them. Seeing that every diseased fish which remains in a river immensely increases the chances of contaminating those that are healthy, there can be no question of the wisdom of the policy now adopted in our rivers of removing and burying or burning every fish infected with the disease. There will, too, be general acquiescence in the wisdom of the Acts of 1861 and 1865, which gave powers to Fishery Boards to erect passes over certain weirs and mill-caulds, below which fish collect and overcrowd, so as to permit of their ascent to the untenanted water above, where the best spawning-beds often lie. But as the value of this provision is very much diminished by the exceptions allowed in the case of weirs erected prior to 1861, it is to be hoped that the Act will be made retrospective, and be extended to all afflicted streams. Even natural obstructions may be overcome, in many cases at least, by the more extensive use of the modern salmon-ladder.[1]

---

healthy fish may be readily infected, they also dispose of the theory that the fish must have fallen into some morbid state before they succumbed to the attacks of the fungus."

[1] "At this moment," says Mr Young, in his Second Annual Report to the Fishery Board for Scotland, 1883, "there are

But besides these protective measures, means must be taken by the artificial hatching of ova on an extensive scale to restock those streams which this virulent pestilence has impoverished; and in work of this description our new Fishery Boards and our newer National Piscicultural Association will find abundance to do. All will acknowledge with gratitude the labours of Sir James R. Gibson-Maitland and other workers in this field, and will look for great results from the latest experiment of Mr Napier, of the Forth Fisheries, by which he has established the fact that it is both possible and easy to incubate the ova not only of diseased but even of recently dead fish. When we are told by the Inspectors of Fisheries for England (in their Report for 1882) that from 2000 to 4000 diseased salmon are annually removed from the Tweed alone,[1] even if we reckon only one-third of them unspawned, we must find it difficult to overrate the importance of Mr Napier's discovery.[2] But to reap

upwards of 500 miles of rivers and lochs in Scotland wholly or partially closed against salmon by natural obstruction; the Falls of Tummel alone obstructing upwards of 100 miles of water."

[1] During the years 1880, 1881, and 1882, no fewer than 22,756 diseased salmon, grilse, and sea-trout were taken out of this river. See Mr Young's First Report to the Fishery Board for Scotland, page 43.

[2] Nearly a dozen fish-hatcheries have now been constructed in Scotland. In Linlithgow Loch Hatchery, as reported in Septem-

the full advantage of all such researches, and to turn them to practical account in the repopulating of our streams, the Government ought, as suggested by Sir James Maitland in his 'Essay on the Salmon-Disease,' to come to the help of the Fishery Boards,[1] and empower them to obtain loans for the construction of hatcheries on a scale commensurate with the necessity.

In the interests of all to whom an abundant supply of wholesome fish is a matter of no little importance, I heartily wish the Boards every success in their endeavours to counteract the ravages of the pestilence; and in the name of the brethren of the rod, I can confidently promise them our cordial co-operation in every wise effort to replenish and preserve our much-loved streams.

---

ber 1884, "young salmon, hatched from the ova taken from a dead fish stricken with salmon-disease, have thriven remarkably well; and there is a tank of healthy-looking ova taken from a trout after being twenty-four hours dead, and impregnated with the milt of another fully four days dead."

[1] Funds have already been placed by the Treasury at the disposal of the Scotch Fishery Board for the scientific investigation of the habits of food fishes; but from that Board's recently published Second Annual Report, it appears that the grant is altogether inadequate.

CHAPTER XII.

PIKE-FISHING.

"Go on my muse, next let thy numbers speak
That mighty Nimrod of the streams, the Pike."
—*The Innocent Epicure.*

"Wolf in greediness, dog in madness, lion in prey."
—*King Lear.*

OF all the names that have been bestowed upon this fish, there is none more significant than the German one of water-wolf. Whether, in the old English name of luce,[1] its nature stands as clearly revealed or not, there is for the angler no necessity to inquire. Of the true character of the fish he entertains no doubt: it is in a firm belief in its greed that he prepares the lures for its death. These lures are, for the most part, fish-baits, for it is upon its fellow-inhabitants of the waters that it chiefly loves to prey. Jack lords it mercilessly

---

[1] *Luce* is generally held to be derived from *lukos*, a wolf.

over the trembling finny tribe, and lays them under heavy contribution to supply his great and frequent needs. No one enjoys immunity from his rapacity, except, perhaps, the tench. Towards that "physician of fishes," if report does not lie, he magnanimously displays his "only virtue." Writers on fish and fishing have, in all ages, expatiated on his ravenous disposition; and even the poets, who have a good word to say for the trout and the salmon, have none for poor Jack. So long ago as the fourth century of our era, the Latin poet Ausonius branded him as

> "The wary Luce, 'midst wrack and rushes hid,
> The scourge and terror of the scaly brood;"

and the muse has hurled hard epithets at him ever since. With one, he is "the tyrant of the watery plains"; with another, "the dispeopler of the lake"; with a third, "a mercenary." There is no possibility that his character has been calumniated:—

> "His greedy appetite will leave your doubts behind."

But the attentions of the pike are not by any means limited to the "scaly brood." Reptiles, rats, and fowls, alike may claim his regard, if they unfortunately catch his eye, and come within range of his terrible teeth—those "serried pikes," that forbid all thought of hope. Even the higher mammalia do not seem to be safe, should they tempt him too far in his native element, for he has been accused of making vigorous assaults upon dogs, oxen, and horses, that happened to come in his way. His "presumption soars" still higher; for without going back to the days of Gesner for the famous story of the Polish damsel, it would be easy to adduce evidence that pike, when impelled by hunger or rage, do not hesitate to attack the human species, and are no respecters of persons.

In these circumstances, we cannot but hold it a light matter that, following the example of other members of his tribe, the luce—

"With ravenous waste devours his fellow train,"

and exercises his cannibal propensities upon his nearest relations. Here is one instance out of many of Jack's love for his brother. It was furnished to Mr Buckland by Dr Burton, of Kelso, in 1880: "Two pike, the larger $3\frac{1}{4}$ lb., the lesser $2\frac{1}{4}$ lb., were this day taken with the hand by a lad out of the Tweed at Kelso, the one nearly half-swallowed by the other. They were both alive, and when with difficulty separated and put into a water-tub, the larger made two attempts again to gorge his neighbour. The lad who took 'em wondered to see 'a muckle fish wi' twae tails.'"[1] Mr Buckland

[1] Natural History of British Fishes, p. 160.

is of opinion that in this, and in other cases, the "accident" was caused by the two fish charging simultaneously at the same bait, which, slipping out of the way (like Baron Munchausen, I suppose, when he was assailed on the one side by a crocodile, and on the other by a lion), brought on a collision between its foes, and caused the smaller to be impacted in the open mouth of the larger. But in this Mr Buckland shows more consideration for the feelings of the pike than, in their subsequent proceedings, they showed for one another; for whatever may have been the original impulse which brought them into such close contact with each other, nothing but insatiate appetite of pike for pike can explain the deliberate and repeated action in the water-tub. What the result would have been had no one interposed, is not difficult to conjecture. Anglers who often find pike in the stomach of pike, have never any doubt as to the manner in which the unfortunate ones get there. Moreover, it is well known that one pike will attempt to devour another of greater bulk than either his throat or his stomach can accommodate, swallow a part of him, and keeping the remainder in his mouth till the first instalment be digested, carry out his original intention by a series of partial operations to a full and final result.

Although the pike has a preference for fish, flesh,

and fowl of some sort, he is quite open to receive contributions from the vegetable, or, if you please, from the mineral kingdom. It is astonishing, on cutting open a pike, to find, in addition to quite a miscellaneous assortment of animal matters, what a variety of foreign substances he has imported— substances which only the sorest need or a literally omnivorous disposition could ever have tempted him to appropriate. But if thus

" True glutton-like his stomach rules his eyes,"

he has need of a good digestion; and certainly Nature has been kind to him in this respect, for she has not given him the desire to devour without the ability to benefit. In his own person he is shark and ostrich combined. If nothing comes amiss to him when feeding, nothing that he swallows seems to disturb his internal economy. His powers of assimilation are marvellous, and dyspepsia is to him unknown. But if he can feast when he gets the chance, he can fast when necessity compels; and we may charitably believe that it is his premonition of a fast, or his experience of one, that whets his appetite for a feast.

If credence is to be given to all accounts of the longevity of the pike, verily he eats to some purpose. Every author on angling feels bound to record the story of the Mannheim fish, which tradition says was put into the Kaiserwag lake by one of the German emperors in 1230, and was captured in 1497, having thus escaped the snares of generations of anglers for two hundred and sixty-seven years. But our confidence in the veracity of the old writers is not strengthened on learning that, some years ago, a clever naturalist discovered that the skeleton of this patriarchal pike, which measured 19 feet, had evidently been tampered with. Whatever amount of truth there is as to the age of the Mannheim fish, there is no doubt that a pike, under even ordinary conditions of existence, attains to formidable proportions; and seeing that its powers of digestion are quite in keeping with its capacity for swallowing, there is no saying what gigantic dimensions it might reach, if circumstances were exceptionally favourable. All who have experience in the rearing of this fish can have no difficulty in agreeing with Walton, that "pikes that live long prove chargeable to their keepers."

Pike weighing from 8 lb. to 12 lb. are common in the Clyde near Lanark. On one occasion I killed a fish 12 lb. in weight with my loop-rod. The largest that I have seen caught in that river scaled 24 lb., but I believe that fish of 40 lb. are to be found in it. The biggest that came under Mr Buckland's observation was one of 36 lb.; but pike attain a greater weight than this in the lochs of

Scotland and Ireland. One fish—to which allusion is made by Daniel in his 'Rural Sports,' and others—was caught in Loch Ken in Galloway, and scaled 72 lb.[1] According to "Ephemera," "the largest pike recorded to have been caught in the British Islands was one taken in the Shannon. It weighed 92 lb."

Walton characterises the pike as a "solitary, melancholy, bold" fish. It does not, however, always swim alone; big fish are often found in pairs, and at certain seasons—after floods, for example,—pike are quite as gregarious as trout. Melancholy they are without doubt, if not sulky; fickle to a degree, and influenced greatly by the weather, they are sometimes not to be drawn from their haunts by the most tempting bait. When in the humour, however, and bent on prey, their audacity is unbounded. They are not to be balked by difficulty or deterred by danger: their courage in pursuit of their game is equalled only by their capacity for devouring it.

Pike spawn in March, April, and May, according to the state of the weather and the age of the fish—the younger ones spawning earlier, and the "dow-

---

[1] This is the largest pike ever killed in Scotland; and Mr Young, in his Second Report to the Scottish Fishery Board (1883), reminds us that it was taken with rod and fly. The head is still preserved in Kenmure Castle.

agers" later. During this season they retire into the ditches or shallows, where they deposit their ova amongst the leaves of aquatic plants, and not, like most other fish, in the bed of the stream. The eggs are about the size of turnip-seed, and exceedingly numerous. In one fish of 32 lb., Mr Buckland found no fewer than 595,200 eggs, the roe weighing 5 lb. When the spawning process is complete, the pike scour themselves in the streams, and then take up their regular stations for the season. Alike in rivers and in lochs these haunts are chiefly the deep, sluggish pools, floored by bulrushes, lilies, and other plants. If the loch is large, they frequent the weedy sides, the little bays, or the mouths of streams where small fry abound; in ponds or small lochs, they may be found roaming more at large on foraging expeditions. In rivers, the mouths of back-waters, dam-heads, and eddies between two streams are favourite resorts,—in fact, wherever there is a weedy shelter and a sluggish water, there the fish may take up their abode. In fine weather they lie just outside these retreats or a little within them; in winter, after the first heavy flood, they retire to the more sheltered deeps. Though trout are found in deep waters which pike frequent, the pike's range is limited to such waters; they are not found in streams and shallows, where trout are at home. The best part of the Clyde for pike-fishing is from the point of its junction with the Medwin to Douglas Water foot.

Pike-fishing was, if not the earliest, at least one of the earliest forms of angling in our country, and the most primitive methods in use were live-baiting and trolling with the dead-gorge bait. In the first English contribution to the literature of angling, and among the first books printed in England—the Book of St Alban's, published in 1486—Dame Juliana Berners thus treats of live-baiting for pike: "Take a frosshe and put it on your hoke, at the necke, betwene the skynne and the body, on the backe half, and put on a flote a yerde therefro, and caste it where the pyke hauntyth, and ye shall have hym." Jack's love for frog has not cooled during the four centuries that have elapsed since the days of the good prioress, and often has his passion brought him pain. Barker, Walton, and many more old worthies held the lure in high estimation; and it is still true that the angler who is bent on sport will be likely to find it

" When a pike suns himself, and a-frogging doth go."

Improvements have from time to time been effected in the tackle for baiting the frog, but many of our modern weapons of war are, more or less, merely modifications of the original forms, adapted to cope with the more wary pike of these days. My tackle consists of four No. 10 hooks. Two, placed back to back, are tied at the end of a piece of fine gimp, and the other two, in a similar manner at a distance of an inch and a half. One of the hooks of the first pair is inserted under the skin of the frog, just behind the head, very much as Dame Juliana recommends, and the barb of the hook is freely exposed. The opposite hook of the second pair is, in like manner, passed through the skin of the posterior quarters, and the disengaged hooks of each set are allowed to lie beside the bait, openly awaiting the attack. It is desirable to select a yellow lively frog for baiting, and to put it on the hooks with as little injury to it as possible, so that it may be able to maintain its natural position, and swim about actively for a considerable time. Remember Walton's famous advice on this point—"Use the frog when baiting him as though you loved him;" and yet be sure the hooks have too good a hold of him to permit an assault to be made upon him with impunity.

For this method of fishing both float and leads are required. The float I use consists of a piece of cork, like the bung of a cask, perforated in the middle. The line is passed through the hole, and kept in position by a peg, which, being easily removable, allows the angler to adjust the float so as to suit water of any depth. The sinkers are

Angling with the Live-Bait. 311

attached to the line about a foot from the hooks. One end served by the float is to inform the fisher of the moment when a pike has taken his lure, but its chief purpose is to prevent the live-bait from sinking deeper than may be deemed advisable. The leads are added to keep the line in proper position under the float, and render it impossible for the bait to swim up to the surface. The buoyancy of the float and the weight of the sinkers must therefore be proportioned to each other, and both to the size of the bait. The position of the float on the line will be determined by the depth of the water, but some regard must be had to the temperature of the season. It is a good general rule that, in water three feet deep or so, the bait should swim about mid-water, and in deeper pools about a third from the bottom. But it must be remembered that, though pike generally keep near their peculiar haunts at all seasons, they swim nearer the surface when the weather is fine and warm than they do when it is cold.

The rod required for this and other kinds of pike-fishing is a stout one of 16 or 18 feet in length, very similar to that used in salmon-fishing. There are two ways in which the bait may be cast. The first is by throwing from the reel. According to this method the angler winds up the line till the bait is close to his side, and imparting to it a slight swinging movement, trusts to the weight of the lure and float and the momentum they acquire to draw from the reel as much line as will cover the water to be fished. In the second, and perhaps the best method, he unreels a good length of line, then holds the rod well back with the right hand until he can grasp the line along with it, takes the bait in the left, and projects it well and boldly into the water, letting free the line from the right as the bait runs out, and at the same time directing the point of his rod towards the spot he desires to reach. In both methods there must be correct calculation of the distance required to be covered and of the force required to cover it, before there can be a successful throw. When the bait has reached the water,

> "The patient fishér takes his silent stand,
> Intent, his angle trembling in his hand;
> With looks unmov'd, he hopes the scaly breed,
> And eyes the dancing cork and bending reed."

If lazily inclined, the angler sometimes rests his rod on a forked stick by the water-side and waits for events. But this style of fishing is unsportsmanlike, and if the attack of the fish on the bait is to meet with a prompt response from the angler, he must hold himself in readiness to give it. The disappearance of the cork is the sign that the pike has accosted the frog and is desirous of becoming better acquainted with it. Some anglers allow a few seconds' grace before proceeding to extremities, but I advise instant striking. The spring snap-hook is considered by many to possess an advantage over the ordinary snap-hook, but if the angler strike at once with my tackle, it will require no spring to lodge the double hook in the mouth of the fish. Live-frog fishing is best when the day is dull and breezy, and the water is low and clear.

Another good live-bait is a small trout. The method of fishing it is the same as that just described, but the tackle is somewhat different. Tie two No. 14 hooks back to back at the end of the gimp, and a single hook of the same size an inch apart from them. Pass the single hook through the skin of the trout, taking a little of the flesh at the dorsal fin, and allow the other hooks to hang undraped by the side of the bait. An equally good arrangement is to have a single No. 10 hook at the end of the gimp, and two of the same size an inch farther up. In this case one of the pair is inserted in the bait as before, and the other hooks hang free. Fixed upon such a tackle, the trout swims easily about and forms a capital lure, while the disengaged hooks are suspended in the position in which they will be most certain to strike when the pike seizes its prey, as it generally does, crosswise.

When the minnow is employed as a live-bait, the tackle consists of a triangle of No. 8 hooks at the end of the gimp. A minnow is fixed on each by passing the hook through the under lip from the inside. Should a pike be on the hunt in the neighbourhood of this lure, the trio of competitors for his attention will all be equally likely to be honoured with it; for to hungry Jack a whole bushel of minnows would scarcely suffice for a meal. The baits being light, the line must not be so heavily weighted as in the previous cases. Live trout and minnow baits meet with most success after a flood, when the water is in the favourite condition between the black and the clear. A good breeze is a desideratum in this, as indeed it is in all kinds of pike-fishing, except, perhaps, when the worm is used.

These are not the only lures used in live-baiting. Falstaff, in "King Henry IV.," has it that "a young dace may be a bait for an old pike;" and gudgeon and roach may do equally well, whether the pike be old or young. Mice, water-rats, and a variety of creatures, biped and quadruped, may all be taken at times as Jack's fancy directs, though fish-baits are to be preferred. But I pass from these to the worm.

A large hook, No. 16, is all that is necessary in the way of tackle. Remembering for whom the diet is provided, do not stint the supplies. Bait with three or four large worms, running each up the line as it is threaded on the hook to make room for the others; and when all are on, bring them close together, for their magnetic influence upon a famishing pike is greatest when in combination. It is chiefly upon their tempting appearance that the hope of the angler rests, as, unlike the fish-baits which swim freely about, they cannot attract by any great display of vigour. Worm-baits secure most sport when the water is "small" and clear, and when the day is bright and sunny.

Live-bait fishing is the easiest and simplest method of angling for pike, but spinning with the minnow is the most scientific. To the skilful angler it will prove also the most attractive wherever circumstances are favourable for its proper exercise. In some weedy waters it is impracticable, and its place must be taken by the gorge-bait. Certain conditions of water and weather are generally more suitable for the live-bait; and the pike being, more than any other fish, subject to external influences, it is not safe to predict at any time which lure will have the advantage. But taking the entire results of an average season's fishing, most anglers will be ready to admit that the spinning-bait produces the best sport. Several reasons may be assigned for this. It may be that the pike is fascinated by the gyrations of a lure which suggests a wounded quarry and an easy prey; or it may be that these rapid movements have the desirable effect of concealing the forbidding hooks when the pike is contemplating an attack on the bait. But if neither of these be held to account fully for the success of the spinning-tackle, there will still remain a sufficient explanation in the fact that, by its use, the angler is enabled to cover a much greater extent of water in a given time than would be possible with either the float-line or the gorge-bait.

This method of angling with the spinning-minnow has been already described. The same flight of hooks, and the same method of baiting, are employed as in fishing for trout or salmon; but gimp is used instead of gut. A small trout will make a good bait, but the hooks for it must be larger than for minnow. As the pike loves the deep water, the minnow must be sunk sufficiently to come under its notice. Place, then, a small sinker on the line, and spin slowly. In this operation have more in view the style of spinning for salmon than for trout; cast across and down, and bring the minnow slowly towards the side. Bearing in mind that pike may follow the lure till it is close to the bank, always be careful to fish the cast out, before withdrawing the bait. In trolling from a boat on a loch, let the line be drawn about sixty yards behind the boat, and row rapidly to secure good spinning. Strike as in salmon-fishing, and strike firmly.

In playing any fish, it is advisable to maintain a strong and even strain upon the line; but it is more imperative in pike-fishing than in any other; for owing to the hard bony palate of this fish, and its vigorous way of shaking its head whenever it feels anything suspicious in the bait, there is great danger that the hooks will fail to hold should the strain be relaxed. If there be weeds in its neighbourhood, endeavour to steer the pike clear of them; but if "crooked fortune" thwart the enterprise, increase the strain on the line as the only means of retaining control over the fish. The pike is an obstinate creature, and shows great reluctance to quit its prey after it has seized it. Sometimes it is drawn almost out of the water without its being hooked at all, simply by its teeth having sunk deeply into the bait. If it make good its escape after being hooked, the angler must not give up all hope of tempting it anew. He should throw again into the spot where he lost it, and he may find that Jack is quite open to a second engagement. The fish often seems as much annoyed at losing the bait as the angler at losing the fish; for, nothing daunted by any scratch it may have received in the first encounter, it dashes again at the insignificant creature that dared to wound and hoped to escape. When there is no doubt that the pike is fast on the hooks, get it into the creel with as little delay as possible. For trolling with the minnow in rivers I have a preference for a low, clear water, with a good breeze.

If an artificial spinning-bait be desired, a good large spoon will perhaps prove as useful as any. The sizes, sorts, and colours to be had in the tackle shops are surely enough to meet the wishes of every angler, if not of every pike, and they need not be detailed here. I prefer one with the outside silvered, and the inside painted red. It generally succeeds best in water passing from the black condition to the clear. A phantom minnow of large size is also a good lure. These, and all other artificial baits, are fished in the same way as the natural minnow. For spinning and live-bait fishing, the water does not require to be so deep as for some other methods of angling for pike; but it is unadvisable in any circumstances to fish in water of less depth than three or four feet.

Another means of catching pike is trolling with the dead-gorge bait. This is the method so fully described by Nobbes, the reputed "father of trolling"; but it need not delay us long. The tackle employed is similar to that formerly described for one method of trouting with the natural minnow. It consists of two hooks, varying in size from No. 11 to No. 14, according to the size of the bait, tied back to back at one end of a yard, or a yard and a half, of gimp, fitted with a loop at the other end. A piece of lead about the weight of a florin is wound closely round the shanks of the hooks. The lure may be a small trout or a grayling—in England, generally, a dace or a gudgeon; and the method of baiting is the same for all. To the looped end of the gimp a thread is attached, the end of which is passed through the eye of the baiting-needle. Enter the needle at the mouth of the bait-fish, and bring it out at the tail. Draw the lead down into the gullet and body of the fish, until the hooks are arrested by the mouth and project very slightly on each side of it. Remove the needle and pass the loop of the gimp on to the swivel, and the whole is ready for action. The method of working is easy. Unreeling a short, strong line, send the bait out with a gentle swing into deep water, and it will

"Sink fraught with fated doom to greedy fish."

When it has reached to within a short distance of the bottom, the point of the rod is raised to bring it again near the surface, when the sinking is resumed. This movement is performed slowly and gradually as the line is drawn home, so as to display the lure to the best advantage, and give the pike an easy opportunity of seizing it. Do not interrupt the action; let it be continuous, but not rapid; and avoid removing the bait suddenly from the water. This last caution is as necessary in trolling with the gorge-tackle as in spinning with the minnow; the pike sometimes makes no attempt to effect a capture till the bait is being drawn up, and then fear of loss rouses to decided action. Fish all spots likely to harbour a pike, but do not dwell long in any. One or two casts in a good place will be quite sufficient to test the mind of the lurking freebooter. Secure every advantage by keeping as much concealed from view as possible; and do not court failure by throwing the bait into the water with a splash.

The first notice the angler receives that a pike has seized the lure is the stoppage or check of the line; but every stoppage or check unfortunately does not betoken a fish. Weeds are common where the gorge-bait is worked, and they sometimes play strange pranks with the line. The interruption they occasion to its motion is scarcely to be distinguished from that produced by the pike's attack upon the bait; but in any case the angler's first step is to slacken the line in preparation for any contingency. A large fish sometimes takes the lure with a dash and a tug that leave no cause for doubt as to its presence and its doings; but generally the only indication that a pike has seized the bait is a slightly tremulous motion of the line, caused by the fish's closing its teeth upon its prey. When the position of affairs is doubtful, pause a second after the check has been received, and then give the line one or two slight pulls. If these be insufficient to determine the nature of the resistance, the tests must be made a little more severe, until the point is settled one way or another. When the angler has ascertained that he is undoubtedly dealing with a fish, he must give it time to gorge the bait, or, as it is termed, to pouch it. The pike generally carries on this operation in its favourite haunt, and no restraint must be put upon it till the business is completed. The time required varies in different cases, but five minutes, seven minutes, or even more may be allowed. Do not be impatient. Captain Williamson has reason with him when he says: "You will find the greatest advantage result from giving plenty of leisure for the fish to swallow the bait; you ensure the prize, because if he has pouched, he cannot escape; and if he has not pouched, you ought not to disturb him."

It is this necessary delay in waiting for the pike to disclose and destroy itself that constitutes one great objection to gorge-bait fishing. If one were sure that a fish was working out its own destruction every time appearances seemed to indicate it, the time allowed for the work could hardly be said to be lost. But, in the first place, the angler may be labouring under a delusion all the while he fancies that a pike is addressing itself to his bait; there may be no pike at it at all. "Never hurry a jack, Tom," is the advice, in 'Punch,' of the old gentleman to his young friend, as he stands, watch in hand, patiently waiting the turn of events; "he has had ten minutes already; I shall give him another five to make sure." But the telling sketch shows the hook fast in a log at the bottom. In the second place, there is no certainty that, even if a pike has taken kindly to the lure, it is doing all it possibly can to carry out the angler's wishes; it may be only playing with the bait. But again, should the case be more hopeful, and the bait actually within the jaws of the fish, there still remains the risk—attending all gorge-tackle—that it may be ejected again "after it has served the pike's purpose, and before it has served the angler's." I have known a pike retain the bait for ten minutes, and reject it after all. It had got a glimpse of the fisher standing on the bank, and didn't like his appearance.

A pike generally begins to move off after it has pouched, and then is the time to strike; but should it show no sign that the gorging has been satisfactorily concluded, the angler must just exercise his discretion as to when he ought to strike. Colonel Venables, a contemporary of Walton, and one of the "great triumvirate of angling," thus counsels the fisher: "When the pike cometh, slack your line, and give him length enough to run away to his hold—whither he will go directly—and there pouch it, ever beginning (as you may observe) with the head, swallowing that first. Thus let him lie until you see the line move in the water, and then you may certainly conclude he hath pouched your bait, and rangeth about for more; then, with your trowl, wind up your line till you think you have it almost straight; then, with a smart jerk, hook him, and make your pleasure to your content." If the reader prefer the Colonel's quaint prose "done" into stirring verse, let him read Palmer Hackle's angler's song on "The Killing of the Pike."

Some care must be exercised in removing the gorge-hooks from the fish, otherwise there may be damage to fingers, or tackle, or both. Having killed the pike, either by giving it a blow on the head, or, as Stoddart advises, by urging the blade of a strong pocket-knife through the spinal marrow, immediately behind the skull, open the gill-cover, cut through the gills, dig out the hook from the entrails, and, disengaging the gimp from the reel-line, draw the bait and hooks through the opened gills. Another method is to make an incision in the body of the fish at the point where the hooks are felt to be located, and draw the tackle out by the aperture.

Dead-gorge bait generally secures large pike. It requires deeper water than snap live-bait or spinning-minnow, and it succeeds well when the river is low and clear. It is, however, of greatest service in waters so overrun with weeds that a spinning-bait cannot by any possibility be worked.

Gorge-bait fishing may be practised with a live bait as well as with a dead one; and by many anglers the former is preferred. Live-gorge may be used in all places where a snap live-bait would bring success, although the method of working it is similar to that already described for the dead-gorge. The tackle corresponds with that for snap live-bait, with the exception of the hook, which, in the case of the live-gorge, may be either single or double: the latter is the more common. Insert the baiting-needle, carrying the gimp and hooks, under the skin of the live-bait behind the pectoral fin, and bring it out near the end of the dorsal fin. Draw the gimp through until everything but the barbs of the hooks is hidden under the skin, and make the connection with the swivel on the trace in the same way as in the dead-gorge tackle. I have not used the live-gorge bait in any form, but it has undoubtedly merits of its own. While it possesses all the attractions which a living bait has for the fish, without the doubtful graces of a train of uncovered snap-hooks, it secures for the angler all the advantages of the dead-gorge bait.

Pike do not often rise to a fly. Still they are sometimes seen to take the large green drakes or yellow flies; and it is not a very uncommon occurrence for the fisher to hook a pike on his salmon-fly. I do not use the fly as a lure for jack; but those who do, prefer a large one, dressed upon a No. 20 hook. For wings they give it two eyes from a peacock's tail; a few showy hackles, and a body of coloured pig's wool, generally red, and adorned with broad gold tinsel. Some employ a pair of large hooks, and make the fly as big as a humming-bird, or even a wren, accommodating it, moreover, with a tail, and two glass beads for eyes.

The best pike-fishing seasons are during May and June, and from the middle of August to the middle of October. In rivers pike do not as a rule "take" well on a hot day in summer, unless when lured by a worm: a blustering day in that season is more favourable for good general sport. The 'Innocent Epicure's' rhyme under this head is not without reason:—

> "Perhaps the day is hot, no breeze of wind
> Is to your hope and vain endeavours kind:
> Rise early then, or try your fortune late;
> Or else till more auspicious minutes wait.
> When keen the winds from any quarter blow,
> The tyrant seldom waits a second throw."

There are many other ways of fishing for jack besides those that I have named. Some of them are unworthy of sportsmen, some are of doubtful repute, and some few are illegal. The unworthy and the illegal need have no notice: of the doubtful methods, that known as "trimmering" is still tolerated in some quarters, and may be briefly alluded to here. It is of very ancient date, easy in practice, and, when all is said in its favour, childish as a sport. Nevertheless, in the eyes of some fishers,

> "Age cannot wither it, nor custom stale
> Its infinite variety."

Trimmering in two of its forms was known to Walton. In its least objectionable fashion, it is a kind of live-gorge fishing with set lines. Part of the line is wound round the bifurcated part of a forked stick and notched in a slit in one of the arms. The stem of the fork is tied by a string to a bough overhanging the water to be fished, and when a pike seizes the bait, the line slips out of the notch and runs off the stick without check. The fish has thus line enough to reach its lair, where it may pouch at pleasure, while connection with the angler is maintained by the string. Instead of being attached to a fixed object on shore, the line may be made fast to a bladder, a bottle, or a trimmer proper—a cylindrical float, red on one side, and white on the other—which is then turned adrift to do all the fishing. This is a stage worse than the once popular method of fly-fishing with the "otter," in which, though the line was attached to the float, the angler kept possession of the rod, and required to exercise some skill in guiding the "otter" to windward, while his flies danced gaily over the water between him and it. But the trimmer-rigger has simply nothing to do, and generally he does it very well, and with wonderful results. Sometimes, however, he imparts variety to the proceedings of the trimmer, though he renders the game even less creditable to himself, when he discards the dull passive float, employs a living agent in the shape of a goose or a duck, and tying the line to its leg, chases it over the water. This is certainly sufficiently exciting for the goose or the duck, whatever it may be for the rigger, but it is an abuse of words, to call it sport for either. Yet the gentle Prioress of St Alban's found it in her heart to style it so, and to say that the sport would lie in seeing " whether the goose or the pike should have the better;"

and Barker, in his 'Art of Angling,' tells us that in his day (1651) it was "the greatest sport and pleasure that a noble gentleman in Shropshire gave his friends entertainment with." To me "trimmering" is a word of evil omen, and in pike-fishing as in politics, is too suggestive of accommodation of principle to profit, to find favour with the "honest" angler. Many, indeed, in their love for true angling, may be disposed to think that Mr Pennell was not less just than he was severe, when, in his 'Book of the Pike,' he thus sarcastically summarised his instructions to any who aspired to the dignity of a trimmer-fisher: "Procure a good supply of old bottles, rusty hooks, and clothes-line, and the assistance of the most notorious poacher and blockhead in the neighbourhood, and the chances are that the angler will find himself exactly fitted to his sport both in tackle and companionship, without 'violating the bond of like to like.'"

There is considerable diversity of opinion in regard to the gastronomic merits of the pike. It appears to have been held in much higher repute both at home and abroad ages ago than it is now. Many of our countrymen at the present day have a strong repugnance to it, and cannot be prevailed upon even to taste and see. Italians like it not, and Spaniards will have none of it. In Germany, too, it has fallen very much in estimation. But some six centuries ago the pike was, according to Yarrell, double the price of salmon, and ten times the price of either turbot or cod. Though this may have been a purely factitious value, arising from its rarity on its first importation into this country, there is no doubt that in Edward III.'s time the pike was regarded as a high-class fish, and was carefully kept and liberally fed. It was no common dish for common folk. Chaucer, to impress us with the easy circumstances of the Frankeleyn, would give us to understand that

> "Full many a fat partrich hadde he in mewe,
> And many a brem and many a luce in stewe."

It continued to be held in high esteem for many generations, and "the rich pike smoked on the board" at many a princely civic banquet. The fact that it has now lost favour with many, if not with most, connoisseurs, is not necessarily a proof of growing refinement in taste: it may be only a change of fickle fashion. But if, in the case of any, abstinence from pike is the result of a vivid recollection of its flavour, I would hint to such that possibly their dislike to the entire genus is based upon their experience of the character of a single specimen, and that an unfavourable one. For it is with pike as it is with people—innate graces aside, the character depends a good deal on the upbringing; and pike, perhaps more than any other fish, differ widely in edible virtues according to the nature of the home influence and the provision that has been made for their growth in goodness. Mr Pennell assures us that "probably the worst pike are those bred in the Scotch lochs." If this be so, we can only lament that certain individuals are always found to disgrace their nationality, and we can now readily excuse the connoisseurs who, naturally believing that "the wale o' a' thing" was to be had in the North, tasted one of its degenerate pike (possibly an importation), and forthwith abjured all pike whatever from that day till this. But there are Scottish rivers as well as Scottish lochs, and the pike of several of the former are excellent. The best feeding for jack in stews was said to be eels; but in the rivers, while the supply of these is not small, there is besides an abundance of young trout and other fry, with which the pike are permitted to fraternise just too freely for the interests of the trout. It is owing to such favourable conditions for growth that the pike of the Clyde prove remarkably good eating—good enough, perhaps, to falsify old Camden's famous report of "Horsea pike, none like." They are best when over 5 lb. or 6 lb. in weight, but they must not have altogether lost the sweetness of youth; for as Walton reminds us, "the old or very great pikes have in them more of state than goodness." Choose one in its prime, and remember that the edibility of an article depends very considerably on the cooking of it. Those who say that Walton must surely have had poor material to work upon when he required no fewer than ten different ingredients to render his pike palatable, forget that this preparation was intended to be, as he said it was, " a dish of meat too good for any but anglers, or very honest men." For others I recommend " kippered " pike; and should any stranger to the dialect or the kitchen ask what that is, and how it is to be prepared, I would remind him that this is a book on angling, and that, as such, it will amply fulfil its purpose if it teach him to carry out, in the case of a fish, the first injunction of the famous recipe for cooking a hare—" catch it."

APPENDICES.

I.

CLOSE-TIME FOR TROUT.

THE pollutions and obstructions in our rivers are evils against which trout and salmon alike have to contend, and to which both alike too often succumb. Trout, however, are further weighted in the struggle for existence, through the absence of any provision for their protection at a time when they are least able to protect themselves, and when the slaughter of one means the loss of thousands. To this cause alone must be attributed a greater destruction of trout than to any other, or perhaps to all other preventible causes combined. Indeed it is not too much to say that unrestricted fishing is, of itself, quite sufficient to effect the depopulation of any stream; and my belief is, that if a close-time measure is much longer delayed, the necessity for it on some rivers will have passed away.

For centuries the leister and the light were—and are still occasionally—used on Scottish rivers with dire effect against the salmon; and now we have the "shabble" and the torch arrayed against the trout. By their means alone whole sack-loads of fish are killed every winter in the tributaries and upper reaches of the Clyde and other unprotected rivers, while no little havoc is wrought by the cleaner hands that ply the rod and line. But though it is the absence of a close season that affords the unprincipled fisher the most favourable conditions for carrying on his nefarious practices, even in the legitimate fishing season there are not wanting those who, "well covered with the night's black mantle," or "trusting to the evil counsel of a desert place," condescend to press into their unhallowed service the deadly double-rod and the still more deadly net. It is within my knowledge that there is scarcely a village in Clydesdale but boasts a net or two, and counts the season's captures by thousands.

The salmon has enjoyed almost a monopoly of the fish legislation—such as it has been—for six hundred years, and its excellence as a food-fish, and consequent commercial importance, fully entitle it to even more attention than it has hitherto received. The trout may not lay claim to all the virtues of the salmon, but it has been treated as if it were entirely destitute of any. Its edible qualities are well known and require no apology; its market price is often not much under that of salmon; and possibly had greater vigilance been exercised in its behalf in years long gone by, it would to-day have been of more account than it is in the food-supply of the community. But far as its fortunes have at present sunk beneath those of "the venison of the waters," it still merits regard, if only from an economic point of view, quite as much as the partridge and the black-cock, and is no less deserving of legislation for its protection. The angler, however, seeks a close-time chiefly in the interests of his craft. He ranks himself with other sportsmen, and expects that, in any measures that are taken for the protection and fostering of innocent and healthful recreations, the rod, as affording lawful sport to scores of thousands, will meet with at least as much recognition as the gun.

But it is unnecessary to maintain the general principle that trout are worthy of preservation, seeing that it has already been admitted in recent legislation both for England and Ireland. The Fresh-water Fisheries Act (England), 1878, declares it to be illegal—

" 1. To fish for, catch, or attempt to catch or kill, trout or char during the close season between 2d October and 1st February following, or during any close season which by bye-law may be substituted for the same.

" 2. To use, or have in possession with the intention of using, any light, otter, lath, jack, snare, wire, spear, gaff, strokehall, snatch, or other like instrument for the purpose of catching or killing trout or char."

The importance of trout-preservation being surely no less evident and urgent in Scotland than it is in England, it is hoped there will be a speedy acknowledgment that "what is sauce for the goose is sauce for the gander," and that we shall have it enacted that, in Scotland not only shall all rivers be closed during the winter months to all kinds of fishing, but that even when they are declared open, they shall still be closed to all kinds of illegitimate fishing. So much at least is needful for the protection of the few trout that remain to us. It will, I know, require more than prohibitive and restrictive Acts, however wise, to restore and maintain trout-life in our streams to the full measure of their capabilities; but it is useless to advocate the construction of fish-hatcheries for replenishing the waters, until there is some security that propagation shall not minister to plunder.

Mr Archibald Young, Inspector of Salmon-Fisheries for Scotland, submitted for the opinion of district boards, river proprietors, and others, the question of a close-time for trout; and in his First Report to the Fishery Board (1882), he thus states the general nature of the replies which he received:—

"The great majority of the answers were in favour of such a close-time for trout as there is in England and Ireland, though a few were decidedly against it, chiefly on the ground that trout are great destroyers of salmon ova and fry, and that, therefore, they should be discouraged instead of protected in a salmon-river.

"There is considerable difference of opinion amongst those who are in favour of a close-time for trout and char, with reference to the period over which it should extend, some being in favour of a close-time the same as that for salmon; others preferring from 1st October to 1st March, or from 1st October to 15th February; whilst some would have it during the months when the smolts are descending to the sea, with the view of thus preventing the destruction of smolts by ignorant and unscrupulous anglers. Considering the lateness of many of the Highland lochs and streams particularly on the west coast, in the Hebrides, and in the Orkney and Shetland Islands, I venture to think that, if there is to be a close-time for trout and char, the best period would, on the whole, be from 15th October to 1st March."

It is of course impossible to secure entire unanimity on any question, but it is hopeful to find that the vast majority of river conservators and proprietors are on the side of trout-preservation. The few who urge or favour its destruction in the declared interests of the salmon, may be selfish, but they are certainly short-sighted. To keep the rivers open during the winter for the avowed purpose of slaying the trout in order to preserve the salmon would most completely defeat the end they desire to secure, as the present state of affairs abundantly shows. Trout may devour salmon ova and fry, but poachers work more destruction than trout; and it is only by closing the rivers against *all* fishing whatever during the spawning seasons of both fish that the existing feeble Acts against the slaughter of foul salmon can either easily or successfully be carried out.

The precise period over which the close-time should extend is a matter which readily admits of adjustment. If not coextensive with the salmon close season on any river, it should, at all events, not fall far short of it; and its duration in each case might safely be left to the discretion of the district Fishery Board. Having in view the southern rivers of Scotland, I should prefer a close season from 15th October to 15th February following—for northern streams it might be later; but if uniformity be desired, I think the recommendation of Mr Young would, on the whole, be most advantageous.

The administration of any Close-Time Act would naturally fall to the Fishery Boards (of which there are upwards of one hundred in Scotland already), and in this work they would, I believe, be most cordially assisted by local Angling Associations on every river. To meet the necessary expenses of watching the streams and otherwise enforcing the provisions of the Act, a rod-tax might be imposed, such as the Fishery Act of 1878 empowers Boards of Conservators in England to levy on all instruments used for the capture of trout in their rivers. On the Severn—as we learn from the Twenty-third Report of the Inspectors of Fisheries in England (1883)—the rate of duty was fixed at one shilling per rod, and the policy of imposing this low tax has been attended with the greatest success. In 1883 the sum of £250 was realised from rod-licences for that river alone, and no less an aggregate sum than £1155 in the last five years. The total number of trout-rods licensed in England in 1882 was 22,755, which brought in £1994; in 1883 the licences amounted to 21,769, and the sum realised was £1913. This gives an average tax, over the whole of England, of one shilling and ninepence per rod—a low price, surely, for the privilege of fishing in a protected stream.

It thus appears that the expenses attending the administration of the Close-Time Act in England are, in great measure, met by the anglers for whose benefit, in the first instance, the Act exists; and there is no reason to believe that the trout-fishers of Scotland are so far behind their English brethren in their regard for their sport that they would be unwilling to contribute one shilling and ninepence each towards its preservation.

II.

SUMMARY OF LURES.

APRIL.

Fly.—In clear or black water: small artificial flies—teal with black hackle for trail, March brown and blaes alternately for the others.

Minnow.—In heavy black water.

Worm.—In clay-coloured water.

MAY.

Fly.—In clear or black water: small artificial flies—teal with black hackle for trail in the early part of the month, March brown, blae, sand-fly, black blae, green-tail, for others. When the March brown is off the water, substitute sand-fly. Towards the middle of the month, teal with red hackle for trail. Evening: small gloaming flies. Towards the end of the month, natural May-fly.

Minnow.—In heavy black water; and towards the end of the month, in a "small" clear water if the day be hot and sultry.

Worm and *Caddis.*—In a heavy discoloured water.

JUNE.

Fly.—In black water: small artificial flies, but less certain now. The natural May-fly the distinctive lure. The green drake, dibbing, if a rough breezy day and no sun. Evening: small gloaming flies. Night: if moonlight, small gloaming flies continued; in the absence of the moon, large flies.

Minnow.—In a "small" clear water with bright sunshine, fishing up; in full black water, fishing down. Night: either with moon or without; best when starry, inclining to frost.

Worm and *Caddis.*—In "small" clear water with sun, fishing up. When May-fly is over, caddis preferred.

JULY.

Fly.—Natural black ant, fished in same way as the May-fly. Artificial flies not of much account, unless on a cold day, or in a black water after a flood. Night: if moonlight, small flies; if not, large flies.

Minnow.—In full black water, if the day be dull; in a "small" clear water, if bright sunshine. Night: conditions as in June.

Worm and *Caddis.*—In low clear water, if bright sunshine, fishing up; or in a black water with sunshine.

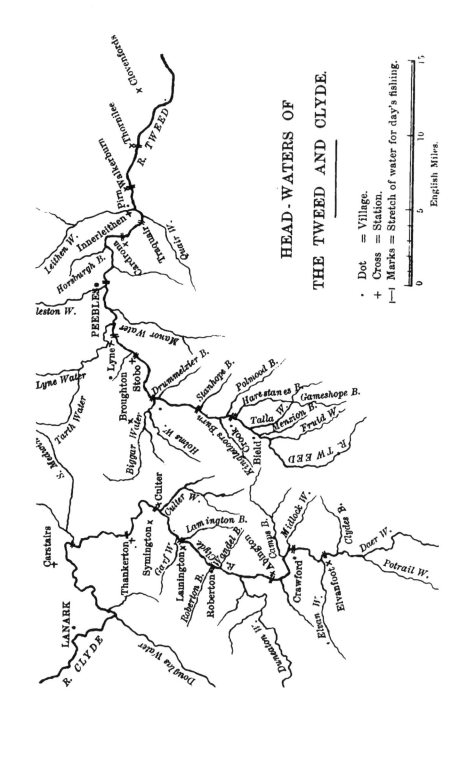

AUGUST.

Fly.—Natural black ant. Artificial flies unproductive in hot and dry weather, but successful if cold and wet, with occasional floods; and in the early morning.

Minnow.—In black water.

Worm.—In a full, flooded, turbid water.

SEPTEMBER.

Fly.—Small artificial autumn flies very successful.

Minnow and *Worm.*—In flooded water.

OCTOBER.

Fly.—Small artificial still good, in the absence of frost.

Minnow and *Worm.*—In flooded water.

Trout getting out of condition. Time for grayling-fishing with fly and worm.

III.

PRINCIPAL OPEN REACHES OF THE CLYDE AND THE TWEED, WITH THE WINDS THAT BLOW UP-STREAM ON EACH.

THE CLYDE.

Section sufficient for a day's fishing.	Wind blowing up.
1. Medwin foot to Thankerton,	Northerly.
2. Thankerton to Culter,	West by north.
3. Culter to Lamington,	North-east.
4. Lamington to Roberton,	North-east.
5. Roberton to Abington,	Northerly.
6. "Graveyard Pool," above Abington, to Crawford,	West.
7. Crawford to Elvanfoot,	North-east.
8. Elvanfoot up the Daer,	Northerly.

THE TWEED.

1. Thornilee to Walkerburn,	East by south.
2. Walkerburn to Traquair (Innerleithen):—	
(*a*) Walkerburn to near Pirn,	East by north.
(*b*) Pirn to Traquair,	North-east.
3. Traquair to Cardrona,	South-east.
4. Cardrona to Peebles :—	
(*a*) Cardrona to Horseburgh-burn foot,	South.
(*b*) Horseburgh-burn foot to Peebles,	Easterly.
5. Peebles to Lyne :—	
(*a*) Peebles to Neidpath Castle,	Easterly.
(*b*) Neidpath to Manor Water foot,	North-east.
(*c*) Manor Water foot to near Lyne,	South-east.
6. Lyne to Stobo,	North-east.
7. Stobo to Biggar Water foot (Broughton Station),	Easterly.
8. Biggar Water foot to Stanhope,	North by east.
9. Stanhope to Crook Inn,	North by east.

The winds given above blow directly, or nearly so, up-stream. With this table before him, the angler will be able, ere he start for his day's fishing, to determine on what section or reach of the river he will have the wind most favourable for sport.

The sections on both rivers lie, in most cases, between one railway station and another. At several of these stations there are no "creature comforts" to be had; but the following places, at or within easy reach of the railway, contain good inns or other accommodation for anglers who desire to stay overnight :—

On the Clyde.—Carstairs, Thankerton, Biggar, Roberton (station, Lamington), Abington, Crawford, and Elvanfoot.

On the Tweed.—Clovenford, Innerleithen, Peebles, Broughton, Crook Inn (reached from Broughton), and "The Beild."

BOOKS ON SPORT.

THE MOOR AND THE LOCH. CONTAINING MINUTE INSTRUCTIONS IN ALL HIGHLAND SPORTS, WITH WANDERINGS OVER "CRAG AND CORRIE, FLOOD AND FELL;" and "RECOLLECTIONS OF THE AUTHOR'S EARLY LIFE." By JOHN COLQUHOUN. Sixth Edition, with Additions. 2 vols. post 8vo, with Two Portraits and other Illustrations. 26s.

SPORT IN THE HIGHLANDS AND LOWLANDS OF SCOTLAND WITH ROD AND GUN By T. SPEEDY. 8vo, with Illustrations. 15s.

"We repeat that we can recommend this volume, with its varied contents, as an admirable handbook to Scottish wild sports."—*The Times.*

"Not only freshmen but experienced sportsmen will find valuable hints in these pages."—*Pall Mall Gazette.*

"The author treats of all kinds of sport to be obtained with rod and gun, in a manner to be of great use to the uninitiated....... Mr Speedy writes with a thorough knowledge of his subject, and the book throughout is eminently practical."—*Land and Water.*

"One of the best books on sporting subjects extant....... Dogs, and guns, and birds, and deer are all familiar to Mr Speedy....... It is a delightful book, and one of genuine usefulness"—*Scotsman.*

RAMBLES WITH A FISHING-ROD. By E. S. ROSCOE. Crown 8vo. 4s. 6d.

"A very delightful book."—*Scotsman.*

"Such books as Mr Roscoe's are our only guides to Continental sport; nor could the traveller who desires to explore the resources of the rivers of Germany and of Switzerland desire a better companion than 'Rambles with a Fishing-Rod.'"—*St James's Gazette.*

"A right pleasant pocket companion."—*Bell's Life in London.*

SCOTCH LOCH-FISHING. BY "BLACK PALMER." Crown 8vo. Interleaved with blank paper. 4s.

"The great charm of 'Black Palmer's' work is its simplicity. He eschews technicalities, and is thoroughly practical. And the angler who takes up the little book will be reluctant to stop till he has perused every word of it, and will only lay it down after mentally resolving to read it again from beginning to end at the earliest opportunity....... 'Black Palmer's' notes abound in practical hints."—*Dundee Advertiser.*

"Both to the tyro and the expert angler 'Scotch Loch-Fishing' should prove a valuable guide."—*Bell's Life in London.*

WILLIAM BLACKWOOD & SONS, EDINBURGH AND LONDON.

BOOKS ON SPORT.—*Continued.*

NORFOLK BROADS AND RIVERS; OR, THE WATER-WAYS, LAGOONS, AND DECOYS OF EAST ANGLIA. By G. CHRISTOPHER DAVIES, Author of 'The Swan and her Crew.' New and Cheaper Edition. Illustrated with Seven Full-page Engravings. Post 8vo, 6s.

"It is doubtless the handsomest as well as the most interesting of all descriptions of the Broads, and will preserve the memory of a paradise for naturalists and sportsmen.—*Land and Water.*

"His book is full of pleasant reading, even for those to whom nature has denied all love for fishing and amateur yachting.......It will be welcomed everywhere by all who can relish healthy writing upon healthy topics."—*Spectator.*

"Mr Davies has made the Broads (or river-lagoons) his special study and pleasure for many years past, and he writes of them both with the fulness of knowledge and with the contagious enthusiasm of the devoted amateur....... Altogether, as a pleasant and well-diversified jumble of sport, science, and picturesque description, Mr Davies's book may be confidently recommended to all who care either for East Anglia, for angling, or for light and breezy writing."—*Pall Mall Gazette.*

"With a keen relish for fishing, fowling, yachting, and boating, Mr Davies, in a pleasantly chatty manner, tells us about all these things as they are followed on the Broads; and his vivacious pen at the same time imparts all the information which any one visiting the Broads for the first time would like to have."—*Field.*

"It is one of the most interesting books of its class we have ever seen, and will be an invaluable addition to the library of the sportsman, whether his fancy inclines to fishing, shooting, or yachting, as it touches upon all three. It is written in a most pleasant, chatty style, and will prove both interesting and instructive to all classes of readers."—*Wildfowlers' Illustrated Sporting Times.*

A HANDBOOK OF DEER-STALKING. By ALEXANDER MACRAE, late Forester to Lord Henry Bentinck. With INTRODUCTION by HORATIO ROSS, Esq. Fcap. 8vo, with two Photos. from Life. Price 3s. 6d.

"A work not only useful to sportsmen, but highly entertaining to the general reader."—*United Service Gazette.*

"The writer of this valuable little book speaks with authority, and sums up in a few pages hints on deer-stalking which the experience of a lifetime has enabled him to put forth....... We can only recommend every one who pursues the fascinating sport of which the author writes, to glance through, and indeed to read carefully, this handbook."—*Sporting and Dramatic News.*

"An interesting little book, alike because of the knowledge which its author displays of his subject, and of the simple style in which it is written. It is a handbook such as sportsmen must have long desired."—*Scotsman.*

THE SHOOTER'S DIARY: FOR RECORDING THE QUANTITY OF GAME KILLED, THE TIME AND PLACE, NUMBER OF GUNS, AND NAMES OF PARTIES, &C. WITH MEMORANDA OF SHOOTING OCCURRENCES, ENGAGEMENTS, &C. Oblong 8vo, 4s.

WILLIAM BLACKWOOD & SONS, EDINBURGH AND LONDON.

Druck:
Canon Deutschland Business Services GmbH
im Auftrag der KNV-Gruppe
Ferdinand-Jühlke-Str. 7
99095 Erfurt